MW01611321

The writing in this book is comprised mainly of journal entries from February 19, 2017 to March 2, 2018 on a password-protected blog site intended for Caroline's family and friends as her journey with her glioblastoma progressed. The posts themselves are totally unedited and appear as they had on the CaringBridge blog. The only posts removed from the narrative are logistical ones, like those arranging playdates for her boys or requests to fill the calendar. The writing here was created in very unusual circumstances: just after her craniotomy, while undergoing radiation on her brain, while taking enormous doses of mind-altering drugs. The posts are kept in their original form to preserve the story's imperfections, its honesty. This is precisely what Caroline's fight looked like in real time.

Forever and always for my beloved Wright boys:
If ever I am far away, I hope this book will
bring my voice to you. Each word is yours.

ALSO BY CAROLINE WRIGHT

Twenty-Dollar, Twenty-Minute Meals
Cake Magic!
Catalan Food with Daniel Olivella
Lasting Love
Charlie the Cook

THE CARING BRIDGE PROJ—ECT

by Caroline Wright

A Note from the Author

I have been a writer my whole life, something I was pulled aside and told I could do by my ninth grade English teacher. He named something inside of me that I didn't recognize. This wasn't a book I thought I'd write, however. In some ways, on the other side of a dream, it feels like I didn't. It manifested itself for my children, a box to whisper into to shelter my voice after my body had gone, after it had been ravaged and stolen too soon by aggressive brain cancer.

The writing—the voice that spoke into this box—was like mine, but not one I recognized in myself before. It was not weak, but strong. It made friends of strangers, rallied support. It spoke the truth even when it was too scary to name. I wrote because it surprised me to do so, because the doctors said I shouldn't have been able to because of where my tumor was, because it felt like *me* when nothing else did. And I wanted to preserve that for my two young boys—aged 1 and 4 at the time—who wouldn't remember me if I had died when the doctors told me I would. They told me I would be lucky to live past my thirty-fourth birthday.

From these words sprang hope, healing and a demonstration of love for my family, my community, and myself. They taught me that there is great power in our bodies, a voice that is deep within each of us that can tell us the secret to life if we listen hard enough.

This book is the telling of that secret I found within me. It is my legacy. I am honored to share it with you.

CAST OF CHARACTERS

Caroline
Garth, the Husband
Henry and Theodore, the Sons
Paul and Glad, the Parents
Allison, the Organizer
The Chorus of Friends:
Sarah, Leah, Sasha, Jonas, Teddy and Gillian,
Sarah Jane, Dan, Heather and Molly,
The Hellegers Family, Jeff, along with hundreds
of other silent voices who didn't write here.

CONTENTS

PREFACE _____

DIAGNOSTIC EMAILS

Lately I've thought about me
separate from your woeful morning
and I can see a light ringing through the sky

It sings of coming glory
strangely tied to this awful story
it lifts the heart and gives us wings to fly

—Abigail Washburn, "Momma"

To: Dr. Deans
From: Caroline Markunas Wright
Sent: 2/6/2017, 7:23 PM PST through MyOnlineChart.org
Subject: Non-Urgent Medical Question

Hey Dr. Deans,
When we had our appointment [a physical about a month ago],
I told you that I have some weird headache type things (sort of
pressure changes, you clarified) when I lie down. You asked if I
had these headaches at other times during the day and I said
no. That—or maybe my awareness of it?—has changed and I
have noticed that I have a headache like that almost constantly
sometimes. I have also had some bouts of being (for lack of a
better word) super spacey. Like it's hard to focus my eyes almost.

I assume that either of these things could just be dehydration
so I drink a ton of water. Even during days when I am drinking
a lot of water, I notice both of these things happening. A friend
told me that the spacey thing could be a form of an anxiety
attack. Is that true?

Are either of these things worth looking into further? Thanks
for taking the time to think on them.

Cheers, Caroline

From: Dr. Deans
Sent: 2/7/2017 7:47 AM PST through MyOnlineChart.org
To: Caroline Markunas Wright
Subject: RE: Non-Urgent Medical Question

Please make an appointment to discuss this further but yes
both headaches and spacey feeling can be related to anxiety.
Can also be related to other things

AD

The email that follows is to Robin, my therapist in New York. I awoke in the middle of the night feeling the need to write her, and then copied the medically relevant bits and sent them along to my doctor. The space between their emails—and roles in my life—are what led me to my diagnosis and, ultimately, saved me from putting myself and my kids in further danger, like getting in a car accident while having a seizure. All of this feels so unbelievable now, but if it wasn't for the connection that I have with Robin I think I would have been in a much scarier scenario than I am even now at the time of writing this, which is having been diagnosed with terminal brain cancer. My family could have been gone, nothing to fight for. What a perspective.

From: Caroline
To: Robin
Bcc: Dad; Sarah; Jeff; Allison
Date: February 10, 2017
Subject: Freaking out.

Hey Robin,

I apologize in advance for the super long email. I do think we should schedule a time to talk, if you can. Here is a verbose explanation of my life lately...

I am having a tough time lately. Theodore has been teething and screaming a lot and the kids are in and out of colds what feels like weekly basis. In short, we are out of a groove right now in a serious way in terms of a schedule. I went to the doctor on Wednesday after I emailed her asking about my development of daily headaches (which she diagnosed as migraines that show up in people in their thirties) and periods of extreme spaciness (after I read on Facebook a breakdown of that being a panic attack for some people). I've since been tracking more of my symptoms, knowing the kind of things she's looking for (data on frequency, physical manifestations of my symptoms that hadn't occurred to me as being symptoms).

...On top of which Garth's stepdad is in town and has been uprooted in our basement because it sprung a new leak that originated in the wall of his room and soaked through the carpet throughout, so we had to tear up the carpet late this afternoon and put a bunch of industrial fans on it in order to dry it out so the carpet isn't ruined. He's sleeping on our couch. I'm not beating myself up over any of this—it's just more dealing with the logistics of finding solutions to these problems today that was just outside of my capability in combination with dealing with Theodore (albeit not even well).

...On top of which, too, I drastically changed my eating habits starting January first. (After testing the matter of my kidney stones I collected after my procedure in October (calcium oxalate), my urologist informed me that I can't eat much of what I otherwise identify as "food"—unexpected things like leafy greens and berries, but most significantly to my life, chocolate. I have basically cut out sugar (an enormous change) and haven't had chocolate since Christmas (also a huge change, possibly even on a chemical level). I rarely consume sugar at all anymore, which occurs to me could be affecting my brain. Today, for example, would have been a day that I would have eaten a lot of chocolate to make it through.

(Another FYI: As a result of going to the doctor on Wednesday, she has ordered an MRI to check on the headaches and get some real answers.)

Here are some things I've figured out...I do have some regular physical stress-related symptoms (in addition to my daily migraines and possible panic attacks): my jaw locks up (I have had bad TMJ since middle school and sleep with a night guard as it is); I have these scaly patches of itchy skin at my temples that flare up when stress gets bad (they're flared up now, as they were on and off last year and throughout my book tour this summer); my right arm was tingly today and has settled into being a pain in my elbow (which isn't the first time it's happened, now that I know to look for it); sleeplessness (certainly initiated by the boys, but recently it was 3:30 after Theodore had been screaming for over 2 hours and I was writing this email in my head instead of returning to sleep and now it's 5 am and I'm at my computer); my hearing (like now) sometimes sounds like a sonogram inside my head, a sort of undulating swelling sound that pulses over the actual sounds my ears are hearing; crazy thoughts (I regularly fantasize/ joke to myself and occasionally other moms about ripping my hair out and running from my house; I also have grown more conceptually/intellectually sympathetic with people who abandon their families); I also find myself reaching for my phone a *lot*, I think stemming from a regular need to vacate.

(I feel obliged to mention to you, even though I think I've told you this before, that I would never kill myself. It has, however, occurred to me that it would be selfishly easier to not be around my circumstances, like on a desert island by myself.)

So, where I am in terms of a solution: I realize I am likely a candidate for anxiety/depression medication, the fact of which I am trying to not let freak me out. (A super funny sentence, I might add, upon proofreading!) I have started to take notes on our family calendar in terms of frequencies of feelings/ symptoms and will track these issues for a few weeks and report back to my doctor so we both have real data to go on. A major part of my reluctance is that I just don't believe in taking medicine hardly at all but certainly not regularly. (For example, you know both boys were birthed without meds, and I rarely even take pain medication, including after surgeries.) It stems from wanting to attempt to treat the source of the issue myself and try to be aware of what my body is telling me, which is something I am not naturally good at. So, my "lifestyle" solution I am vowing to myself to try, if my actual life will let me, to find some ritualized calm in my life (my ideas have included waking up and doing a guided meditation in the morning before the kids get up—though usually I soak every last second I can in the morning to sleep; or getting in bed shortly after the kids do and reading until I fall asleep). This is on top of my regular, already started (also since Jan 1) pattern of regular exercise and more sleep. (We also hired a cleaning lady I'm told we can't afford because I can't handle survival in a house that always feels like a crisis and results in only being able to find a single sock for either kid.)

This is all to say I am becoming acutely aware that I need to relax and I don't know how. It isn't something I find cute or a badge of being tough anymore, like I used to. Not with two kids and a marriage to manage. I know I need your help and I'm guessing at this point of the email you probably agree.

Anyway, sending you love all the same. Oh and I'll be in New York right before my birthday. Hope to see you then...

I am going to try to go back to bed now that this is out of me.

xo
Caroline

To: Robin
From: Caroline
Date: February 10, 2017
Subject: re: Freaking out.

Caroline,

I am going to throw the old, "if you had diabetes or heart disease would you refuse medication?" I think having all the issues with your house over the past year or so, stress with garth, stress with having two young children while trying to work—need I list more?—have all come together and now you are depressed and anxious. I don't know why you wouldn't get help via medication if it would help you. And it would help you mentally and physically.

We can find a time to speak next week about this. But you are too smart not to do whatever is necessary to help you and your family.

Robin

Co-Director, NIP C & A Program
Associate Editor, Journal of Family Social Work

To: Robin
From: Caroline
Date: February 10, 2017
Subject: re: re: Freaking out.

I know you're right about the meds as you always are. Xo

Sent from my iPhone

To: Caroline
From: Jeff
Date: February 10, 2017
Subject: Re: Fwd: Freaking out.

Gurl. Your life.

Read this email twice, without tons to say in response other than I wish I were near by so that I could be more concretely helpful, and cook you and your family some meals and babysit and give you lots of hugs. Glad you're reaching out to Robin and that you're considering psychotropics. I think you and I share a (maybe unfair) fear of medication and a (sometimes punishing) sense that we can just bootstrap ourselves out of the shit, but I really agree with Robin that anything that could be helpful at this point should absolutely be on the table. And you're already doing all the boot-strappy stuff already! I love you. And I really believe in you. Let's talk this weekend.

Xoxo

To: Caroline
From: Sarah
Date: February 11, 2017
Subject: Re: Fwd: Freaking out.

Hey girl...I am checking my email in the office of a production company about 30 miles from Belize...I am playing with an artist and am pretty much MIA until Wednesday next week as we don't have cell service. I got on specifically to check in with all of this. I love you so much and I am SO FUCKING PROUD of you for saying " hey, something's not right with me" and taking steps to figure it out. I love you and I will call you on Wednesday when I get back to town. In the meantime, I will pray you are just the strong person I know you are and that the docs can put something together for you to make life a little easier for now.

I LOVE YOU
S

To: Dr. Deans
From: Caroline Markunas Wright
Sent: 2/10/2017 4:30 AM PST through MyOnlineChart.org
Subject: Visit Follow-Up Question

Hello, Dr. Deans:

I am sorry for emailing again so quickly after my last visit. I truly don't want to bother you. However, now knowing the sort of information you need to know, it occurs to me that I have more things going on symptom-wise than I realized at our appointment a few days ago.

Today was a super horrible day stress-wise. My right arm was tingling from about mid-afternoon on and now has settled in a feeling of something I imagine tennis elbow to be (said by someone who doesn't play tennis or really know what that means).

I do have some regular physical stress-related symptoms...
[I go on to tell her the same symptoms that I told Robin before, about the headaches and jaw pain, numbness in my limbs.]

So, I realize I am likely a candidate for anxiety/depression medication. I have started to take notes on our family calendar in terms of frequencies of feelings/symptoms and will track these issues for a few weeks and report back so we both have real data to go on.

Another question I had for you: how will I know when I have the green light to make my MRI appointment, insurance-wise? You mentioned to wait a couple of days to see if it was approved or not, but I didn't know if someone from your office would reach out to me to give me a thumbs up, or if I needed to call someone to check, or if I was safe to assume by Monday or something.

I apologize for this amount of information and level of neurosis and verbosity that you have to wade through to get to the actual point of what I am saying. I am a writer, after all! I really appreciate being able to write this to you, however, all the same. I send my sincerest thanks along with all of this crazy.

Cheers,
Caroline

To: Caroline Markunas Wright
From: Dr. Deans
Sent: 2/10/2017 1:03 PM PST
Subject: RE: Visit Follow-Up Question

Caroline-thanks for the email. Your description of symptoms makes me think even more your headaches are stress-related. In regards to the MRI I will have my staff reach out to you when it is approved. I am out of the office today and back on Monday. I would be happy to see you again in clinic if you are worried

AD

I had the MRI a few days later on February 17, 2017 at 10:45 am. The experience of the MRI—the noises that triggered an overwhelming headache, the interactions with the tech that were disturbing because I sensed she fumbled around some new knowledge as I put my shoes on—left me disoriented, unable to find where I'd parked my car. The machine had triggered a seizure, I'd later learn. I drove home, as if holding my breath, and clung to the directions spat from my phone for the two turns it took to get me home as if they were my lifeline. I felt drunk and confused, so much so I didn't know to be scared. Dr. Deans tried to call me a few times and I missed each one.

To: Dr. Deans
From: Caroline Markunas Wright
Sent: 2/17/2017, 3:59 PM PST
Subject: Test Results

Hey Dr. Deans,

I tried to call the number you left—your cell—but got the recording that told me not to leave a message as a patient.

Can you call me back please? I believe you wanted to tell me something about the results of my MRI this morning.

Thank you,
CW

The Call.

It was dinnertime. I had just placed a pale roasted chicken and squash on the table for us and the kids and we had only just begun to poke at it. It was a pallid, lifeless meal, not fondly remembered or properly cooked, which should have been a warning sign in itself. I had lazily taken it from the oven in the haze of an afternoon seizure, too soon. The skin, still flabby and pink, clung to the bones when it was sliced into. Our dogs eventually ate it days later. I excused myself to answer the phone.

"Hi, Dr. Deans." I am anxious, eager and sweaty, as if called into a meeting with my boss or a revered professor from college. I had never received a phone call from a doctor before, much less one who is on vacation.

"...I can't believe I am about to tell you this," she says. I trail off in thought.

"...It's actually quite large," she says. I trail off again.

A mass. No answers, just words and ideas that swell to fill my brain. I pace around our living room to keep from falling down. The kids are swirling around my knees now, Henry begging me to read him a book and shouting at me that he loves me. I am numb and my world is swimming. Garth took the phone, relaxing his clenched face as details poured through the receiver. He spoke calmly and evenly, collecting himself the way he practices at work with clients even as a storm brews inside. (He only let himself dissolve with me hours later, as if my puddle of emotions seeped into his solid earth and turned it to mud before my eyes.)

While Dr. Deans informed Garth of the plans for the next few days, the warning signs to look out for, I sat silently in the large armchair I had mostly used to nurse Theodore in. *Okay, brain surgery. People survive brain surgery all the time. How could I have a mass in my brain? I feel pretty normal, except, well, maybe I've been a little extra odd lately. Dr. Deans sounded scared, intimate, like a parent who opens a window of vulnerability to their child out of a desperate need to feel part of a team despite being the only one in the room with any power.* I thought of her pointed shoes and lab coat for the first time of a million to follow.

I guess I have to start telling people.

What do I say?

The moments that followed were a flurry of phone calls and emails, trying to reach family and take care of the kids: my last acts as a primary caregiver for what would be a while. *Help would be on its way soon, all I had to do is ask.*

That night, during the phone calls to friends, I noticed that the right side of my lip had been going numb, along with the right side of my soft and hard palette. I had been feeling some deep laziness in my right eye for some time, as if I could feel it in my ocular nerve, but I thought it was a pre-existing condition I had as a lifelong glasses-wearer. (I also told myself that no one can feel their ocular nerves so I must be crazy, obviously. Turns out that with a tumor pressing on it, you can.)

I would eventually decide to go to the ER, even though I hardly knew how to describe what I was feeling. *But I'm not worried about being neurotic anymore. Something is actually wrong. This is really happening.*

There I saw my results and some positivity for the first time since learning of the news—that it was operable and not likely an aggressive form of cancer. Only part of that sigh of relief actually turned out to be true. The difference that spread between the diagnosis (a mass, operable) and the prognosis (cancer) that would come about a week later is the strength that allowed me to fight. There, on that same field that sprouted strength, I sprawled out and began to write these pages—the sunshine and water to germinate the seeds.

The following night, after the kids had gone to bed and the last of the phone calls were made, I wrote two letters: one to my boys, which I've saved for them someday, and this other one included here. I wrote it to my closest family of friends to ask them for help with holding my love, come what may. Writing this and getting their responses was the beginning of my healing, I see now, so I think it's a good place to start this story.

To: Jeff, Jonas, Gillian, Teddy, Sarah, Sarah Jane, Amy, Sasha and Allison
Bcc: Garth and Robin
From: Caroline
Date: Friday, February 17, 2017
Subject: All my Feelings

To the loves in my life, my clan of "best friends" that are not one person but my blood and air and family—

Jeff, Jonas, Gilly, Teddy, Sarah, Sarah Jane, Amy, Sasha and Allison,

All of you know now about the tumor after we've spoken. I am scared of the unknown, as you might imagine, but I am choosing to nurture the kindest and bravest thoughts that come into my mind about my situation. Part of that is writing you this sort of morbid email, but I hope you know it comes from a place of not leaving anything unsaid before we move forward, rather than worrying about defeat (which I am actually managing to avoid somehow).

I am feeling empowered, oddly, by this state. I cried to most of you last night about hating that I am putting my boys in this place of defining part of their childhoods by something that's happening to me and not them, that I would be bringing weakness and fear into their worlds in a way I don't have any control over. However, because of a really helpful conversation that I will never forget from Jonas in Switzerland as he cared for his two sick kids in the background, he reminded me that this is actually an opportunity to show them my strength and be their superhero, and I intend to do just that. If anyone could make it through this, I know it would be me.

The reason why I know it is because of each of you. You guys have given me the kind of love of and belief in myself because you all have seen me so clearly and supported me, despite distance (or in Sarah's case, never actually living in the same place, ever) and timing and my own life narratives that have seemed to cruise forward before anyone else was ready to join me (marriage, kids, an move to an isolated place). I love each of you so much and am so thankful for you. I hope you have an idea, but now feels like the moment to forget a fear of redundancy. You each hold a really big and valued part of me that no one else knows.

On that note, and this is the sad part, but if for some reason I don't end up with the outcome I am determined to have, I really hope that you guys would step in and show my kids the parts of me that only you see. I need my big, crazy love to be in their lives, even if I am not there in the capacity that I am imagining now. Each of you could pass that along. Care-wise, in terms of them being fed and sheltered and taken to school, I am less worried about (except maybe in the short-term during any acute recovery period); we are very fortunate and they have a lot of people in their lives who are seriously invested in their upbringing in practical terms: Henry has a great school, we have devoted friends here (old and new, very fortunately for us in such a short period), and people are already lining up to bring us food and help with the daily business of having kids.

Anyway, I don't really have anything else to say other than that. I hope it doesn't freak you out that I am writing this to you and I honestly believe I will be fine. I need you to get ready because this sassy bitch is going to get sassier when I get to drop "oh yeah, I had a brain tumor" into conversation about my future broken and mended wishbone tattoo on my arm to match Jeff's and possibly my eventual sheared head with the nose ring I intended to put back in today but didn't because of writing my will. (Right?) Get ready for that shit.

I love each of you so much. Thank you for building me up, through this and every day.

Love always,
Caroline

My loved ones—the forces in my life that make me feel like me, my chosen family—responded with resounding support. The all visited me in the months that followed, helping me march forward on a path that was already written for me that night even though I didn't know it yet. (Protocol, I was eventually told.)

Over the weekend, Garth and I rushed around to find copies of my MRI images and bring them to a new acquaintance, a head of neurosurgery, for a friendly second opinion. At our meeting, he snapped images with his cell phone and texted them to two colleagues who would turn out to be my surgeons only a week later. "A glioma," he insisted, throwing theories of juvenile tumors gone awry to explain my young age and atypical symptoms. Keep smiling, *I thought.* Believe him.

A few days later, I had to tell everyone else, solidify this swirling cloud of emotion into a concrete thing, something with a form, a shape, a name, even though I had none of those things to give. Even though it was going to be cut out of me sooner than I realized then, holding its secret (cancer or simply unwelcome, confused biology?) for another week or so.

To: Garth
Bcc: My list of contacts
From: Caroline
Date: February 19, 2017
Subject: Some News.

Dearest family and friends,

I have some crazy news that I wanted to share with you. Email feels like such an impersonal way to tell someone something like this, but since I found out the news, I have had trouble finding ways to tell people I care about as personally as I would like without feeling exhausted and away from my two little kids by being on the phone constantly. I'm also trying to hold onto any quiet or calm moments that come my way to process stuff myself, as you might imagine after you read what's up. I know, however, that is important to me to have a community surrounding my news and that I will need help and love as I move forward.

I have a 7 cm brain tumor in my frontal lobe. I found out on Friday at dinner, after my MRI that day.

I know you will have questions and some of you may want to know everything I am going through, so I set up a website that both Garth and my Dad will be able to update on my behalf as I approach surgery (this week, though not yet confirmed precisely when or by whom).

This is the link: **www.caringbridge.org/visit/carolinewright**

Thank you for the caring you send my way, even if it is thinking about me now as you read this email.

Xo
Caroline

To: Robin
From: Caroline
Date: February 20, 2017
Subject: nonsense

_____

Hey Robin,

I am also having silly nonsensical worries (that Jeff and I have laughed at) wondering if this tumor and where it is is actually the thing that has made me so emotionally intelligent. Is that possible, do you think? Could my self-awareness that I take such pride in go away after the surgery?

Caroline

To: Caroline
From: Robin
Date: February 20, 2017
Subject: re: nonsense

———————————————

Absolutely not!! Your emotional intelligence is internal and part of the hard wiring of your prefrontal lobes!!!!

Co-director, NIP C&A Program
Associate Editor, Journal of Family Social Work

———————————————————————————————

To: Robin
From: Caroline
Date: February 20, 2017
Subject: re: re: nonsense

———————————————

That's what the sane part of me assumes. But still the idea that the shape of who I know my brain to make me could change freaks me out a little (not too much, I think) right now.

———————————

Caroline
To: Caroline
From: Robin
Date: February 20, 2017
Subject: re: re: re: nonsense

_____

Your doctors will tell you specifics of what to expect post surgery. From what I have read, people are extremely tired for a month or two so you may have to put some projects on the back burner for a bit—that seems to be the biggest post surgery side effect.

Robin

Co-director, NIP C&A Program
Associate Editor, Journal of Family Social Work

To: Caroline
From: Jeff
Date: February 20, 2017
Subject: re: Steroids Suck

Found a new spot in Prospect Park. (It feels like the highest spot in the park, but who actually knows, and the pics don't do any justice.) Prospect Park at sunset has been my altar for atheist prayers and rituals for you. Along with my stove; I make batches of chicken noodle soup and frittata and imagine healing steam floating your way. Thinking of you as always and sending lots of love. Happy to read on your blog that your parents are with you and that you've made a decision about your surgeon. Heading to bed with you in my thoughts.

Xoxox
Jeff

To: Jeff
From: Caroline
Date: February 20, 2017
Subject: re: Steroids Suck

I love you. This and you are beautiful. I like the idea of altar stoves and you there thinking of me. I miss you and am going to be fine. Just got off the phone with my neurosurgeon who said my surgery- exact details to come on Wednesday—will definitely be Friday.

Xo
C

Sent from my iPhone

1 _____ PRE-

SURGERY

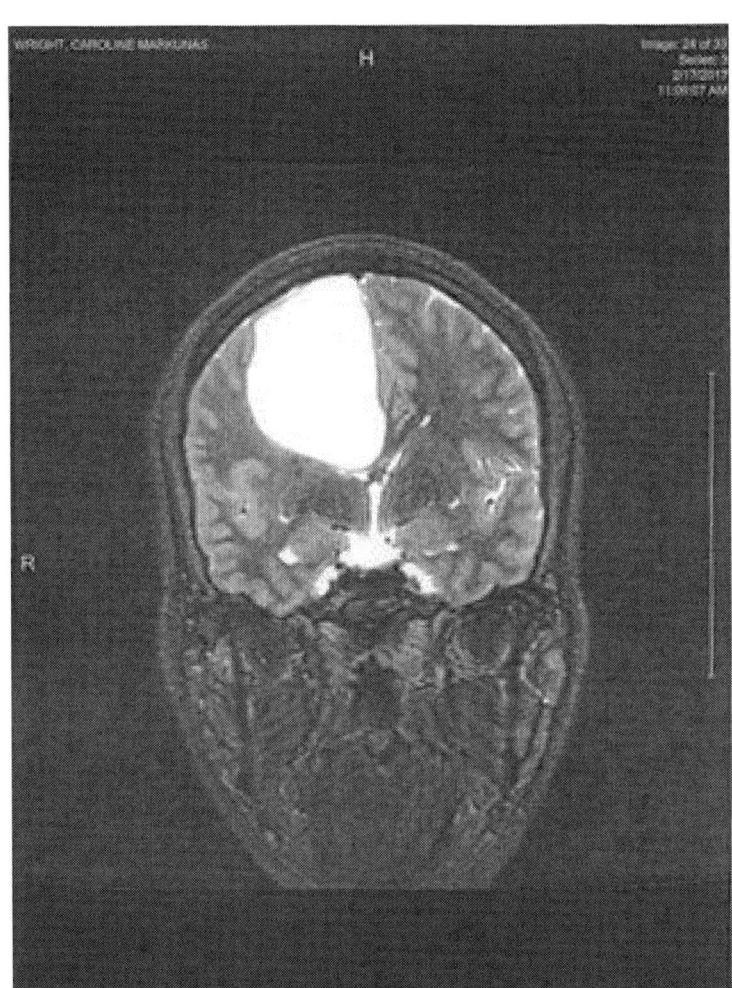

R

FEBRUARY 19, 2017

An Update | Caroline Wright

I just had a very encouraging meeting with the first
neurosurgeon I will see this week—it seems of about possibly
four (a sentence I honestly never thought I'd say!).

Other than my full confidence in this doctor and the
team he wants to put together for me, I can say there are some
weird pieces of information that I am processing:

- He was shocked I hadn't lost motor function because of
  the place it was and how big it is.
- He thought it had been growing for some time, likely
  around a year.
- I mentioned that I had had high blood pressure for over a
  year (they weren't going to let me leave the hospital after
  giving birth to Theodore, actually), and he said that when
  tumors grow, your blood pressure goes up and your pulse
  goes down. I found that fascinating.
- He thinks they won't shave my head, but rather braid my
  hair and slice in between the braids.
- He thinks the two surgeons will put a strip on my motor
  functions and activate my brain to be able to operate
  around any activity that appears, which he assured me is
  the safest practice they have out there now.

· The current timeline that they are discussing—I say "they" because the doctor we met with referred two other senior attendants who only operate on the type of tumor I have (but Garth will post some notes about that shortly since I feel tired), and both want to operate on me, side by side—is meeting them on Wednesday and a surgery on Friday. He said with a smile that he bets I would be home on Monday.

What We Learned Since. | Caroline Wright

I went to the ER on Friday night because of nausea
symptoms. What happened there:

- The ER doc went through the notes from my internist,
  and the notes from the neurologist she consulted to
  review the scans before contacting me (and who my
  appointment is with on Monday), and showed me the
  actual images.
- We learned that it is a very round and clean shape with
  very well-defined borders, which is encouraging in terms
  of its removal and could be an indication that it is slow-
  growing, not intermingling with my brain tissue, and not
  cancerous, which we will confirm with a neurologist.

I started taking a steroid in hopes of decreasing the
inflammation caused by the tumor (also the reason for
my headaches).

A Scary Night. | Caroline Wright

I am here to purge at 3 am in hopes I can drink tea and head back to bed. Last night, a few hours ago, was super scary. I came home from our encouraging doctor's appointment, high on the confidence that the rational part of me still feels (in good care, being monitored, discovering the edges of this and the behavior it's giving me that I didn't realize before), combined with some meds that are making me totally crazy (these strong steroids that are meant to shrink the swelling of the tumor, which can really mess with your thoughts I am learning). I texted the new doctor after I realized I was having a lot of trouble tracking my immediate actions—and called seizure meds into the pharmacy right away. I took my first pill last night.

He reassured me that I am going to be fine and that I will feel so much better when this thing is out.

I called one of my oldest friends and she just let me say all the things I was scared of and told me rational thoughts behind them and reassured me. I was eventually able to quiet down enough to read a book and fall asleep, which is really what I know I need to be doing well right now before my surgery.

Trick is, I've always had a really strong capacity to manage my feelings and fight adversity in really profound ways. Always.

Right now I am faced with a moment that I lack any control of, including my emotions and brain activity, so I am realizing that I may not actually be able to do a good job with that this week. I may have to lean here on this space and on friends to talk me down from times that feel really overwhelming.

I hate that I am feeling scared right now because a huge part of me is just not scared of what's ahead, but really excited to feel better. My parents are coming early this morning (in a few hours) to take over with the kids, which is huge, but I also know they are processing that their beloved daughter has a fucking giant mass in her head and I am afraid I can't take on any of those feelings right now, to protect them, while I am also trying to protect myself from my thoughts.

The other crazy piece of information I found out last night while texting (followed by a call shortly after) with the doctor is not only that these spacey feelings I've been having for some time have likely been seizures, but also that some of the weird things I have going on in my face—my jaw is locking up on the right side and some numbness in my lips and soft palette—could actually be because my tumor is apparently very close to the motor function for my face on the right side. He reiterated that the mapping they are going to do during surgery is very important, which is blowing my mind and giving me a new host of fears about my fucking face.

Anyway, so any support you guys can lend here could artificially help me get through some of these dark moments that I know are ahead (thanks, steroids!), I would really appreciate. Writing always helps me in life, so this space is already proving to be invaluable. Thank you for that.

These early posts are included here unedited, even in their meandering nature, because they are products of how I felt then: manic, swinging from the heights of adventure to the depths of the unknown. They also were written while effected by steroids, which removed any filter I have. My brain actually couldn't shut off. It was truly exhausting, but I was too busy to realize it. Note the volume of the posts—not just their length or content, but also what I felt necessary to have spill out of me. I was unstoppable, overflowing. And very sick.

Henry's Brilliance │ Caroline Wright

My sweet Henry is four years old. He's a very bright, articulate, and emotionally capable boy already. Those of you who know him well can see that clearly right away.

Yesterday at lunch we knew we had a doctor's appointment at 2 pm and that a neighbor friend was bringing her son over to play in our basement together with our boys, so I was trying to prepare Henry for his afternoon.

We told him that I had to go to a doctor who was going to talk to me about my brain tumor. He asked what a brain tumor was—and Garth and I aren't looking to hide anything, but also strike a balance of what we know he could possibly understand right now (which we know is a lot, especially him, though we don't want to push him further than needed)—so we spit out a few phrases about having an unwanted thing in my body that a doctor needed to help figure out how to take out, things like that...

And HENRY (not us, I swear, with zero prompting) said, "so your body is like a garden and you have a weed in it."

WHAT. Eloquent and perfect. Thank you, Henry, as always, for giving us the language to parent you and never ceasing to amaze me.

Thinking about Last Year and Symptoms |
Caroline Wright

I am sitting here feeling so thankful that I have the support structure I have right now, despite my last year being so challenging.

I know many of my loved ones have seen this already, but I want to repost a Facebook message that I wrote on December 2 after turning in my manuscript for the Spanish cookbook I had been working on. I've been thinking about it because the obvious punchline is "...oh yeah, and I had a brain tumor during this, too, that made me feel disoriented and crazy":

(Posted on Facebook on December 2 after my December 1 deadline)

Last night I turned in the manuscript for my most recent project. I took a shower and went to bed at 7:30 pm while all my friends texted me champagne bottle emoticons. It was physically the heaviest document I've ever written in my life thus far, including being an honors comparative literature major in college and having written two previous nationally published books.

*I woke up almost 12 hours later feeling such joy that I am using
this space to express it. I cannot possibly explain the garbage
year (of still such incredible privileges, I realize) I've had—and
I don't want to change the subject, so I don't want to dwell on it
here too much, but the highlights may suffice merely for context: I
moved a new city with a 2-week-old baby and his vulnerable and
suffering 3-year- old brother, bought and renovated a 1906 house
in Seattle (every word of that is a massive challenge), was already
on deadline for the most challenging project of my career that
involved international travel and collaboration between multiple
time zones (I think 5 time zones is factual for just the key players),
went on tour for my second book which came out somewhere in
the middle of this mess, on top of just a terrible year in the world
(to quote John Oliver, "fuck 2016"). It was hard, and I am not
someone who says that out loud that much.*

*I have turned in my project feeling incredibly excited about its
possibility, knowing how good the pages are going to feel in my
hands when it finally comes out. (Not just because it's my third
book and I always genuinely feel that way, but also because
This. Book. It is going to be something wonderful, I just feel it,
as I have since the beginning to merit all of this hard work.)*

*So, this is all to say, waking up right now in my house that is
almost—almost!—done and makes me smile for the most part, to
my two loving little boys, the older of whom screamed "Yay, we*

get Mommy back!" last night just after I emailed my manuscript to my editor and agent and we cranked up a dance party in the kitchen as I hopped around with my truly wonderful husband, and that this clarity and joy is aligning with the start of December, when visits from my loving family and cards from people I miss deeply from around the country and world will be sent to my house and delicious food and memories will get crammed in to my body, is just too much to hold in.

I swear, if a person could actually explode from joy, thankfulness and excitement, this moment would be mine. I feel like George Bailey. (And what a fun, socially appropriate moment to feel like George Bailey!)

Also, how life can be all these wonderful things and how it still is also so daily, that I will still have to change diapers today and probably get a call from my contractor who is has attempted for the third time to fix our basement leak this week by jackhammering out part of our recently finished basement. And that there is still so much more work ahead to do, socially and politically (and certainly creatively).

It's really fun to be a human today.

Anyway, I know that there is a good chunk of you following here who I have taken with me wherever I've gone in life.

These connections are solid as anything I know in my world, like the air that fills my lungs. I know, however, too that a lot of you are new friends and neighbors looking to find ways to bring me food and take care of my kids and do the things I don't feel sane enough to do in my daily life, little glimmers of kindness and comfort. Both of those presences feel so important right now, and I am deeply thankful for both.

To the new ones, thank you for taking on the friendship of a very vulnerable and weird person last year. That I can have a brain tumor and feel comforted and loved after moving to a new place with a new baby and living through some crazy isolating shit is really huge.

Parents' Arrival | Paul Markunas

We are here (Paul and Glad) after a week-long vacation to Maui cut short by six days. Ironically, we had a connecting flight in Seattle from Orlando and spoke with Caroline on the phone as she was heading in to her MRI; by the time we arrived in Maui, I had an urgent message to call her and found out about the tumor.

Change of plans. We spent our first night of two in Maui on the phone with her East Coast friends crying, explaining and worrying and trying to get the next available seats out on Delta. We got out on the redeye back to Seattle and arrived at 5 am this morning.

Now that we're here, things will be easier for all of us. The grandchildren are happy to have us back and we can be a big help there and keeping the house and meals organized.

Caroline seems fine on the outside, save for small noticeable symptoms such as fatigue, dizziness and irritability (not sure if that's a symptom!) but it is a real relief for her and for Garth to have us here.

They have finalized their decision on her surgeon this morning and will be proceeding with pre-operative consultations on Wednesday and surgery most likely on Friday. I will post when Garth or Caroline cannot.

Second Opinions | Garth Wright

Today we went to a different neurosurgeon for a second opinion. He very quickly convinced us - to go with the first doctor we met with! Not only did he fail to note our appointment (even though we had a piece of paper telling us when and where), his staff giggled as they told us his office was closed and he had no appointment slots to reschedule in.

Frustrating.

But the day got better when the first doctor called Caroline as he left the hospital, following an 8 hour surgery, to check in and give us some more information about our week's schedule. We will have an initial meeting on Wednesday with "the glioma guy" and then surgery will be Friday morning. If everything goes according to plan, he said, Caroline would get to go home Monday night.

I'll update on Wednesday with any further discoveries.

Kindnesses (Or Luck/Privileges) So Far
Caroline Wright

So Theodore woke up just now at 12:30 and it has been hard lately to get back to sleep when a thought wakes me up. That's true when I have a creative outlet in general like this one, but I also I assume that the heavy medication that I'm on makes it harder.

I have been thinking about the abundant kindnesses that have been shown to me since my news and I want to share the kinds of energy I have in my life right now, both so I can remember later but also so I can show my loved ones the kinds of incredible thought that has flooded my way since my news on Friday:

- Little things, like...Because of a tip that Garth read about brain surgery healing, I put a search out on a "Buy Nothing" Facebook group that I have come to love deeply since living in Seattle for old pillowcases. It has actually been a place for community that has represented a lot of the feelings of sharing and love that I have felt for this city and my community on a larger scale, almost immediately after moving here, and this is one little practical example has made a difference to me. We have dozens of pillowcases now to use and even discard after use if necessary. Someone even threw in a wedge pillow for my time in bed that may help me read!

- Best friends from cities I have lived in like Paris and New York have offered to send me LaDuree macarons, pizza and bagels. This is not an empty offer to me and something I would really look forward to during recovery, even if they arrive in the form of very tasty crumbs. My friends get me...and my stomach!

- My closest friend here in Seattle took me for a walk around Green Lake and just literally let me talk at her for a whole hour because the one-and-one conversations I am capable of having (she and my mom were the recipients of this yesterday) right now end up being a verbal dump of the information I am wading through and thinking about, quite literally without much pause for breath. I appreciate the veil of understanding they have shown me, despite what I'm sure is physical exhaustion on the part of my mom who traveled overnight to see me from Hawaii and my new, fierce friend who has other shit to do than listen to me talk in circles and drift and lean softly into her as I walk off-balance. She brought me magazines that I could flip through when feeling wired, that I will turn to after getting these thoughts out of my body.

- Tea. I am not much of a tea-drinker but I have enjoyed it a lot since Friday, because it seems like something that people do to relax while also hydrate (and avoid wine, which I can't drink on these pills!).

· Cookies. My silly chocolate chip cookies that so many of you have eaten throughout our friendships (old and new, they are my "party trick" and sign that I am feeling adjusted if I have dough stocked in my freezer), I made for my brain surgeon. He credited me as giving him the fuel to get through another brain surgery yesterday (something that isn't meaningless to me right now for someone else) and told me how talented I am as a baker, both things that have nothing to do with my state other than the fact that it brings the normal version of myself a lot of joy over the ten years I have been working on that recipe and share that with someone who has a significant role in my life.

· Phone calls. Yesterday I spoke on the phone with one of my very best friends in New York, Teddy, because he is an epileptic who has the exact kind of absent seizures I had been having and he offered me tips on how to avoid them; a high school friend who has turned out to be a highly ranked dermatologist and all around level-headed and amazing mom called me just to talk about the kind of care I was finding. Friends have been calling and leaving messages while I've been reading to my boys or just sitting quietly and prefer not to talk. These things feel significant to me right now, even if I pass the calls to voicemail and don't call back. I joked about it with both of them but I really feel like my life has brought me a sort of crack squad of people I love who are uniquely suited to help me with aspects of my coping right now, but I really do feel the comfort of that statement.

· Henry's School. We were very lucky upon moving here to be recommended to a school that literally embodies any hopes I could have had for my kids in terms of their pre-schooling—a loving, open, play-based space run by like-minded people. I came to Seattle from Dallas, where kids don't really go to preschool but rather wait for kindergarten and even then it all felt like more of a status symbol or unloading of your kids to give you free time rather than putting their needs or personalities first. The smiles and love for my son that I felt immediately last year upon putting him in school meant a lot to me as I was wading through so many feelings about being new to a city and managing all that I had going on. It was not empty to me then, nor is it empty to me now. So many of you parents who I don't even know yet really at Henry's preschool are reading here just because you want to support me and find a way to take away a small need, even with just words. That is also not empty to me. His school took care of my family when I was overwhelmed (and, now, I realize, definitely managing symptoms of my growing tumor). This support came in the forms of being greeted with hugs by teachers who swept Henry up in whatever state he arrived at school to take over the deficits of whatever I couldn't manage that morning (clothes, gloves, forgetting lunches and emotions, among them) without judgment.

- My husband. Of course there is an expectation and an understanding that is implied here, but you guys don't know my husband. He, obviously, was the first person to know about the tumor and the first person to process my (significant, overwhelming, scary) emotions in their most raw state. He translated it all into oddly comforting terms, being a lawyer and a very smart person, and things that have felt like differences since our meeting at age nineteen have fallen away into feeling like truly perfect strengths for this situation. I couldn't be more thankful to have him by my side, even in the middle of the night like tonight when he begrudgingly wakes up when I want to talk for a few minutes. He is grace, kindness, love and calm personified. I have been reminded now how incredibly lucky I am to have chosen him decades ago not knowing that this could be part of our story.
- My parents. My parents are wonderful people, a fact I consider often, because in no way could I have survived last year without their help. (Symptoms aside—I mean just logistically, really, with all that I took on which was my own stupidity and lack of judgment of not knowing what

having a second kid would be like, let alone the *complete* lack of understanding of the idea of relaxation or self care. The latter deficit I credit to my youth, blind optimism or craziness depending on the day. Their help was especially necessary in the face of the logistical turmoil of moving to a new city and working on the most challenging book project of my career so far that necessarily required a lot of travel and care of my kids to make it happen, while also being on book tour for my second book.) Oh and renovating our house, too, of which my very eager dad is literally a master (and carefully watched from the sidelines, thankfully, to allow me to create my own vision for a home I loved very much and saw for the lifetime of my family and still do!). Like yesterday, for example, he knows that we have a second leak in the past few months in our newly refinished basement and he climbed up on a ladder in the rain in a fucking cashmere sweater and cleaned out our gutters, hoping that would prove helpful. These are the kind of parents I have, who love me with all of their especially generous hearts. This is not something I take for granted, even if it seems like I might because I can't possibly catalogue all of the wonderful things they do for me and my kids (who they love beyond measure) on a regular basis without my asking.

· My doctor connection, which I feel like I have already referenced separately, but I think about this stroke of luck almost every minute because *who is one phone call away from the best doctors in town based on a personal favor after just moving to a new city just over a year ago. Why does that person get to be me right now?* Especially in the face of the fact that the doctor, who I was supposed to see just yesterday and was recommended by my diagnosing internist, didn't show up to our appointment and is involved in some major neurosurgical-specific drama at Swedish Cherry Hill (Garth won't even let me Google that shit).

So this is all to say that I am really in a good place right now. The kindnesses that are finding their way to me are holding me in a thick blanket and making me feel very safe and positive. I am soaking up everything with gratitude and deep appreciation for the fact that no one, especially here in a new city, owes me any of this. Including my very own brain and the perspective it is helping me nurture.

ASMR | Caroline Wright

One of the amazing qualities I feel I am equipped with today, my profound network of love, I attribute in great deal to my amazing husband who I met at the age of nineteen. We are very markedly different, we joke as different as we can get.

However, because we met so young I have this theory that it left time for me to get to know myself and other important people in my life because I already had "the boyfriend" part figured out. This, combined with his lack of feeling threatened by my friends and need for other sources of love in the way of getting to know myself better, is the reason I have a very loyal tribe that I often allude to here and is seen in the emails I answer and texts to my phone. People who are taking pictures of the views they see at the most beautiful parts of Prospect Park in Brooklyn at sunset and ritualistically making my recipes as a form of a healing altar, wafting steam in my direction. Making my cookies with their children that I love. For those of you who know me well, you know that these people are my everything, almost as much as Garth himself or my kids.

So, back to ASMR. I had been telling one of my best friends from New York that I am having trouble sleeping, Dan, and he emailed me a bunch of weird links that I remember only from hearing Ira Glass talk about it on This

American Life in a very interesting episode. A few things come to mind alongside his recommendation, as well as King Ira's implicit one:

- Even thinking of this makes me remember talking about this episode in my Park Slope kitchen, while cooking dinner for my closest friends and it reminds me of them coming up to me and giving me hugs as I chopped and talked about This American Life. Those are easily some of the happiest memories I've ever had and I cling to them daily. They are the well from which I write my books, then and still.
- I remember volunteering in the local Winter Park library as a fourth grader or so and that I loved the sound of the thud and crinkle of the plastic-coated books turning over as they were being checked out. (ASMR is exactly that— people who find certain sounds relaxing and interesting.) My older son, Henry, I know also possibly senses some of this stuff because he talks about noises in a way I thought about as a kid. Acknowledging that this weird, possibly slightly fetishized, mode of relaxation could hug that little girl inside my brain made me feel nice, too.

So, back to ASMR (again, sorry): This shit was brilliant. I had spent a few hours writing here and then wanted to get back to sleep if I could and I thought that the magazines and reading

I had lined up would actually be more stimulating than relaxing. Hypnotizing apps that people have sent my way seem like they could be helpful, even though not exactly my style, and still required me to find and download something at 3 or so in the morning. So I turned to my dear friend Dan's recommendation—I found a pair of headphones and turned off all of the lights. I clicked a YouTube link, feeling slightly pervy, but decided to lean into it.

The first video that I will include here was completely transformative. I feel like I am almost quoting Ira's piece now as I attempt to describe it (or warn you, or defend myself) when I say that there is definitely something odd about it. (But I am in a place to try odd right now if it works and I trust Dan with my soul.) It is at once kind of "porny," which I definitely feel like Ira said (and I definitely had to reduce the brightness on my screen so I couldn't see someone talking to me), but it is also so intimate and caring and relaxing. It completely transported me and—no shit—*actually made me feel like my brain tumor was shrinking* with how relaxed I was getting, which I haven't felt since I found out.

It's totally wild and I'm positive is not for everyone. But it really helped me and made me so happy, once again, that I have friends who love me so much who I can trust with feeling vulnerable and weird. I will absolutely return to the collection of videos that he sent if this pattern of late nights/ writing at screens persist. And I do implore anyone reading here who might struggle with relaxation and may have some little "brain tickling" thing (like my best friend Jeff would say) with noises to give it a try.

I wonder if my tumor actually shrunk last night. Thanks, Dan, I love you forever. As I was sitting in the darkness with these weird sounds tracing the border of my skull with headphones in and my eyes closed, tears of gratitude were squeezing out from the closed lids of my eyes for this and Dan.

My Beliefs Right Now | Caroline Wright

When you are diagnosed with a brain tumor, a lot of big questions come to mind. Mostly, so far, this tumor has seemed to continue the kind of thinking I have already set up in my life up until now. I feel compelled to share some of this with you here.

One of the things I've been thinking about a lot is religion. It's just something that I know people lean on in crisis and a natural (understandable) lens through which comments are filtered in terms of well wishes. To be perfectly plain, that behavior or language doesn't make me uncomfortable. What other people believe is a beautiful thing and it makes them say and do kind things for others. I have no issue with that. My belief structure isn't in something divine. It is in something concrete—all of *you*. All of us. This. Writing about humanity, giving and sending hugs and love and meaning it. That has been my lifelong belief and that is how I have built the love in my life that I have, something I am thinking about every second of every day since Friday.

I am an atheist and have been my whole life. That might make some of you in my family and outer friend circle uncomfortable—and I promise, I'm not trying to, I'm just trying to be honest with myself and my thoughts. I wasn't particularly raised with religion (sorry to my grandfather and the people who loved him and the idea that we were somehow church-going), despite having some religious historical background in my family.

In fact, I have always been drawn to the rituals of religion because of the social component. I grew up with many Jewish friends and loved their Passover traditions (probably the food and sickly sweet wine and the family and the hunt for the *afikomen*). I went to Bible Study with my childhood best friend Sarah Jane because it was the only time she wasn't too busy with school. I was a dork who liked hanging out with people who liked to watch movies rather than make out with boys who were kind of mean (and boys didn't seem to want to make out with girls who had feelings or things to say like I did, anyway).

I have been thinking about all of this because this is actually a big reason why I think I am so strong right now. It isn't fake, my calm and joy, and that is something I need all of you following here to know. I am truly inspired by the kindnesses that are in my life because, for me, that is what some people may see as God, even if I don't. I am feeling that, whatever *that* is, every minute. It comes from me and from my friends and from you. Small things as much as the big things. Notes here on this site, texts and emails I may not respond to. Missed phone calls. Jokes sent to me by friends trying to make me laugh. They are all in my skin and I am taking them with me every step.

Thank you for showing me a new level of my own beliefs. I am truly thankful.

Family | Caroline Wright

Family is something I think about a lot. I am a mom, as you all know, and I come from a mixed group of people in my life (as so many of us do). I have struggled with people I am related to and fallen deeply in love with people I am not related to, who give me my "blood."

I don't hide it, but I have an estranged brother with whom I was very close to growing up, which has been a highly contested subject within my family for many years. I get his reasons for needing space and I don't begrudge him of his process to finding happiness. I mean that. I contacted him (and ferried messages to him through people who do speak to him) about my brain tumor and it makes me sad that, even now faced with this challenge, we won't be able to consider a narrative that could give either of us any comfort or resolution. That is actually okay with me because I get it.

My family is comprised of a select group of my friends who have found me throughout my life, buried themselves deep in my skin and my meaning. Soul mates. I have way more than my share and I am epically grateful for them all the time. They have shown me who I am and are reminding me throughout each day. They are my bravery and my love and I am holding it in me like the light that it is.

So, the idea of my brother not being in my life right now and missing this (which feels like a point of no return, not just in terms of something mortal but in terms of something like a plot point that can't be caught up in a few sentences... clearly!), feels calming in its way. I have my brothers and sisters. They know who they are and why. They are the family to my children. Come what may, even though I *really* am not feeling worried about that now. Knowing this just gives me the peace and comfort to look forward to brain surgery and not be scared.

Caroline's Doctors | Garth Wright

We are going to meet Caroline's neurosurgeons tomorrow morning. She is lucky enough to have been slotted in this week—the usual wait is 20 days!

So far in Seattle, Caroline has found a urologist and internist that she likes; both are competent and direct with her. When her internist called us Saturday afternoon, she had found us an experienced neurosurgeon so we could get answers as soon as possible. Although her referral didn't work out, she has followed up every step of the way with Caroline. She has only good things to say about the UW neurology clinic and says Caroline will get "amazing care" there.

I will give another update tomorrow breaking down what we've learned and what the game plan is for Friday.

I Slept! And Then Thought... | Caroline Wright

I slept for a few hours! Then woke up needing to pee and, in
a shocking bit of normalcy that is actually very comforting,
my writer's mind began to turn phrases. When I get to this
point of phrasing, I have to get out of bed and write as the
only solution. This is true of non brain-tumor me. It's a curse
I have with my books and all the stages that lead up to them
(their proposals, the brainstorming even before proposals).
I find it very hard to shut off regularly, and find it actually
impossibly so now on these steroids. What got me out of bed
this time are two thoughts of things that are working for me
right now:

- I went to bed with an essential oil diffuser burbling
  lavender oil in my face. I got into essential oils with my
  best friend in Dallas; lavender oil has ferried me through
  other periods of (usually creative) insomnia. Even
  reaching for an essential oil and diffuser reminds me of
  someone I love dearly and who I know is hurting terribly
  right now because of what I'm going through. It got me
  thinking about how isolated I am right now (I'm avoiding
  the phone, not wanting to re-tell stories right now to
  keep seizures at bay) but still manage to have these little

presences in my life that remind me of people that I know want me to feel loved right now, like my beautiful Sasha in Dallas, who I sat, partly ironically but evidently somewhat earnestly, in a stranger's living room and participated in an essential oil trunk show of sorts. Even that memory brings me joy and a smile.

- Writing here. I had a kind of emotional hangover yesterday that was making me feel guilty for sharing such huge ideas in such a beloved yet weird space on this website, wondering if I am doing the thing where my brassy and unapologetic nature can get in the way of kindnesses and connection on the part of the person I'm speaking to. It's not a quality I'm proud of and it's one I've tried to round out as I've gotten older at the encouragement of my softer, smarter husband. (But then the mouthy girl chimes in, "fuck, you have a brain tumor, when can you let it hang out if not now?" I love her, too.)

So, these ideas—thinking about even the books I read to the kids before bed and the essential oil diffuser and the next video of Dan's I am looking forward to trying after signing off here, and even the construct of writing itself—are conjuring an image of messages in a bottle. I have long since been confident in my gift to allow people to affect me deeply and change me (something that was kind of funny when I was little and even not-so-little, and has led me to get my heart broken many times), to let people show me their stories and really envelop them in my nature with gratitude, and have always known that this is a huge part of my personality. My Henry is the same and it makes me worry about him and be happy for him at the same time.

This exact quality, however, is making me feel like the ways that I have let people touch and see me are like messages in a bottle right now, sending me little tokens to wash me across a sea of uncertainty and what could otherwise be fear. Garth tells me that it is repayment in some way to some investment that I've made, and while those aren't the terms I use, I see the thought in that. I feel like these tokens of parts of my beloved life are carrying me across this unknown sea, truly like messages in a bottle, and bringing me to a safe place.

This is to say that if you love me and are sending that my way, I feel it, even now. Thank you for being a part of that. None of it is small or lost on me.

Pre-Op Appointments | Garth Wright

Today was a big day. Caroline had 3 pre-operation appointments: neurosurgeons, anesthesiologists, and blood draw.

At the first appointment we met the two attending neurosurgeons—Dr. Ko and Dr. Silbergeld. These doctors were kind, thorough, and direct with us. It was a reality-based conversation in which we learned (in no particular order):

- They are going to cut a large piece of bone out of her head to get to the tumor, then put the bone back into place with a titanium plate
- She will need to shave all or a portion of her head so the large incision can be made
- The surgery will not be "curative." That means that some part of the tumor will be left in the brain, simply because they can't keep cutting and cutting to get a margin around the tumor
- In surgery, they will use ultrasound, the MRI taken the morning of the surgery, and their eyes (using magnifiers) to look at the tumor
- The surgery should last for approximately 4 hours, with an update every hour from a nurse

- Because the area of the tumor (and cutting) is in Caroline's sensory and facial movement area, they are going to use electrodes to map the functions of the brain in real-time and (hopefully) avoid removing anything important
- There is a common syndrome called Supplementary Motor Area Syndrome that occurs after an operation in which there is no volitional movement of the opposite side. So, because Caroline is having surgery on her right side, this will affect her left side. A patient affected by this cannot initiate movement on that side, and usually moves the functions to the other side. The recovery can take anywhere from 1 hour post-op to 4 weeks, though a usual recovery window is 1-2 weeks. As long as Caroline is affected by this, she will remain at the hospital. It's only once she has recovered from this syndrome that her strength and motor skills can be tested against anything that might have happened in surgery.
- If all goes according to plan, she will be in ICU for 1 day, then a regular floor room until she goes home Tuesday.
- Once the tumor is out, it will be sent to pathology. The turnaround time is 7-10 days until she will know what her next steps for treatment are.
- Even if there is no cancer diagnosis, she will be consistently monitored for the rest of her life.

The other two meetings were straightforward. We are supposed to report to the hospital at 5am Friday morning for pre-op meetings with her anesthesiologist and the surgery team. She will be going into surgery sometime between 8:45 am and 10 am.

My Mom | Caroline Wright

Today was a hard day. I see now since I went to bed at around 8:30 pm that Garth has written about it like I had asked him to and I am very grateful for that. Reality is something I am having a hard time with grasping right now.

On that subject, I had been wanting to write a post about my mom all day but my time became filled with managing a lot of other feelings and I never found the quiet.

My mom and I haven't really been close throughout my life. My dad tends to get a lot of emotional credit because he takes that space naturally and we are more outwardly similar. (Loud, controlling, demanding, defended and insecure, among all the beautiful things I love about myself.) He is one of my favorite subjects and can be (and often is) quickly described as a "force" by anyone who meets him. He raised my brother and I, you see, while my mom worked really hard to provide the privileges that I have come to understand as an adult. My dad, in his way, was the basis for the bleeding heart, open person that you have been reading about here —he showed me from the time I was a little kid that this kind of honesty and truth is the only real currency in this world, sort of how I realize I do with Henry in my way. He is fierce and kind and I could say a million things about him that stem from deep, profound love and gratitude from the very fibers of my core. My mom isn't really like that—it doesn't make her bad or unfitting, it just makes her terms and vocabulary fall outside of the language that I was taught to speak from a young age. It didn't make growing up easy with these push and pull forces in my house or the intentional (or unintentional) allegiances to the open flames of love and language. I think it is a true statement that she and I are very different moms to our children in many ways.

I have so enjoyed as an adult the spaces where I have seen and loved my mom for who she is. It makes me feel like a real grown up and the little girl in me gets a less confused each time. One of those times was today. I am also realizing that there is some thinking that people choose their fathers in their partners when marrying, and I've chosen my mother. Loving and seeing Garth in this new, profound way since my diagnosis has made me see this about my mom and I send even more love and thankfulness to their (somewhat shared) spaces. I wouldn't be able to do this without either of them, nor would I want to in my scariest nightmare, and that is a very important thing to acknowledge to myself right now knowing some of the complicated feelings of my past.

Mom, I know you're reading this and my writing this would make you very uncomfortable. But I need to write it and I hope you understand, which I undoubtedly know you do after today even if it is weird for you to experience.

I was looking forward to your joining me in the hospital

room today to meet the doctors. To bring your note pad and have a sense of purpose and use your brilliance in a way that might clear some of this muck for me. To let Garth maybe be as present as he can be as my partner because you would be there thinking similar thoughts essentially on his behalf.

Instead, you were scared and silent. Stunned. Watching your (now somewhat only) child get a less-than-rosy rundown of the process without frills or even much hope to cling on to. Seeing your feelings scared me and made me sad and it took a heavy afternoon for me to process that.

The things my mom has done consistently since being in town that have really struck me as deep, healing kindnesses: picked up laundry off the floor, done a steady supply of dishes, read every journal entry here with empathy (including the weird video ones!), given me an endless flow of mugs of tea and glasses of water, reminded me to take my pills, held my squirmy little boys she also loves with her whole self, called me beautiful after I shaved my head (more on that in a minute).

Thank you, Mom. The parts of me that I am clinging to now in comfort are combinations of you and Dad—practical, logical elements that are processed with bottomless feeling. I love you very much, see you very clearly now, and am very grateful for this opportunity to do so. Feeling this way gives me hope that this circumstance has a greater purpose in my life and actually helps to make me feel lucky. Thank you from the bottom of my scared soul and thank you for being so strong.

My Hair │ Caroline Wright

Today at the meeting with the two neurosurgeons that was diligently outlined by Garth (thank you again, my love), I was told that the idea that my hair could be braided and the incision could be made between the braids was not, in fact, going to be true. I dwelled on it as the timeline washed over me, imagining exactly what I would do. It had been suggested to me by the well-meaning nurse practitioner to shave to the right of my hair part and keep the second side as a sort of comb over. The idea of a stylish hat or scarf was offered up as some sort of consolation sounded tinny as it kicked around in my head.

As the weird and depressing meeting came to a close and I began to process feelings of being scared for the first time since my processing of all of this really started, I turned in on myself with the kind of arched brow I usually save for idiots in traffic or those who use bronzer: *It's only hair. Let's not make this a thing.*

In the back of my mind I was thinking, okay, if this could be cancer (something I genuinely am still trying to push out of my mind as a low variable), will I want to deal with losing my hair later and re-negotiating my appearance with my kids after it has become clear I didn't have a choice in the matter and it was made by the progress of my health? And will I want to actually come up with hairstyles that involve a sad comb-over? (For those of you who know me well, I am lazy and unskilled when it comes to my appearance and even the idea of femme-ing up this look with lipstick feels foreign to me, though a trade-off I think I could manage only in exchange for no hair.) And is there a way I could use this decision to bring some control to my day and Henry's narrative of this process?

My first reaction was to pull out the clippers and set up in our then briefly sunny backyard and have Henry shear off a few ponytails. Garth agreed that he would shave his head, too, in solidarity and, if he was interested, allow Henry to join in the tribe of cueball Wrights if he chose to. It felt fun and normalizing in a way. Then when I told my dad right after returning home from the doctor's appointment, he brought up the very astute fact (something which my mom was trying to the whole time, but I kept pushing it off assuming she just didn't want me to shave my head for her own reasons) that it was passing Henry maybe more involvement than he could process right now.

Instead, I called my regular hair stylist (a badass and kind woman, a native Seattleite whose stories of 90s Seattle and her dating life of mostly construction workers and indie bandmates I cling to as a boring mom) and made an appointment for about twenty minutes later. I also called my best friend here, Adair, a professional photographer goddess and asked her to grab her camera. Garth and I hatched a plan to pick Henry up from preschool a few hours early and take him to the salon.

It was actually kind of perfect. I beelined it to Jamie when I first walked in the store, grabbed her by the shoulders, and said something like this, "Listen, Jamie, I have a brain tumor and I need to shave off all of my hair. Can you do that?"

She held me close and tears filled her eyes. "I would be honored. Let's do this. Henry, grab that step stool over there and ask Lisa for her clippers. Can you help me shave Mommy's head?"

It was an unexpected moment of grace and control in an otherwise hard and strange day. And I got to shave my head, which I honestly never thought I would be brave enough to do as a person who, despite being super lazy and rebellious and a mom, is also someone who weirdly has to be on TV and in front of strangers for parts of her professional life as some image of a woman who makes cakes in your neighbor's kitchen.

Adair snapped photos as Henry gleefully ran the clippers under each of my 5 or 6 small ponytails; Jamie caught them as they fell. It was a blend of fun and weird for him, I could tell, but he kept saying that he was going to make my hair the shortest it could be, shorter than his. I kept asking him for tips on how to be still and wear my hair that short, since Mommies don't usually know how. We briefly went for ice cream afterward at Jamie's suggestion to a soda fountain spot nearby and we joked about having opposite day, like Henry and I do sometimes when Garth is on a business trip.

There are a few unexpected thoughts that have come into my mind without the protection of hair:

- I weirdly feel kind of beautiful. And empowered again. I see my features on my face (not like I think about them ever) differently. I look more like my brother and that's okay with me right now.
- Garth has promised that he will never take it lightly again when I jokingly complain of his Saturday morning stubble on my face. It's a real thing.
- Having no hair in February in Seattle is kind of cold. It also feels more like sandpaper than I was expecting. And I have a rounder head than I worried I might.

February 23, 2017, 8:45 am
Text from Sarah Andrews to Caroline

SARAH:

Man your posts really got to me this morning, sweet friend. I know how deeply some of that stuff with your mom flows and it just made me really emotional—it was beautiful. I also took a second between tears and laughed at the part where you said she would be very uncomfortable lol

Then I don't know why but I lost it at the part when you walked up to your hair dresser. I'm not telling you this to upset you—just want to let you know that I'm processing with you, crying with you, laughing with you and finding such thankfulness in the new friends who are close and who surround you in the real, real ways that the rest of us want to be.

Things that Are Important (and Not) | Caroline Wright

I have been thinking a lot about what is important to me right now and, conversely, what is not. I wanted to write this down so that future, hopefully healthier me, can hold tight to this space that I wonder may be only tied to the clarity of standing at the edge of this abyss. I hope not because I am finding it very beautiful.

Things That Are Important To Me Right Now:
- Love
- Connection
- Friends
- Writing
- Family
- Breathing
- Listening to My Body
- Small Pleasures
- Today

Things That Are Not Important to Me Right Now
(In No Particular Order):
- Semantics (both metaphorical and linguistic)
- Awkwardness
- Personal Drama
- Food (weird for me to say, I know! The good stuff, the stuff I really love like one of my cookies that I have been baking for my neurologists or a treat brought to me by someone with good flavor and craftsmanship, falls under the "Small Pleasures" thing, I think, more than this here. I mean food right now is more about biological function than I have really ever experienced before and mostly a vehicle for taking insane amounts of drugs and giving me strength to fend off symptoms)
- Politics (I mean, I literally just can't...)
- The Past

I really do feel like I am being given a gift to continue to write and process the beauty of my world in the way that I honestly do in my regular life. These lists are an attempt to hold on to this feeling for as long as I can in the future.

Help. | Caroline Wright

The topic of help is coming up a lot through emails and texts
from a wide stretch of people so I thought I would write
about it here for a second.

All I can say with confidence is that I *know* I will need
help as a likely somewhat incapacitated mom of two little
kids, I just don't know exactly the parameters of that help just
yet because of recovery and the other unknowns right now.

To combat the actual practicality of logistics and to
appreciate and channel this help, I have appointed one of my
dearest and most beloved life-long friends, Allison.

To give you a bit of background about Al, she is the wife
of my high school acting teacher who lives in Shoreline and
gave me those books for Henry and some amazing thoughtful
gifts the other day. She is also the woman who talked me
down from what I think might have been a seizure—*see* "A
Scary Night"—because she is so practical and honest and has
known me since I was, I think, twelve and they since they
were around 26. She and my old acting teacher at my middle
and high school in Winter Park, Florida, her husband Tom
(who is now Garth's closest friend here, an unexpected twist
to the twelve year old me that lives chubbily somewhere
inside my body), were huge parts of my childhood, young

adulthood, marriage, children and now life as a Seattleite. They are unparalleled in most any respect I can explain here and occupy a huge part of my soul. They are both brilliant and have often since given me the model for which I have chosen my wonderful, creative and smart friends throughout my life, of which I—again—have more than one person's lifetime allotment. Their children are people I love deeply, too, which is wild since I babysat the both of them from the time they were infants. We have oddly lived in Orlando, Dallas and Seattle together and I always joke that they warmed up the cities before our arrivals.

Among some of Al's unassuming superhero qualities is that she is incredibly organized and type A, unlike literally anyone else I've known in my life. I've invited her to be an author here and she wants to take over the logistical aspects of this space. There is no better shepherd than her, I can assure you, and I will make it known how we can gratefully and gladly accept help from our beautiful community here in Seattle as I figure out the scope and timing of my needs.

This is not to stand in the way, however, of my deep gratitude for all the messages and individual offers of ideas to help that I have been getting. I am taking those messages as the little flickers of candle light that is lighting my way when times get dim. Thank you.

February 23, 2017, 8:50 am
Text from Sasha to Caroline

SASHA:

So I know it was a really quick moment when you were here and we started singing "I go on walking / In the middle of the night." But since then I've thought how funny it was and how I wish it had gone on longer. So today I took E and Jack to the doctor for ear infections and at CVS getting the prescription while I was walking around sad about the ridiculousness of what you are going through, that song came on. I'm taking it as a good sign.

CAROLINE:

Thank you. I am too.

SASHA:

Thinking of you and how much joy you have brought to my life. Hope you can sleep some tonight. Love you so much and I know it will go well.

An Apology to my Body | Caroline Wright

So I actually meant to write this yesterday but decided to take another lap around Green Lake in the sun with sweet Adair and her floppy dog Earl instead with the rays bouncing off of my dewy, bald head. I have been thinking about it and will share my thoughts here so I can hopefully get back to bed (and maybe listen to my last tumor-shrinking embarrassing video) as fast as I can. I have a tumor's butt to kick in a few hours and would like another wash of lavender and a cuddle with Garth before I get up and take another weird shower, so let me get on with it.

I hate that I've spent so many years being so mean to my body out of insecurity and also possibly out of being a woman. Saying mean things about it in my head, letting other people say mean things about it, feeling justified in letting boys or mean girls in my younger and weaker life joke about it and get away with it. I really hate that I've done that to myself and I am going to do everything I can on the other side of this to change that narrative.

After all, my body grew and carried my two beautiful boys to me. (Without pain medication, actually, so a few staples in my head at the end of tomorrow don't seem as scary to me as they might have otherwise.) It holds my brain and for now my tumor, but not for long. I have to trust it and work together with it to get through this next step. I have to listen to it differently than I will have ever had to before. This experience has made me endlessly thankful for the ways my body has maintained function during this sickness, including allowing me to write here and function pretty well (take care of kids for the most part, make friends, cook, drive as safely as possible given the circumstances, share my soul and write books, among them) during the growth of this tumor without loss of my sense of self or even that surprising of an amount of motor functions. Thank you, body, for that strength and I look forward to tapping into that gumption and stubbornness tomorrow as I recover. I hope to start to own the fact that I need to give you more of what you need and listen to you before you have to turn to shouting at me. I will try to breathe well through this as repayment as best as I can. I will also find a way to return to eating chocolate, if that makes you feel loved.

That's really all I wanted to say. That I am thankful for my body and wanted to send it a big hug and high five because we have to cling to each other in strength to move forward in these trying coming hours. My mom and I are choosing to believe that my endlessly beloved grandfather will be standing there with me to teach me how if I falter.

Thank you to each of you, too, for reading here and sending me flickers of strength. I read all the comments, notes, texts and emails and it has brought me the well of power from which I feel strong facing this now. Love.

2 ____ SURGERY

AND

COMING

HOME

This we have now
is not imagination.

This is not grief,
or joy, not a judging state,
or an elation, or a sadness.

Those come and go.
This is the presence
that doesn't.

—Rumi

To: Teresa
From: Caroline
Date: February 24, 2017
Subject: What I Did While Waiting To Leave

Teresa,

I tried on the hats [you lent me to warm my bald head post-surgery] while Garth took a shower. I was so touched by your gift and note but yesterday was a little flustered so I didn't get to appreciate it as much as I wanted to then. I was going to sit down and flip through a magazine to pass the time. Instead I opened your wonderful hat box, truly the nicest thing I think anyone has ever done for me in my life, and fit each one on my head as I thought of you. I don't really know how to wear this one [a bedazzled, braided red wreath], but I think it's my favorite and I like the fact that it feels like a crown. Thank you.

Sent from my iPhone

A Father's Prayer | Paul Markunas

This is my post as my daughter heads into surgery this morning, and I hope it will be as healing for her and those who read it as it is for me to write it.

I am amazed at what Caroline has become. I have seen her grow in strength, courage and determination with each passing year. I have seen her talents bloom and her capacity for love increase as she has tackled obstacles of family, home and friends—and, most recently, health.

It wasn't always this way, although, in fairness, she has remained the essence of what she was as a child: bright-eyed, inherently optimistic and happy, and with a capacity for empathy and understanding that surpassed her years.

Tumultuous times in childhood with dysfunction in the family stemming from generations of dysfunction brought her to a crossroads. She chose forgiveness. She chose love. She chose compassion. Those choices have made her who she is today.

For even through tears as I write this, I see very clearly that forgiveness brought healing which opens the airways to love. Forgiveness resolves anger, which leads to healing, which leads only to love. And compassion is only available to those with an open, healed and loving heart. And it is a deep and vibrant compassion that touches the heart and souls of anyone who is lucky enough to be a part of her life.

The benefits of her choices for her parents are obvious to everyone—deep and abiding relationships with two sensitive, smart and lively grandchildren and fair, honest and loving relationships with their parents as adults.

I couldn't ask for more.

So now, I need my prayer for my baby heading into serious and risky surgery to be to ask for all the forgiveness, compassion and love she has put into the world to protect her in her most dire moment of need, to guide those responsible for the work to be done, and to give us all the same strength to endure and help her heal as she so effortlessly shows to others everyday. I know deep in my heart it will be so because universal law demands it, but, nonetheless, I want to recognize and embrace this call to protect her openly and honestly. She is a gift to be treasured and has so much more to do and to give. As Lin Manuel Miranda recently said, "love is love is love is love is love." May we all in this moment of urgent need consciously call forth the love we feel for her and ask that the healing she has given to so many others now, more than ever, be truly her own. Amen.

To: Caroline
From: Mom
Date: February 24, 2017
Subject: Yeah it's Over!

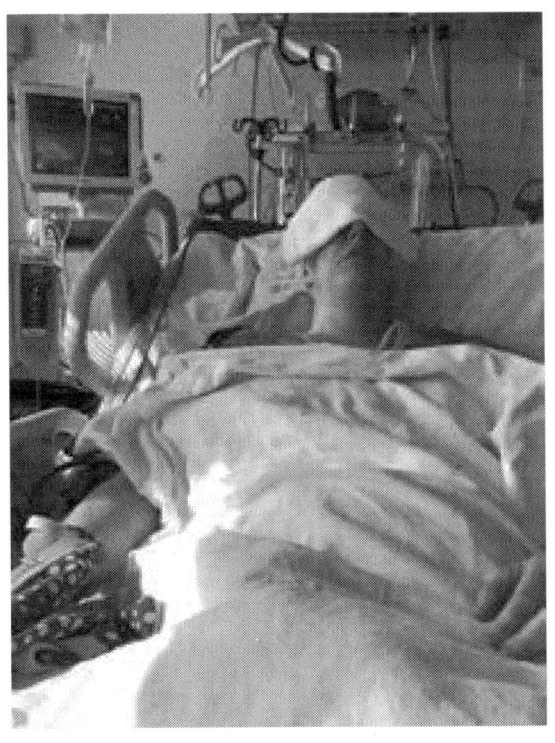

My mom took these pictures and emailed them to me from my hospital room. The first image was the time I was wheeled out of surgery; the second was her first vision of me, eyes shielded from the light and clutching my son's blanket toy, Dido.

Update—Surgery Over | Allison Taylor

From Garth:

We just spoke with the surgeons and everything went well. Tumor is out and she is in the immediate post-op process. She will be moved to ICU and kept overnight (this is usual practice). If she has any surgery-related adverse effects, they will usually present themselves within 12 hours.

Just Spoke with Caroline!!! | Paul Markunas

Glad just called from the hospital so that I could speak with Caroline in the ICU! All her motor skills seem to be working and she is talking just fine...She said she has a little headache and that's all! (I don't doubt that.)

So thank you to all for your kindness and prayers and thoughts. Maybe the worst is over.

Let's all keep our fingers crossed for the next few days.

February 25, 2017, 1:55 am

Text from Allison to Garth

This exchange, which happened in the middle of the night while I was in the ICU, was the nicest compliment I've ever received in my life. I smiled so hard when Garth read it aloud to me from where he lay crunched on the window seat.

ALLISON:

> Will they do something to make her sleep?
> (So you can sleep?)

GARTH:

> No. She is really jazzed up

ALLISON:

> If she is ready to party, why the fuck am I tired?

GARTH:

> ICU nurse will come around
> every hour anyway.

ALLISON:

> She is a terrifying alien in human form.
> Give her a kiss for me.

My night nurse on the longest night of my life, I may forever come to call it, was as close to an angel I think my atheist beliefs can bring me.

I learned she is married to a bartender and she recommends Slave to the Needle for my upcoming tattoo. That her nurse pet peeves, bodily function speaking, were sputum and flop sweat.

And that the steroids I was on, she assured me, were going to make this the longest and hardest night of my life, she informed me before the clock had even turned 11 and my turban (a source of great pain) wouldn't come off until 7 am.

What It Means to be Weak, I'm Learning.
Caroline Wright

So I am now at home, sitting in my bed where I usually lie next to my loving husband, writing to you to clear out a very scary experience from the darkness of my mind so maybe I can ride over the wave of the drugs I am on and find a little bit of comfort to meditate (as apparently sleep isn't even likely on the menu according to my night nurse last night until they reduce my steroids, which won't be until Monday at the earliest).

I went into surgery at 5 am yesterday morning and, powered by all of your words and emails, I just thought that it would be, you know, one foot in front of the other and marching toward a surgery that made me feel better. A risk, sure, but I had been holding positivity and luck in my favor, after all. It did not occur to me—and is only creeping into me now in scared and dark places—that it could actually be cancer, even though obviously that is an intellectual end to this week-long mess. The army of love I have behind me will save me because I am stronger than most, I deluded myself.

I need to tell you here that I'm learning that this is just not true. I saw it on the faces of my kind nurses who have clearly believed in their patients before. The calming, beautiful nurse who held my hand and let me cry as the anesthesiologist put me under, like she had done it before, whose name I made Garth write down because I was sure I would make her cookies someday very soon. I am realizing in this moment that I may not and it's just too much to process.

The experience of being a patient—a real, infirm patient—has been nothing I could have imagined in my most vivid nightmares for someone who projects and believes in strength like I always have since I was a fierce little girl who bullied the bullies. I don't know how to do anything halfway. I am the picture of an over-achiever with straight teeth who thinks and hones every angle. I have always projected excellence, sometimes confused as a striving for perfection (which is actually something I fear about even this space, which is just not my intention—I am really just trying to process complicated things with the only lens I know how, through writing here and feeling). I am now starting to wonder if that is the reason why I am here with a foreign matter in my brain in the first place—that I should have listened to my body and needs sooner.

I am *not* a superhero, that's the scariest thing of all. Coming out of brain surgery has shown me that. It's dark, lonely, and the night is very long. Strangers checking in on you every hour in ways they have been trained to in order to keep you as comfortable or safe or cloudy as they can so you don't panic.

The only thing I can say is that I was having this recurring image of tiny little men with white gloves running around like ants on the inside of my body, checking every little corner to see if their object was last where they left it. (All the things that were relevant to the doctors—my motor skills, pupil reactivity—were doing so well that I was constantly heralded as almost a miracle.) There were things that were missing to me, though, like the sensation in my palette and teeth and the right side of my face and I, too, was hoping that a nurse could give me something to make me comfortable, safe or cloudy so I stop being terrified, which I just don't know how to do.

Like I said, I am just not good at being weak. I'm not bragging. I actually think of it as a character flaw. I'm learning here, tested with this darkness that the sassy me refuses to even put words to, my resolve has little cracks that break open. In those cracks are where my thought slips in, hardens, and removed by force of a scalpel or radiation.

In this moment, the *only* hope I can cling to other than writing is what the doctors tell me. Wait and try to really listen, believe them and lean into my strengths.

And then the resilient, sassy girl in me wonders if this is what fighting looks like—if it's dark and human and scary and ugly. Not as a means to paste over the fears, but if in my life of great luck and privileges that this is what it means to *truly* struggle. With tears now rolling down my newly somewhat lazy face, lying in bed with squeals from my two wholeheartedly beloved little boys coming from under the door, I sit and vow to learn my struggle. I will fight, for both my kids and for myself, and I guess that's all I can do to find peace in this moment. I guess that has to be good enough for today. It's not okay or even able to be packaged into something that makes any sense at all to the people I love most.

It doesn't mean I will prevail. Or, I'm realizing, that the road ahead isn't any brighter than now.

I know that all of you here are sending hope, love and support for my family who are taking care of my kids while my heart aches to be able to. That means something to me in this fearful darkness, even if only to hear my boys laugh because they deserve that and not a sick Mommy. Keep it coming, even though in this moment I'm not sure it will make a difference. Hope for luck on the pathology and, if some version of cancerous, that I am strong enough to do yet another super weird thing I never thought I'd have to do like brain surgery.

Or hope that these drugs I'm on and the experience I've just had are making me so crazy depressed that after I lessen my steroid dose (more than 3x the amount that any doctor has told me would make me feel completely witless), rest and relaxation will follow and I can begin to hear what my body really needs other than family, tea and kindness.

Abigail Washburn | Caroline Wright

So in one week I went from never having an MRI to having three and a brain surgery.

They had to do one right before my surgery so they could provide a brain map—actually, a feature of this whole surgery process that brought me a lot of calm in how medical and scientific the care is—to know precisely where the surgeons had to work, guided by these stickers that Garth kept joking made me look bionic (which I now am!).

The only other MRI I've ever had in my life was the one that had diagnosed me—and I later found out I was having a seizure throughout—only a week earlier. Then there was yet another after the surgery as a double-check.

I mentioned the uncanny timing to my MRI tech and he offered to play me some music through earphones. Any music, he offered. I arched my brow, like I told you I can do when it comes to bronzer, and said "Any?" and asked for Abigail Washburn, the long-time spirit muse that my best friend Jeff and I share. Her voice, as well as clutching Dido—my son's blanket toy he's used since a baby—rolled me into the large, white, screaming box for yet another MRI of my "new" brain.

I'm Very Good at Being Drunk. | Caroline Wright

For those of you who know me very well, I am a very convincing drunk person.

I have this thing that if I am acting drunk, I need to be wheeled off to the hospital for poisoning. I only came close to putting myself at a health risk—sorry Mom and Dad—once in college before Garth and I started dating.

These are the things I was thinking about as I recovered. As in, is my punishing and shameful nature about saving face standing in the way of masking neurological symptoms? Or is that what this process is—lifting my left leg because I know I should be able to?

I'm telling you, brain surgeries are weird.

...And so are steroids when you feel it necessary to explain this exact theory to every nurse you meet.

Am I A Singer? | Caroline Wright

Many, many years ago a dear friend and I had a conversation that I carried with me to today. Ironically, it has been over this health news that the two of us have reconnected, for which I am deeply grateful because she is a spiritual pillar and rock-solid woman. I remember a conversation that she and I shared while sitting on the floor of her Lincoln Center-adjacent housing where she was spending most of her time. I wonder if she remembers this moment like I did today.

Anyway, I had been gaining a reputation of being verbose (*impossible!*) and incessantly descriptive about my symptoms in a way that apparently was unusual to the other doctors and nurses, but not wrong. A new neurosurgeon I hadn't met on the rounds—that's a totally weird thing, by the way, when people stand around you and talk about you in third person like you aren't there—smiled wisely at me and asked me if I was a singer.

I croaked something about, "Oh, why because my voice from the intubation tubes sounds so great?"

And he said, "no, actually, that there is some theory to how singers have a greater intuition to do with both sides of their brains."

That is the exact conversation I remember having with Sasha years ago, about how she could sense she was getting sick really far in advance because of the lilt of her soft palette. It was actually the lilt of my soft palette that drew me to the ER on that first Friday night. The neurosurgeon confirmed this theory from the floor of that Lincoln Center apartment, and, helped oddly remind me that yes, I used to be a singer with some degree of aspiration. It was also a beautiful way to bring Sasha to me in that moment.

Isn't that wild?

My Decision to Go Home | Caroline Wright

Another decision in the middle of that dark night, shepherded by ICU angel Kate, was that I wanted to go home as soon as they would let me.

If, in fact, I was a medical miracle and was surpassing all expectations for my motor skills, then I needed to stop telling people that I am very good at fooling them and just let them send me home.

At home, I figured, in my bed and no longer being an infirm patient, maybe with Henry snuggled up with a book, would be the best way to weed out which of my symptoms were actual symptoms and which were actually my idiosyncrasies reading into my symptoms. (Namely, I thought, with a good dose of normalcy, distraction and perspective would help sort out the severity of my symptoms; those that could shout over the boys would have to be loud!) So I stopped trying to make excuses for myself in the hospital room and let them convince me of my capability.

Is that what health progress looks like, I wondered?

Being Liked. | Caroline Wright

It would be dishonest of me if I couldn't acknowledge that the life I have built for myself as a writer, even though it truly isn't put in this place in a way I'm in control of, is that I have gotten by due to being liked. A performer of sorts. Even here. There is that part of people where they want to believe in you—that's the part that makes me employable and marketable in addition to talented, which I didn't ask for. It's comfortable for people in their healthy lives and ideals to have a mascot. You would have to know me well to know that I don't identify with this in terms of vanity at all, but that I am honest with myself enough to know that this is obviously a factor in how people work.

The scariest part of being in the hospital was that I realized that being charming or a favorite patient doesn't matter. Cracking up the nurses or making fun of my butt hanging out in my dressing gown wasn't going to save me from dying if that was the timing. It's a dark thought, I know. But nice people die. It isn't fair. My having two little boys and a handsome loving husband I love with my whole, bright spirit isn't going to make me heal faster or better. I'm still reduced down to just a body. And understanding that I could be one of those people was important to me in the hospital, as scary as it was.

Then I wondered, however, if it does matter somehow in the very smallest way. Even writing this makes me wonder if I am saying it for me or for you.

Maybe if showing myself to the nurses, people who understand my care better than I do as professionals, allows me to crack humanity open a little bit and find that grain of sand with which to rebuild my life. I literally mean a grain of sand, that's how small and how invisible it felt in that hospital bed.

But, again, I'm wondering if this is what learning to fight or survive looks like. I don't know how to do it, it doesn't look like the manual for how to be liked on television. Or maybe it does in some very small way: being open. Being vulnerable. Being naked. Being scared. And finding a way within all of that to still feel like a person and not a patient.

I at once acknowledge that none of this matters—writing here, feeling supported—in the big scheme of things in terms of mortality and odds, but maybe in that same space it does matter too. Writing yesterday from a dark place was the only thing that brought me back to myself after a few hours, like my mom standing next to me and quietly rubbing my swollen forehead in silence, pretending deep inside my scared mind that I am a little girl and she will make me feel better. The joys are so small right now, but I have to collect them because I don't know what else to do. How can I find the strength to fight if I don't feel like myself? Before my experience in the hospital, I thought that these same pillars of my life would be enough to get me through—the big things, like my kids and my loving husband, these ideas of security that entitled me to a healthy and happy life. It's true, those pieces are huge in the support that it will take going forward. It just isn't as clear, charming or as written as any of us would like to think. I'm seeing it now as going to take all of those things and *then* also a lot of work (and luck) on top of it. Work I know I still believe I am capable of because I am not just a patient but also a writer and a mom and people believe in me. It doesn't just come from one place, so I am gathering together those grains of sand.

Thank you for being here with me in this scary place. It does help somehow, even though I am having a hard time recognizing myself like this. I don't know what hope looks like from here, but I am still willing to look in the smallest places and open myself up to people who might be able to show me.

(As an important side note, I am writing this now from my bed at home where I SLEPT FOR THE FIRST TIME IN A WEEK UNMEDICATED and caught a glimpse of the space in which healing can happen. Real sleep, even though I wake up in shock and pain, negotiating the space between what my brain and body can integrate.)

The Noise. | Caroline Wright

I don't take medicine usually. Ever. I am a highly cerebral (I've always joked neurotic!) person and I like to be aware of my faculties. I'd like to pretend that I've had some sort of participation in my integration between mind, body and spirit or even that I have some sort of control in that space. It's the hope I'm clinging to now, that I can listen to my instincts and rebuild someday. Simple things, like breathing well or drinking water and being kind, regardless of circumstances.

The thing that happens when you get sick like this is that this balance gets all messed up and I can't hear my voice right now. Writing helps, for sure, because I have to commit to thoughts and words in order to share them. But then you have complicated, deep factors like family—my beloved dad, for example, telling me that I'll be back at it in no time to stay positive, which I get, and the guilt of being a sick mom to my perfect, unknowing boys—coupled with the fact that I am on very strong drugs which have very real, scary side effects especially for an emotionally connected person.

Help me keep finding my inner voice. It's so noisy where I am now.

Pop Rocks | Caroline Wright

So this wild thing has been happening to me all day.

I can feel my brain readjust its fluid levels. It feels like carbonation in my skull, at the base of my neck, and occasionally in my sinuses. I was wondering about this sensation when Garth mentioned that some people can feel it. He offered some anecdotes from his research, that some people say that it's like the vibration of bowling balls being knocked together in a caddy. Mine feels like Pop Rocks, who knew.

What's also wild is that I have been doing my physical therapy exercises, following the pamphlets like a good student with Garth, my good teacher. It gives all of us purpose and it makes me feel a little less like a patient and more like I'm kicking ass with my motor skills! Feeling braggy about exercise is funny to me, who formerly would have considered exercise as walking to the refrigerator.

Getting Caroline Back Home | Garth Wright

Yesterday afternoon Caroline was discharged. After passing every strength and motor test they required post-surgery, she was deemed healthy enough to bypass another night in a regular room and go straight home from the ICU. She was exhausted and sleepy and overwhelmed.

Late last night I called her doctor to double-check some prescription information and he gave Caroline a huge break - he is allowing her to cut her steroid dose by 75%. It is no coincidence that last night Caroline slept for the first time in a while, sleeping about 5 straight hours. With the steroid dose lessened, she is better able to control her moods and is less constantly jazzed; she's able to relax.

This week the focus is on getting her as close back to 100% as possible. Our next post-op appointment is this Friday March 3.

I Knitted! | Caroline Wright

Knitting is something I really love to do—it is meditative and it produces something beautiful. It helps me with my blood pressure. And it's a two-handed, quiet activity.

I pulled out my knitting today, the first time in over a year. I used to knit nightly and both boys have hand-knit sweaters that I've lovingly made for them. (Theodore less than Henry, it won't shock you to hear, I'm sure! Poor second kid.)

And you know what's weird? I could feel, just like with the physical therapy exercises (for example, I noticed when I lifted my left leg I had a sensation behind my right ear, things like that), that my brain was reintegrating through knitting. I know this makes me a crazy person but I also kind of like that.

Now I am making up a blanket. It makes me happy, thinking about this blanket being on one of the boys' beds someday. So there's that.

My Kids | Caroline Wright

Those of you who know me well know that being a mom is a really big deal to me. I would turn myself inside out for my kids to give them anything they needed from me, a trait I think I inherited from my dad. Being here, where they are, for them is as much as a part of myself as anything I can think of.

It makes this moment hard, too. Being vulnerable and scared and also physically swollen, but wanting to break it down for my sweet Henry and Theodore that I am still here for them just like I always am.

I know I can't control anything or even that my being available to them won't necessarily change anything. That makes this scary, even though I don't think it is worth it to focus on what I don't know right now.

All I can say is that because I would turn myself inside out for my kids, the next steps (likely radiation, I'm told from a slip from an attending surgeon at the hospital) seem less impossible.

Then the positive, possibly delusional part of me says that they won't even remember this version of me (swollen, scared) someday. Henry might remember that week where he partied at school more than normal and neighbors brought him Legos to build, but probably not. It makes me feel hopeful that there is narrative space here in which the future—theirs—could be rewritten regardless of what happens.

Things I Am Thankful For | Caroline Wright

In my current state, I am constantly thinking about certain skills that I have accrued that are helping me out right now. I don't imagine I am special in this—right now, from where I stand, my goals are simple and my means of getting there feels very clear. I am struck by a few things in my past that have prepared me for this moment and I wanted to give thanks to them here.

My breath. I am so thankful that I took voice lessons as a middle and high schooler. While I am doing my physical therapy exercises now, I have been reminded of the image of my vocal coach—a puffy and very kind opera singer without age or wrinkles at Rollins College—putting my hands on his diaphragm, feeling his lungs inflate and belly swell. I remember being embarrassed in that moment by how noisy real breathing is as well as how physical it is. Good breath is not silent, nor is it without effort. I am so thankful that he taught me to breathe like this, because I have used my breath as a regulatory force throughout my recovery so far. Breathing well—from the bottom of your lungs—requires work, as does healing. I am so thankful that I took voice lessons for this reason—something I have wondered about in my adult life, questioning the purpose for those efforts, other than to sing to my kids.

Pilates. In vapid moments in which my bodily condition felt very important—I probably don't need to outline that this coincided with a certain white dress and my handsome groom—I got very into pilates. Pilates and its micro movements (that involve mindfulness and repetition) have been incredibly important to the success of my physical therapy exercises today. I don't know that I would have paid attention to the exact direction my toes were pointing or the alignment of my spine had I not gotten into pilates years ago. It helps me to know that a strong body is ahead for me, even though the steps forward now are a bit shaky.

I am feeling more like myself today and am encouraged to wait for my diagnosis with thoughtfulness and, in the meantime, rely on the love from my family and these basic life lessons of listening to my body and giving it what it needs. The love you here are sending my way gives me encouragement in the moments that bridge the gap between mind, body and spirit as I wait.

Oh, and I ate a burger today. Which helped, too.

The Idea of Miracles | Caroline Wright

A friend of mine who has lived through her fair share of spiritual awareness—this lady knows what she's talking about and may be one of the few people who could actually meet me where I am today—texted me that she thought I was a living miracle.

I laughed, texted back, and said that I thought miracles were much shinier than this. Just like the idea of healing or fighting, the idea of a miracle seems so tidy and clean from the outside. From where I'm standing now, miracles, if that's what is happening now, are very human: made by drinking a glass of water, the comfort of a warm compress or mug of tea, taking a poop, getting rest. These things when accumulated in a very non-human place, are the making of a miracle.

Permission | Caroline Wright

The idea of permission—as a connotation of consent, kindness and responsibility—is a strange one in my current state. I feel like I am in the mode of doing things in which the idea of permission is totally irrelevant, including in my own being. I don't know what's going on and have to trust that other smarter people do.

My best friend Sarah, whose story is unique and one of my favorites to tell, gave me the idea that I needed to give myself the permission to understand that steroids were doing really bad things—as close to an allergic reaction as she could imagine without the physical danger—to my body. This hadn't occurred to me, even though obviously I was terrified of them.

Allow me to tell you my story with Sarah because it shows just how lucky I am as a person. We met at summer camp at the age of fifteen, an arts camp in Michigan that is already so unusual to explain because it involved uniforms and a bugled 6:45 am wake-up call around a flagpole. Stranger still is that Sarah and I weren't even in the same cabin, which were these large collections of artsy kids in a variety of serious disciplines—hers, classical piano and mine Shakespearean acting. (You know, summer fun for ambitious art nerds.)

Meeting Sarah was the closest thing to the divine I've ever experienced. As with all my closest friends, I can tell something about them that is just meant to be, like they glow differently. Sarah said hello to me and I knew she was going to be my best friend for life. The lucky part is that she somehow felt the same and not that I was a stalker, which would have also been fair.

Next thing I knew, she pulled me aside in the lunch line, and said something like, "Hey. I have to tell you something. I am really allergic to a lot of things, so I am supposed to tell someone how to stick this thing in my leg if I disappear to the bathroom for a long time."

And that was it. We have never lived in the same place, but this woman has held a huge part of my soul for so much of my life. We became the symbols in each other's lives, and our families that knew us, for faith in so many ways. In fact, she was the only person other than my dad that was worried that something was physically wrong with me as my tumor symptoms mounted because of how well she knows my personality. She had seen me face a lot of obstacles in my life without anxiety, depression, or even too significant overwhelm, and about a week before the MRI I had been considering going on some form of neuro-regulator drugs. When I told her about the tumor, she told me she was relieved; she had feared I had experienced a stroke and had been having the strong inkling that something physical was wrong with me. Just from emails and phone calls.

So when someone who has spent a lot of her life on steroids tells you that maybe you're having a bad reaction to them, that is a powerful thing, and makes me think more critically about participating in the dialogue of the next steps of my treatment.

Not Being Afraid | Caroline Wright

It's hard to explain right now, and I am aware that any attempt in doing so may imply that I have a self-awareness or stake in feeling "brave" or something, but I am having trouble feeling afraid of the unknown right now. I know I should be, but I'm not really and I'm finding it interesting.

That is not to say that I am ready for an aggressive treatment plan. I am not. Nor am I ready to stop living. But being afraid of those things in this moment seems like so much energy. There is also a lot of beauty that is happening around me right now—the purity of my children, incredible and otherwise unimaginable systemic healing with my parents, strength and love from my husband, a community of almost strangers in a new city that have risen to hold me up on uncertain ground in a time of need. Flowers. Notes. Kindness. Quiet. Sleep.

So, I know I should be afraid and I know that a lot of you out there are holding that for me in a sort of universal way. Thank you and keep doing it. It's working for me and I think it's part of what is bringing me some semblance of peace right now.

My Beautiful, Beautiful Family | Caroline Wright

I was awakened in the night to write this, sleeping blissfully, after a really transformative evening of baking cookies with my mother. It sounds quaint, I know, and might give you some idea of what that would look like based on some sort of conventional wisdom of what mothers and daughters (especially ones who bake) do together, but I can tell you that there is nothing conventional about this.

My father, a great cook whose passion for creative outlets have sometimes surpassed his skill, makes great pasta. Pasta, especially in the decade since my becoming a food professional, has been one dish that he approaches with care, rules and planning that is an outlier to his cooking style. His method has changed since the pastas of my youth, grown more sophisticated and more comforting still. It is objectively excellent. Last night's dinner was a hearty *ragú* ladled over fresh rigatoni, thick with glossy gravy and sat slouched in a pool in a shallow bowl. My kids devoured it with joy—something they reserve only for quite good pasta, really, the little snobs—and it was exactly what I wanted to eat in this moment. (Healing, as it turns out, makes me very, very hungry as if I had just gone for an exhausting run, but all the time.)

My profound love for my father is something that I have alluded to here and he has returned in the form of his beautiful prayer to me the day I went into surgery. He is an exceptional person, a fact that anyone realizes within seconds of meeting him, regardless of which side of the fence they choose to see him from. I have long since believed that our connection is spiritual. He is the well from which I am drawn as a person, the blood in my veins, the beginning and end of every circle I could draw as an illustration. Even an attempt to describe his wonderfulness or beauty is like trying to grasp at light or sand—the energy slips from my fingers in trying to hold it. He is a force. He is most things I recognize about myself (sick or well, it turns out), like my creativity, hope, positivity, generosity and joy. Because of his character and his own journey into his skin, he also has been made (and earned, if being truly honest) a villainous role in more than one narrative in the lives he has touched because of the way he learns and changes out loud like he does. I can promise that you have never met a more dynamic (or talented, or lovely) person. There are edges to this, ones that I grew in the light of, and ones that most people find it easier not to embrace because it takes forgiveness and love to do so, especially in the face of someone who needs help and can't find the words to ask for it. The kindnesses that my dad has shown in the past weeks have been ones that are typical for our closeness— optimism, honesty, clarity. Loving my kids as much as I do while still getting them to bed on time or making them the perfect kind of scrambled eggs they like before he even has the chance to brush his teeth in the morning. Being endlessly generous and patient and loving. That is the dad I have been blessed with and know with my whole being. I couldn't be more grateful for him in this moment. He is my constant and brings me the life I loved before my tumor.

The healing my mom and I have found since my diagnosis has been the most incredible experience of my life, and definitely not one I thought was possible for me before my tumor. As I mentioned before, my mom and I weren't close growing up. My dad and I have always been, for reasons I understand to be both practical and logical. My mom and I didn't speak the same language and there were blocks in our spiritual flow based on the kinds of reasons that stack up over decades in families brimming with complicated, passionate people who learn as they go and try to face their issues and fail. My mom and I weren't exceptional people in these moments, even if respectful to each other's spirits and loving in our own ways over the years. The way my mother has chosen to support me in the past few weeks, without the fear or blockages I witnessed from my childhood, has brought me a kind of healing that I can't really find the words to express. I can honestly feel the broken parts of my childhood soul being knit back together and I can literally see it as tissue that was stronger than what was there before. This is not an experience, it is a truth, and I am endlessly grateful for it. And her bravery to meet me here. Her willingness to stroke my swollen, sore face just after surgery in the hopes it would help circulate the fluid from my face and put eye drops in my enveloped tear ducts. To bring me tea and water. To hug my children and me and acknowledge my fears before her own.

My brother, despite not being in our family or choosing to acknowledge this experience I am going through, is still in my house and helping me heal in his way. I look like him without hair. Both of my sons have his goofy soulful laugh that I remember hearing from outside the halls of our high school as he joked with friends. I have found people who take the practical space of his love, of brotherhood, like my Jeff and my Jonas, so I have not been lost despite an underlying loneliness. I am holding him close now, though, and wishing he could listen to Mom like I am experiencing now or eat Dad's pasta. I know that the kind of pain from our childhood wasn't easy (or even clear or something diagnosable) and that I took a long-term path to lean into healing over many years; I am feeling the benefits now, certainly, as euphoric but I am not so silly to believe it came without choices or work on my part. Having him here with me now brings me healing. I send him genuine love and hope that the path he has chosen brings him the kind of peace I am finding now, even if only someday. I respect his process and the space it takes to find the words to ask for what one needs to heal. No one can do (or prescribe) that work for you, so if his distance is what helps him to find those words, I genuinely understand it. As I have for the past twelve years, Philip (if you are reading this, which I know you are not), I will continue to love you and respect this space of yours. We will always be family and I will always be here for you if you need me. I want this joy and peace for you and you have my word that I will always do whatever I can to make that happen, even though I doubt I have anything other than swirly anecdotes to offer that come from very different roads.

I know in part I can survive cancer, if that's what I'm experiencing now, because I already have. Thank you, my beautiful family, for showing me the way and making me strong and aware and humbled by your love in this moment. We are truly in this together.

3 _____ PROGNOSIS,

OR

NAMING

THE

BEAST

*You may not control all the events
that happen to you, but you can decide
not to be reduced by them.*

—Maya Angelou

News... | Garth Wright

It's not good. Caroline has a stage IV astrocytoma (or glioblastoma).

In about a week she will begin the initial course of treatment: radiation and chemotherapy for 5 days a week for 6 weeks. There is no cure so their goal is to have it grow back as slowly as possible.

The median survival rate is 1 year. Caroline wanted me to note that one patient of her surgeon's lived 22 years with this tumor and she wants to beat that.

Know that Caroline reads all the comments, text messages, and emails sent her (our) way. She is very thankful to have such support, and so are we.

Before we received the news Caroline had 41 staples taken out after her surgery. She says she intends on bringing this up in the future as evidence of her "bad-ass"-ness.

On the Bright Side | Paul Markunas

I know it seems like there is no bright side at a moment
like this.

But in all the tears that are flowing madly in this house
right now, there is a determination that Caroline's life WILL
NOT be defined by her death, that her death is only one of
the possibilities within the next year or the next several years
(or more) and that we all know that if anyone can roll back
odds with hope, love and determination, she can.

We only ask for time to make a plan and to process this
sober news. But we need love and positive energy to flow into
this house. Love can, and will, beat this cancer, one way
or another.

So Scared. | Caroline Wright

I am scared right now in this moment. I honestly cannot believe the news that I was just told—it feels like groundhog day (but so much worse) of the very first Friday I heard the news of the tumor. Phone calls, pacing around the floor. Worsened by holding my wailing father and shaking mom, holding hands with my beautiful and beloved husband. But better, too, because of them.

I have a few positive feelings that are breaking through my trembling limbs. One is that I am thirty-two (almost 33 in about a week!) and giving up is physically not an option. I have to let this sink in, be sad and get it out of my system, and make a plan to get strong and fight with every invisible grain of sand in my body. They're in there, I know. I don't see them yet but I know I will find them.

And if not, I will die trying to find every extra minute I can with my boys. My beautiful family has my word. Please lift me up in this time and help me change the subject of my scared brain.

Oh, and practically speaking, I've made a few decisions about how I want to find my focus. I would like to unplug from my phone completely. If you want to get in touch with me, I prefer letters first, emails second, then texts and phone calls which can be ferried through Garth. I will certainly appreciate visitors—I want to hold to things that make me feel like me, like great conversations—but not until I start my treatment and see the kind of strength that takes.

As far as writing and my work goes, I am moving forward with the idea of turning this journal into a memoir and having it funded so that I can have it printed for my kids, whether or not it turns into a charity venture at this moment. I am also placing my creative energy in *Charlie the Cook* and loving every development of the characters and drawings, looking forward to knitting the pages and images together as soon as possible.

Right now I know I'm scared and processing so every idea I have feels desperate and raw and, in the light of my palpable fears, a little more cliché then they did without them. I look forward to a new day where the light of these projects will lift me up when I need them.

High Points for Today | Caroline Wright

Clearly, I have had the scariest afternoon I could have imagined and was really struggling to feel like myself after a few hours. A close friend here (our former architect, in fact) insisted I call a friend of his who is the chief of radiology at UW. Our conversation mostly circumnavigated bits of advice about oncology treatment in general and confidence in the team that had been assembled for me, rather than specific ideas about my prognosis (which I actually found comforting and way more relevant rather than a second opinion type scenario). Imagine her soothing Mary Poppins-sounding voice as she gave me these little nuggets of hope:

First she began by saying that you have to decide where you fall on the scale of willingness to go after your treatment. I assured her that I am willing to turn myself inside out to find any weak cells for my boys and do whatever necessary to give me any time with them I could. She picked up immediately, fortified with this knowledge, and the tone of her voice assured me that this was something she saw as a key to success.

"We wouldn't be wasting all the money for oncology treatment if there weren't people who could pull through." Okay! Good enough for me right now!

She recommended physical activity to deal with the agony of chemo and radiation. Little things, like walking around the block. I actually imagined how thankful I am going to be that Seattle's spring will start to bloom when I am going through this nightmare treatment. (The camellias in this town are incredible, for those of you who don't know.) That thought made me almost smile, which was definitely not nothing after my afternoon of writing goodbye notes to my boys.

She walked me through my care team and gave me the confidence that I have the best possible crew on my side. It made me firmer in the resolve that 1) I am lucky to have found the team that has done such a good job with my care so far and 2) having faith in my team going forward is another extension of hope and trust in the process I am already involved in. Second-guessing (or second opinions) is not where I am now. This is my ride, let's go.

She reminded me to see an oncology counselor if the ups and downs of treatment get to me. (I didn't even know this was a thing! Of course I would want to see a specialized therapist for cancer treatment! For those of you who know me well would know that YES OF COURSE I would want to talk to someone who can help me understand my cancer! And then I can tell people how awesome my oncology social worker is at dinner parties and make them uncomfortable for years to come!)

She named the "oncology rollercoaster," something that I obviously am aware of personally since this three-week process from diagnosis to prognosis with a brain surgery in the middle. But naming it and acknowledging that it was going to have its ups and downs (and be physically exhausting along the way in addition) was really helpful and honest in this moment.

These were my little glimmers of hope today that somehow stitched together the incredible heart-wrenching wound of holding my beautiful Henry and telling him that Mommy is dying but going to find every possible way to fight that weed that might want to grow back. Oncology rollercoaster, here I come.

Floating Bridges | Caroline Wright

Today, on a day where the boys have been sent off to be with Aunt Allison and Uncle Tom for a bit of normalcy while we set aside to process some very real conversations together as a family and when I launched the Kickstarter for this memoir, I didn't think that today would turn out so magical.

In fact, if I'm being honest with myself, I am starting to show some physical signs of deterioration (though again could be fatigue or anxiety based, due to our stressful day yesterday) and am having some trouble breathing as well as I usually do. But breathing I still am, make no mistake.

And then it was a beautiful day and I went for a walk with my precious Theodore and Garth and saw crocuses spring from the ground.

And then two wonderful friends came by just to sit and give me their truths because of how much they care about our family.

This humanity and beauty are the floating bridges that I glide on from one moment to the next, finding the language to fight through the smiles and genuine love each and every time it shows itself to us in a new way. That is the miracle, right? Not just the breathing today, but that. And I feel small and humbled and proud to draw air into my lungs, not sick at all.

New Territory | Paul Markunas

Never thought my lovely wife and I would be talking about a funeral for our daughter...but we did that today and talked about so many other, equally important, tasks and objectives and thoughts and wishes and hopes.

This sucks.

We are grappling with the unknown on every level.

The disease. The daily needs. The children's needs. The husband's needs. The patient's needs.

Am I the best person to give her the care and solace she needs?

How are we going to get through the months and, hopefully, years ahead?

It is sad and baffling and, for tonight, I will let the unknown linger, hoping to make a better choice in the day that is coming. I will let my sadness go the way of my dreams, not to remember much of them tomorrow. Each coming day. May they go on forever.

Fighting for Today | Caroline Wright

I think it's fair to say that I've been honest here in my writing in this space. It has functioned to show me the true shape of my inner self through writing it out to you, and it has cracked open new places for hope and humanity in having my most honest thoughts reflected back at me through the love and community that has grown around me here. That is the shape of fighting and strength for me, I'm learning. This is part of my power that will allow me to live as long as I can—and as richly as I can—given my prognosis of certain death.

Right now I am processing a very real, deep physical anxiousness until I start my treatment and can be monitored by my care team. The thoughts I have running through my consciousness are that the MRI they showed me at the end of my prognosis meeting with my two surgeons—the one I left shaking in the arms of my mother and husband—was "clean" and that is supposed to be comforting to me in this moment. It was an MRI image of my stapled head without a tumor inside, though they know that there are millions of cells in there because of the nature of brain surgery and human capability. So that an image shows it to be clean doesn't mean that it is. It just means that the aggressive cancer I have in my head has been weakened in terms of its mass size, but not in its ability to grow. And that this MRI was a week old doesn't provide comfort to me either because no one knows the rate at which the cancer is growing because it hasn't been monitored yet.

So, until I can get to my care team on Monday and start turning myself inside out to stop the growth of these cells, I don't think I will be able to find any deep comfort in my situation, other than I get to spend another day with my loving family and my kids, which isn't nothing. It's today.

In the spirit of honesty and acknowledging this deep anxiousness, I can be honest in saying that I have been scared since my prognosis because I am feeling symptoms again not unlike some of the weirdness that I felt last year during what I now know was a period of tumor growth. I am having some headaches—not terrible or disorienting ones, but headaches still—and my capacity for breath is changing. My vision is blurring. But, same as the rich life I held last year despite my tumor growth, none of these symptoms matter, right? I have to keep living with a refusal to being defined by this thing or my fears. Which involves acting like myself, like writing here or launching a Kickstarter or collaborating on a book project with other artists.

I honestly went to bed last night thinking it could be my last. I don't really know why I felt that way, but I had this deep acceptance all day yesterday that I needed to get my work affairs in order so that my legacy—*Charlie the Cook* and this writing being the most critical ones to me right now—is intact and my voice lives on for my kids. It's a very morbid point of entry that is not my usual personality, but it feels important to acknowledge that I don't have control over my situation right now. I will have some more control (and support) starting tomorrow and I just have to be okay with that.

And then I tell myself, again, that this is what fighting looks like. It can be fearful and still strong. It is living with intent and love and knowing that I don't have control of my timeline but I do have control of its meaning. That is as true in living as in dying—the difference between them is a matter of perspective.

Growing Versus Nurturing | Caroline Wright

It is a very weird thing, this process of having something in your body that is growing from you but not being able to love it. Even though in a weird way, I kind of do, because my tumor is my life right now.

The only other times I've had something growing in my body, I was pregnant with two of the greatest loves of my life, my two boys. I would sit in chairs and imagine their toes wiggling and sing them songs and fill my body with hope because they were growing there.

It is a very weird thing that these instances of body awareness and growth capacities are the only sense memories my body has. They are so diametrically opposed, yet somehow linked in the experience of my body. And spiritually connected, in some way, because being in my children's lives for as long as I can despite this growing tumor is what will motivate me to seek the most aggressive and constant treatment possible while still fighting to be myself throughout it.

This is so strange. I am so thankful to have this space to talk about how strange it is and that the smart, kind people who have found their way into my life are finding little ways—little floating bridges—to take me from one moment to the next. That's the part where faith—mine in humanity—comes in.

Getting to Know My Tumor | Caroline Wright

When this kind of thing happens to you, everyone tells you a story. (I find that when you bake cakes for a living, people tell you stories about that too. This is significantly less fun.)

And that is beautiful. It gives me hope to know that so many people I know also know other people who have survived my precise kind of tumor. People who have lived much longer lives than expected.

It's a totally weird thing to say, but all of this just makes me want to get to know my tumor. To meet my team tomorrow and figure out exactly what my tumor is like and what it's going to take to beat it. Because until then, all I keep thinking is that my tumor has my DNA in it and we don't know how that will respond to treatment until we know.

In the meantime, I am hoping for the best and trying to stay me. It's working well so far—I actually had a wonderful walk today with my beautiful Garth, holding hands and talking about our big life together and the places we would like to travel when I get well. We talked, too, though of if I die I want a grafted apple tree (I hear there are kinds that grow three kinds of apples here in Seattle, called "combo trees," one for each of my boys) planted in the yard with my ashes underneath. Then I came home and built the greatest

Lego airplane Henry and I had ever seen and managed one lap around our big dining room table at my usual fast-paced revving speed that somehow still manages to have me come in second place after Henry every single time (even when well). I joked with little Theodore and savored his sweet smirk, knowing what a handful he will be in high school and wondering if I will see it.

To: Caroline
From: Sarah Jane
Date: March 5, 2017
Subject: questions.

Hi, I saw your most recent Caring Bridge post and I hope you are unplugged and not reading this until tomorrow, but now that I am home from trip and back to reality I just wanted to share some thoughts and ask some questions. My thoughts are all over the place right now, which I am sure you will pick up on quickly.

I have been the worried friend the past 2 weeks and while I will continue that, my nurse practitioner side of the brain is having a hard time staying quiet.

First off, please use me not just as a best friend but also as a resource since I am an oncology nurse practitioner. While I am in an unfamiliar place having never had a sick friend, I see cancer patients every day and help them go through exactly what you are going through. I even have a patient with your type of tumor. She is 6 years out from her diagnosis and she had no problem proving us wrong when we told her she had 18 months or less. I know you are getting ready to assemble the dream team up there and that they will provide all the support you need but don't be afraid to ask stupid questions about treatments/side effects, etc. I promise, I have heard it all

Next, I just have questions. Do not feel pressure to answer all or any but I think I will feel some comfort knowing a little more about what is going on. I can even just talk to your dad if you prefer?

-Are they calling the tumor a high grade astrocytoma or are they referring to it as a glioblastoma multiform (GBM?). Did they have "clear" margins or was the surgery more of a "debulking" procedure

-Are you going to see a regular "medical oncologist" or are they sending you to a specific neuro-"oncologist"? Both can treat GBMs but some people prefer one over the other. I saw that you were already referred to a radiation oncologist which is good. He/she will be a very important of your team

-I know you haven't seen the oncologist yet but did your surgeons mention the plan? We usually give a chemo pill for treatment of GBMs (during and after radiation) so not sure if anyone mentioned that yet?

-How are you feeling? Are the headaches better? Do you absolutely hate the steroids? I hope you are able to taper down soon. The side effects of steroids can be worse that the underlying disease sometimes

-Are you googling things about your tumor? I tell patients not to because there is a lot of crap on the internet but if you want legit sites I can send them to you and I can give you my professional login info if you want access to NCCN guidelines (that is our "Bible" in the oncology world)

-Not a medical question but has Philip reached out yet?

Sorry I am all over the place. Wish I was there to meet these docs but it sounds like you have been in amazing hands and you seem to have full confidence in your docs so that makes me really happy

I love you so much and I hope you enjoying your time healing with your boys, G and your parents.

SJ

The Space In Between and A Few Beliefs |
Caroline Wright

As of writing this, my Kickstarter to fund The Caring Bridge Project is fully backed and I spent the morning feverishly trying to cull content that felt relevant to the manuscript that no one else would see if I didn't put it together. That brings me peace and, I hope, the ability to get some rest.

I spent the afternoon unplugged with Garth, then the kids, as I already mentioned.

And now, in the middle of the night, I was compelled to get up and write each of my boys a letter in the case of my death.

It's strange to have to live a double narrative right now, in which every thought and action I have has two meanings. One that has to believe in my current strength and will to live (which is very strong and deeply protective of my normal, positive self and any approximation at normalcy in terms of motherhood especially) alongside another that also acknowledges that I have no control over my timeline or treatment (and, so, have to prepare goodbyes and do weird things like appoint people to work on my open projects, sign wills and talk about my funeral). That I have to live both narratives feels dishonest to the both, like they cancel each other out. I guess in a way they kind of do, except for the fact that I have a very real hope and will in positivity despite my realism. This positivity bridges that space, and I know how strong my hope and will are as I have proven it before.

The space in between, where this hope and will lives in the face of two versions of reality, is the space I am choosing to spend all of my energy. It is the person who is trying to live for today and bask in the now because that is literally all I can know with certainty. It is wild to realize that this is always true in life, but not something you can actually feel until you are facing death. It's amazing to see this perspective and it makes small things feel so mighty. I am sitting here, facing death and hoping for recovery, while also bottling this thankfulness knowing that I will have to live out my days (regardless of it being 6 months or 6 years) in its essence.

I am sending each of you all of my love right now. I really do believe that if I have a shot in hell—as in, my DNA responds to the treatment I am going to learn about tomorrow, which feels like yet another piece of luck that I just don't have control over and blind hope feels vain or dishonest—I will fight with every inch of my being to get through this for as long as I can. I am willing to turn myself inside out and be scraped clean, face surgeries and pain and exhaustion and more testing, with the hope of being well, even if for an undetermined amount of time. If, however, I give it my all and the path leads me to being sick and weak, then I will accept that my time has come and my family needs to move forward without me. That's not where I am today, but I acknowledge it could be a part of the path ahead. Today I am ready for the fight.

I also believe that if hopes and wishes and connection could carry me to luck (even though you know from here that ultimately I really don't believe that, as I learned in the ICU), then all of you would be bringing me there. I am very fortunate indeed.

4_____ THE

WAIT

Before you know what kindness really is
you must lose things,
feel the future dissolve in a moment
Like salt in a weakened broth.
What you held in your hand,
what you counted and carefully saved,
all this must go so you know
how desolate the landscape can be
between the regions of kindness.
How you ride and ride
thinking the bus will never stop,
the passengers eating maize and chicken
will stare out the window forever.

Before you learn the tender gravity of kindness,
you must travel where the Indian in a white poncho
lies dead by the side of the road.
You must see how this could be you,
how he too was someone
who journeyed through the night with plans
and the simple breath that kept him alive.

Before you know kindness as the deepest thing inside,
you must know sorrow as the other deepest thing.
You must wake up with sorrow.

You must speak it till your voice
catches the thread of all sorrows
and you see the size of the cloth.

Then it is only kindness that makes sense anymore,
only kindness that ties your shoes
and sends you out into the day to mail letters
and purchase bread,
only kindness that raises its head
from the crown of the world to say
It is I you have been looking for,
and then goes with you everywhere
like a shadow or a friend.

—"Kindness" by Naomi Shihab Nye

Meeting Caroline's Tumor | Garth Wright

Today we met Caroline's radio-oncologist and her neuro-oncologist.

Caroline's treatment won't begin until March 20, at the earliest. More likely it will be the end of that week. Before then she has to get fitted for her radiation helmet—a plastic head/face molding that locks into the table and makes sure that the radiation hits the same spot for each treatment. She will be locked into the table for 20 minutes while they irradiate the tumor resection bed and the margins. No decision yet whether it will be photon or proton therapy. The M-F doses of 2 gray radiation for the 6 weeks will result in a cumulative 60 grays (right below the "problem" amount).

There were some inconsistencies in her pathology, so the doctors are still waiting for the protein sequencing and the MGMT methylation results—her IDH1 stain was negative. They want to determine the total makeup of this glioblastoma/ GBM because it has a tendency to be a rapidly growing cancer.

Her chemotherapy will begin the night before radiation begins and end the night after radiation ends. It is taken orally.

Caroline can expect her worst fatigue to begin around week 4 of the 6 weeks. Once the 6 weeks of radiation and chemo are over, she will have to wait 3 months to know next steps (because radiation can cause false images of tumor progression on the MRI).

If the cancer responds to the chemo, Caroline will follow with another 12 cycles of chemo (5 days a month for 12 months). There will not be any more radiation because she will be close to the maximum amount.

Caroline is feeling more positive now that she knows the plan. So are we.

"Prayer" Food | Caroline Wright

So I woke up this morning having decided something that I think you guys could help with.

We have been managing here at the house fine in terms of food, but we have been eating a fair bit of takeout because of the logistics of managing the kids and the busy, truly exhausted evenings we are having. And takeout also has felt, thus far, to be a weird kind of treat that makes me feel like I live in New York again and just want to grab something on the corner because it will taste salty and good. So it's been okay and soulful in it's way, but I woke up feeling a philosophical shift.

I am aware now that I need to eat things that grow from the ground. Fruits and vegetables. Things made by people I love with love, with soul in it. I have some foods in my freezer of my own making that will bridge the gap as momentum of meals could be brought our way or even as I decide to cook a little bit (a goal I would really like to do soon because it also is what makes me feel like myself). But I feel like even soups from PCC (what I basically lived off of in the earliest days of my post-surgery recovery) are made by a talented stranger, which feels wrong in my house.

I would love for people to make me homemade soup, really. They can be frozen and eaten as needed, paced according to our needs and individual daily issues that come up. Soup and a piece of good bread feels like the food that will make me well and with enough variety, I wouldn't get sick of it. It also feels like a way that my body understands and accepts love, which feels like the right moment to be listening to it.

No. More. Takeout.

(I am sure this is going to send Al into a frenzy. Sorry, lovely woman, for posting without warning. I love you.)

The Team │ Caroline Wright

Yesterday I met the two doctors that are going to spearhead my cancer treatment. Two bright, competent women whose care and skills made me transform from honestly walking into their appointment feeling symptoms and fear to feeling seen and listened to. Having them assess me and tell me more about their theories and goals based on what we do and don't know right now (which is still missing some key points of pathology for a few more days, we're told) was incredibly calming. As was both of their concern with my hyper speed energy level on steroids and needing to relax in order to heal.

I went into the appointment steeled with the reality that my tumor could be growing, since my symptoms that I now recognize from the growth period—seizures, blurry vision, among many others—had appeared with gusto over the weekend. I began to panic with this vision that I would need another emergency surgery to remove another mass before the treatment was to begin—total nonsense and purely side effects of my meds, but definitely a very real feeling all the same.

That's the trick about having a problem with your brain, especially for someone who feels like they have pretty acute control over it most of the time. It can be hard to parse out what are symptoms, what are emotions, what are emotions based on the fact that all of this is just objectively overwhelming and what are emotions based on the fact that I had a growth in the portion of my brain that controls my emotions. I trust my instincts with my whole being and have lived my life in the glow of that emotional clarity. To have an experience that derails that—a traumatic, physical one no less but one that also happens to mess with your emotions on top of it—has been deeply jarring to say the least.

So this is where the trust of my team comes in. All I can do is be terribly honest about every thought I have and hand it over to them to dissect and diagnose. My ability to communicate emotions might be the thing that saves my life.

It is definitely the thing that is making me feel alive right now in these moments and for that I am deeply thankful. For each of you, too, for helping me process this space and for being willing to see every angle ("real" or nightmare and reading along as I figure out the difference) with support and kindness. It is making the biggest difference in terms of my experience of these feelings, which is really the only thing I can do from here.

Mom's Leaving | Caroline Wright

My mom left on a redeye flight last night after tucking me into bed. She had been crying for two days straight and I could tell felt wracked with guilt and sadness over leaving. She had spent the day with me meeting my oncologists and nurses and tallying questions and answers in ways I am not capable of right now. She held those details before she left along with my hand.

I know she didn't want to leave. I wish we could have continued to bask in the joy of being close and vulnerable for longer. Just because she isn't in this house and making ice packs for my neck doesn't mean I don't feel her here with me now. Or that I won't be seeing her soon when it becomes possible for her to visit again.

This is an important part of the strength I can feel in facing death, I think. That connection doesn't have to be in front of you to be felt. I love you, Mom. We'll talk soon. Keep kicking butt and so will I.

To: Caroline
From: Katy
Date: March 7, 2017
Subject: Lots and lots of love to you today!!!

There is something I thought of when I was wondering how I could support you best...When I was in my deepest moments of grief, there are just so many things that people can say that are the wrong things. Like, why would you even think you could say that to me right now kind of things, why would I want to hear that or that is really all about you or that is so dismissive or how presumtive of you to think that that would help or deep spiritual things all about themselves...a million things.

One thing that really helped me was that every time someone said something deep or meaningful (for them) to me, I'd put myself in the place of: *okay, it is very courageous of them to talk to me about this topic.* Sometimes random people say really helpful, insightful things. But if they'd say something that was any of the above, kind of off the mark things, I'd try to think: *Okay, they really needed to say that, this is probably a part of their own grief process. I don't need to take any of this on.* I figure I'd compile it into a blog post, "Shit people say to a grieving widow", and would try to laugh about it later.

People want to help and engage with you. They really don't know what to say sometimes so default is to say something they think is relating to you or supportive. But really I know it's nice to just not have to say anything, for people to really listen, to hold you energetically. I wanted to say this because I feel at a loss maybe for what to say to you and it reminds me of this time I was in. I don't know if you've felt any of these above things regarding "shit people say to people with cancer." It can feel isolating when no one really knows your insides unless they listen to you talk.

I remember one of the first grief groups I went to, we all went through a litany of the shitty things people had said to us as widows and it was incredibly refreshing to be able to complain with people about my situation that I didn't have to then take care of afterwards. Or worry about someone thinking they had to say something as a follow-up to the load I'd just dumped out. Sometimes you just need to say the darkest things to someone who really understands or is neutral enough to hold that space for you.

I hope you are finding some of those things, deep listening spaces. I'm glad you are such a beautiful writer. It's a gift to everyone.

Love to you, sweet friend.

A Story from Today | Paul Markunas

I went down to the best cake maker in Seattle today to order a cake for Caroline's birthday (in case the homemade one from Caroline's *Cake Magic* doesn't turn out the way Garth hopes!) and I was behind a lady in line who didn't have quite enough cash to pay for her piece of chocolate truffle cake. It's a cash or check-only place (go figure for techno-centric Seattle!)

She was a dollar short.

I heard her say to the woman behind the counter that she took the five dollars out of her wallet that her father had told her to always keep in reserve but didn't have enough to make up the rest of the ninety-seven cents needed.

I told her I had a dollar and would be happy to contribute so that she could enjoy her piece of cake. She thanked me and was touched and grateful. Then I said to her, "you know I heard you say that your dad always wanted you to keep a fiver in reserve for whatever so I'd like to give you your five back, too."

She teared up a little. She said she couldn't accept it and I said to her that I wanted to pay it forward a little bit. I told her I was suffering emotionally from the news of our daughter having been recently diagnosed with terminal brain cancer.

At that she really teared up. She told me that the reason she teared up originally when she gave the five dollar bill to the woman behind the counter was that she thought of her dad always telling her to keep that five in reserve.

She had just come back to Seattle from burying him. He died of a brain tumor.

At that we hugged. And both cried.

Miracles exist and do happen everyday.

As A Parent... And Thanks | Paul Markunas

I've been thinking about this a lot since the news.

I've thought about it even more because of the amazing notes and emails from other parents who feel our pain and suffering and offer words of love and support and kindness that warms my soul and feeds my strength.

Why couldn't it be me? I WANT IT TO BE ME.

No 32 year old should ever have to suffer and possibly die soon leaving a 4 year old and a 1 year old and a wonderful husband and a life so filled with family of all sorts that it shames everyone of us to be better, more loving, more gracious, more giving, more thoughtful.

It IS almost too much to bear.

But reading the notes filled with love and hope and kindness (does anyone under 60 ever remember talk of being a "kinder, gentler nation"?) make me realize that we all have our path and our path is the same. It is to love each other and to be kind to each other and help each other along the way.

It doesn't take the temporal suffering away, the intense pain that you feel at the threat of a loss so dear, so unique that only a parent can appreciate, but it does make my story our story which lifts the load, spreads the weight.

But still, I would rather it be me.

The Boys | Paul Markunas

Tonight must be a night of purging. This is my third post and second box of tissue.

Glad (for those of you who don't know her: my wife, my love, my better, my self) is short for Gladding (not Gladys, thank you) and is Caroline's mom.

Since the day Henry, our first grandchild, was born, we made a pact to him to see him every month of his life for the first two years. We lived in Orlando. He lived (with his parents) in Dallas. We kept our promise.

It was a pact our daughter and son-in-law lived through. It wasn't always easy or convenient. But it was karmic.

The bond we made with him is like a second skin he wears so proudly. He is gifted. Smart. Sweet. Irascible. Tenacious. Sad. Exuberant.

Glad and I took the boys to Bellevue Mall last Sunday. Henry loves the Tavern Hall because of the thousand tv's, one of which has Formula One race cars on it at all times. Theodore loves the company, the ketchup and the bacon.

I was just so struck by our closeness with them, how comfortable they are, that it gave me comfort for the news we are bearing and endure.

They will be safe. And loved forever and ever.

I'm Not Dying | Caroline Wright

The thing about being told you're really sick and that you only have the odds of living a year is that, you know, it's scary and makes you immediately think about the boundaries of your life.

My experience since my terminal prognosis, however, has been nothing but bliss. I laser focus on my kids and the joy they fill me with, the sound of their laughter and the pride I have in being a version of "normal" with them and being able to be out of bed and chase them around a little makes me blissfully happy. I know I should be scared, but I'm just not. If these somehow are my last days, I don't want to spend them being scared or hiding from the love and truths in my life. It's not how I've lived a day of my 32 (almost 33!) years so far, so I don't know why I would start now that the timing really seems to matter.

Friends from around the globe are coming to visit me starting on Sunday, the people who have given me the shape of my love for my whole life and floated me through past traumas. I see us laughing and crying and taking walks (hopefully) in the sun and sitting in the house that I designed so they would visit someday. This isn't even a shade of dying, it's truly living. I can't control the path of my body, but I can control the path of my spirit. And that is living to its fullest.

I have a strong feeling that I will survive my given year and longer, I really do. It's the closest thing to faith I am feeling right now, my gut telling me that I have some good odds because of my age and drive and the love and competent doctors behind me. But if it doesn't work out that way, and I do die, I will have lived a fortunate, beautiful and grateful life until the very end. Unafraid.

To: Caroline
From: Jeff
Date: March 9, 2017
Subject: Happy birthday, love

Hey Gurl,

There's a package on the way for you, full of things that Michael and I gathered together, hoping they'd bring bring you some joy and pleasure. He's a better gift buyer than I am, and helped me manage and move with (and sometimes out of) my numbness and paralysis, in a time when making any choice about what to send you on your birthday feels just impossible. (There may be chocolate in there, which is not meant to be sadistic, but with a hope that you could enjoy chocolate a bit on your bday!)

You probably already know it, but you've been with me in my office, especially when patients talk about grief and loss; I can sometimes feel into their experience (when I feel a little more alive, maybe after a cigarette) in a way that couldn't have been possible before your body introduced us all into this experience of the chaos of life going in unimaginable directions.

I love you! I cherish you! You just sent me a picture of your wishbone tattoo. I feel so happy to share this brand with you, and to share your belief in the courage it takes to make wishes, to make a life that feels as close as possible to what we want, to ask for what matters. The risk and pleasure of finding hope in something broken. There are so many wishes to make now! For now, wishes for miracles and good sex come to mind.

Oh gurl. I don't know where we are these days, but you're in my cells, in all the food I eat, in my being a therapist, in my being a partner and a guinea pig daddy. I think we will just have to keep breaking wishbones and blowing out birthday candles, since what else is there to do?

Michael is going to make pasta with zucchini and mozzarella for us tonight. You may remember I made the pasta with Alston, too. I ate it on Gillian's back house stoop that windy day when you had pictures taken for your first book. I guess we'll just keep eating pasta, too. :)

I love you and will be celebrating you today!

Love for always,
Jeff

Sent from my iPhone

My Birthday | Caroline Wright

My birthday was an absolutely gorgeous day. It was too full, I learned at the end of it in the face of a cake-fueled meltdown from Henry who shared a missed bedtime with me, but really magical all the same.

My favorite part was going out for lunch with my three best friends here in Seattle, three hard-working and incredible moms who left their babies and children with loved ones and put on leather shoes and jewelry so we could have a beautiful, quiet lunch with my father. It was so meaningful and I will never forget our conversations or the thoughtful, empowering gifts. Or the fact that heart-shaped balloons are maybe still at the time of writing this on the ceiling of a homemade pasta restaurant in Fremont thanks to sweet Katie who forgot to tie them to a chair as we sat down.

Yesterday was a valuable lesson for me, though. I've noticed in the past two very busy days that my energy, which I am not good at protecting because it has always felt bottomless, is very sacred right now. It is affecting my breath and my capacity to draw it in, even. I have to learn to prioritize self-care in a way I have never done before, because this reckless energy spending of mine is just irresponsible right now for me and my loved ones. This is a permanent life change for me, however long my life may be, and it has to start now. I have to relax and take care of myself and tell people how to help me and let them. I have to find the places where kindness rests in a focused way, rather than dispersed outlets. I am suspending my social media accounts today until future, recovered Caroline makes the decision to rejoin. (She gets to call some shots, too.)

Thank you from the bottom of my heart for all the birthday love. (Especially the drawings from Tara's Tots and FCS, which I will write about and include some images of later, which changed me and my Henry, I think. And the Ladurée *macarons* and *palmier* shipped fresh to me from Paris by my beautiful Amy, which I actually ate in lieu of cake last night. The friends who gathered for cake—the first one in recent memory that I didn't make!—and brought their families to hug me. And, and, and.)

I realize that my love is like Katie's balloons from lunch. It can be released and will rest in a corner somewhere until gathered up and passed on. I have to do all I can to tie it to my chair right now.

Highly Sensitive and Living with a Terminal Illness
Caroline Wright

I had long since suspected that I am a "highly sensitive person." I mean this in an actual diagnostic way, not just that I cry at some of Google's commercials around the holidays. It's a person that feels every sensation more intensely and processes their world differently. My father definitely is, who is the one who raised me knowing about this kind of worldview.

I became more interested in researching the highly sensitive person when our son, Henry, seemed to not be moving out of the tantrum phase (and that his "tantrums" were much more extreme than the kids of our closest friends, triggered by sensory overwhelm). It is clear upon meeting Henry that he is different and deeply special. He is incredibly expressive and aware of his feelings (we call it a "superpower" in our house that sweet Garth attributes to me, which I wear proudly like a cape). If you think your kid might be highly sensitive, the book *The Highly Sensitive Child: Helping our Children Thrive in a World That Overwhelms Them* by Elaine N. Aron, MD, is truly transformative and so helpful in seeing your special kid. In reading the book on Henry's behalf, I confirmed not only Henry's nature, but also my own, Garth's, and basically all of my friends (possibly an unwritten standard in the code of how I've sorted my closest friends in my life, because of our shared language.) The very light that I described Sarah to have, in addition to all of my friends. Highly sensitive, indeed.

The hard part about being highly sensitive and living with a terminal illness is that I am processing everything—as I do anyway—closely but with an additional temporal and emotional lens, which makes already intense feelings more so. Emotional processing is basically a hobby of mine, shared with my now therapist best friend, Jeff. I am very grateful that I like to experience life this way, as it grounds this surreal experience into something intellectual and curious for me.

For example, every person I have met and fallen in love with in the past year—many, many people, I am fortunate to say—immediately call tears to their eyes when they see me. That is the hardest thing about all this, actually. It makes me feel like the walking dead, when I am trying to live in the present, full of life. (As I've already mentioned, I am learning that dying is a state of body, not mind.)

Being a highly sensitive person and being truly alive, however, is kind of magical. I notice every blooming flower, hear the soul in every laugh from my kids, taste textures and flavors of foods better than I did before. It's incredible. I'm so lucky that however long I live, I will soak up every little drop of life. It's an adventure and it's weird to say, but I feel lucky to be a part of it. And have an emotional brain that is into that.

To: Caroline
From: Tara
Date: March 11, 2017
Subject: Miracle

Today at lunch I told the children about a miracle I had with a goat I named Billy the Kid. When he was a baby his mother starting kicking him away from her when he wanted to nurse. I called the vet and she asked me to bring him in. We found out he had pneumonia, and it is a common characteristic of animals to want to protect the healthy baby, that's why his mother would not allow him to suckle, as he was a twin.

The vet told me clearly, "He's going to die."

After finding out that animals just give up when they are sick, I asked the vet what I could do to help him recover - basically I had to force feed him every hour or two, and keep him warm and calm. So I brought him back to the farm, built a fire in the fireplace, milked his mother, filled a baby bottle and tried to feed him. He was so weak by this time he would not suck, so I cut the tip of the nipple, held his mouth closed, tipped his head up, and rubbed his throat so he would swallow. (I wish you could have seen the kids faces as I told this story.)

Billy and I slept together by that fire for days until it was obvious he was better, and after a return to the vet my suspicions were proven correct. He was healthy.

I brought him back to the farm, reintroduced him to his mother who licked him all over and let him nurse: A MIRACLE!!!

I love you Caroline. XOXO

Conversations with Henry | Caroline Wright

Watching my sweet Henry grapple with the new state of our lives has been so beautiful and painful for everyone in our house. He is deeply sad right now and processing all that he can understand and acting out when he doesn't. He is relying on the love of those around him (so many powerful forces of love in his life, he is very fortunate) to guide him.

We have chosen to tell him the complete truth about everything we know. Because of the book that Al brought to us within days of the initial diagnosis, *How To Help Children Through a Parent's Serious Illness*, which I sincerely hope none of you reading here will ever need, we were immediately focused on protecting our bond as a family over shielding Henry from the pain of the reality of losing his beloved mom. The book makes the great point that children are resilient and capable of understanding far more than parents think they do, and that the part that damages them through the loss of a parent is not the adjustment itself (they will end up fine, ultimately, as long as they are loved and cared for) but how they are treated through the process of the death of their parent. If they are lied to and the trust is broken, and the sick parent ultimately dies, then the bond that they had with that parent is broken forever without the capability for healing. That is the damaging part more than the loss itself.

I might have come to this conclusion on my own anyway, but it was very helpful to provide actual talking points and language to get us through those early days as we figured out how to talk about what was happening. The other rule that is important in this book is that, while we have open conversations about what we know, we try not to push him to reach a realization before he is ready. We are available to talk to him about anything, but forcing him to talk about death or his feelings isn't how we are trying to go about it. What results are random, sad moments in which it is clear that Henry's understanding is breaking through and time stands still. I wanted to share a few with you here; they are gut-wrenching but comforting to me ultimately, because I think Henry will be as beautiful forever as he is today, whether or not I am here to see it.

[I am in the early days of recovery, sitting in the nursing chair in the very early morning and writing. Henry comes in holding his Bunny, his favorite friend other than Dido who was given to him a few years ago by Grandma Meliza and has been inseparable since. Henry, groggy from sleep, comes into the dimly lit room and climbs into my lap.]

Henry: Mama, Bunny has two tumors in her head. She is really sick and needs to go to the hospital. She's really scared.

Caroline: Let's zoom her to the hospital then! She will have the best doctors we can find and we will help her be strong so she can do everything she can to get well. Even though it sounds like she's pretty sick and there's a chance she still could die, even if she fights really hard. We just have to do everything we can to make her feel okay. What could we do to make her feel cozy?

Henry: Tuck her in and hold her while she sleeps. She wants to cuddle.

Caroline: Okay. I've got her right here, she doesn't need to worry. We'll help her in every way we can, okay?

Henry: Okay. I'm going to go get some yogurt while she sleeps.

[On the basement stairs a few days later, after playing together downstairs, as we climbed together in silence.]

Henry: Mama, I will love you forever. Even if you die.

If that is how he feels, then I am proud to know that I have done my job—even with him at the age of four—to show him the space of my love and that he feels confident in his way that he could hold it with him forever. Until recently, I don't know that I could have said that about my own mother. So that's a gift I've given him and I have to be at peace knowing I've done the very best I could, even now.

The "What Ifs" | Caroline Wright

This is a game I don't play often because there is no point to it. In that spirit, I am going to unload all of the "what ifs" that I have kicking around in my head so they can get out once and for all. In tired or baffled moments, the "what ifs" can settle in and they sound something like this:

What if I had waited to go to the doctor for a symptom that seemed more real to me (I had already peed my pants in broad daylight without urgency or the ability to stop it, which in retrospect was a seizure for sure) and it took another month before I figured it out like having a car accident or something and hurt my kids or someone else's and I would have still had a stage 4 glioblastoma being someone with a ruined life anyway

Or what if I had not had Joe in my life who handed me to Dr. Ellenbogen and the team at UW and told me to not read the news and get a second opinion which actually turned into the first and that meant I was still referred to a clinic in which the doctor didn't show up to my appointment and I wouldn't have been able to get into surgery for the better part of a month while my tumor was still aggressively growing, after which it could have been inoperable

*Or what if I hadn't emailed my doctor that day for that
headache and what I thought were panic attacks and she
dismissed the headaches because of my lifestyle choices, or I
hadn't come in because I'm too busy or my kids were sick or*

All roads lead me to right where I am now—that path doesn't
seem like it could have changed. Even not knowing how long
it could have been growing (you have to have "two pictures
to tell time," Dr. Tseng tells me, because you have to have
a baseline image and the discovery image, yet that never
happens because no one is going to wait for treatment once
a tumor is discovered), I know that this was unavoidable
for me. (I didn't cause it, it isn't genetic. I am afraid of
microwaves, preservatives and never did drugs. Cell phones
don't cause this.)

So, in the grand scheme of things, I really do believe with
my whole heart that this is the luckiest possible outcome. I
mean that. In the face of possibly hurting my kids (I had been
driving and having seizures!) or a tumor whose progression
could have been inoperable or too involved with my brain
tissue to resect well, this truly is the best possible outcome.

I had a tumor that, though scary, was completely resected
and I am starting from cells that the tool used to detect
them can't even see. I have a team created through personal
connections that care about me as well as are the very best in
town at their work. That my sons are totally taken care of and

my family and friends (old and new) have lifted me up in a light I can only compare to a religious experience because the kindnesses I've been shown are unlike any version of human I've known so far in my life, and I've picked good ones over the years. I am 20 years younger than a normal glioblastoma patient and have strength and youth and everything worth fighting for on my side.

The best of all, though, is that I am still me. Even now—I am writing, talking, walking, quilting, chasing my kids. What if I had waited and that wasn't an option today.

The Idea of Perfection | Caroline Wright

My dear friend Katie came over just after my surgery, armed with a box of croissants and the brave question of how I would possibly return to regular life (mostly in the context of trusting my brain again). The conversation eventually turned to my insufferably high standards and how I was going to have to adjust them with this new perspective I've been given. To learn to rest and find contentment. And even that this experience itself—my writing about it and how well I've done medically—is an expression of a perceived grace and willfulness that could be viewed as perfection.

I have gotten a similar comment throughout my life—an attempt at compliment, I sincerely trust—that I am graceful and make things look easy. ("Graceful," for those of you who know me well, is hilarious because to me it conjures an image of a ballerina. I have always felt lumbering and clumsy in my body, which is something I want to change going forward.) "Perfection" is the moniker I hate most because it couldn't be further from the truth of my experience, and I certainly am not trying to hide my experience from those around me. Two pillars of my understanding of myself are that I've always lived my life out loud—authentically, honestly and in the open—and, too, that I have faced serious struggles (often self-inflicted, though not always). So, when I hear from friends or family, even in jest, that I make things look easy or that something I do is "perfect," I bristle.

Firstly, I am just not perfect and have no idea what that even means. I am human, I make mistakes, and I work really hard to figure out how to do something that feels like a good job to me. I try. Saying I am perfect means that it removes my very real effort to do better. I'm not doing it for someone else, I am doing it for me and those I hold dear as an almost extension of myself. I am not a saint. I rarely consider what other people think of me, truest in matters of moral standard or my kids.

It bothers me, too, because one thing I have learned that I truly love about myself is that I am a teacher. (I think I may have always been a thinker who likes to talk and have conversations about the way the world works, even as a little kid. Maybe that's why I didn't have boyfriends in high school?) I like to push ideas around in my head, turn them over, find a new way to look at something. This is why, when perfection comes into the conversation, it means that there is a necessary distance between my choices and those of the person who is talking to me. That what I am doing is unattainable or impossible.

Furthermore, I spend my career as a cookbook author, a most sincere extension of my inner self, trying to deconstruct the idea of perfection. In my work, I attempt to dissect things that seem impossible and make them easy and even *empowering* to someone who might have been intimidated to try something new.

Today Garth and I had a session with a clairvoyant that was so powerful that I can't actually write about it now. But this theme came up as one of the first things she said—that I need to try being less "perfect"—and I had been thinking about this post already because of my sweet Katie. So here we are.

We're in this together as imperfect humans. I'm trying hard in this hard place. You're helping me find my way and I am thankful for you.

During this time, since my post about a week prior calling for homemade soup, we were receiving multiple drop-offs daily from a wide range of friends. Mostly new ones or ones I'd never met. A cooler sat outside our front door and it would empty and fill, as if possessed in aid of my healing. Soup was a balm to my soul, as was having my community cook for me; homemade food appeared, conjured as if through magic. The cooler became a conduit for sympathy in its only palatable form.

The Meaning of "Terminal" and Some Changes | Caroline Wright

I've been thinking about what the word "terminal" even means. It's a scary word, for sure. But realistically, instead of it being the shape of death, which is what it immediately calls to mind, it is just the shape of my life for the rest of it. How long that is, we don't know. But no one does, right?

In that spirit, I've decided to make some changes to my lifestyle that could help compliment my experience of chemo and radiation, I'm told. I know so many of my beloveds here in Seattle subscribe to this "better living" already, so I would love any recommendations for the outlets/guides to make this transition easier. I need to be taught how to do this stuff and fast. Help, my progressive tribe!

- **Yoga:** I want to find a walking distance studio that has an awesome teacher who has a very beginner class that focuses on the mindfulness and body integration part really well. I'm not looking to break any personal bests. Just a place to really focus on being in my body, my mind, and expanding the boundaries of both as I heal. Recommendations?
- **Naturopath:** Through speaking with a clairvoyant yesterday, I found out I need to examine my gut and

its ability to absorb trace metals and minerals, which apparently will be important for my treatment as well as my timeline in general. Why not? She specifically mentioned that acupuncture is less of a concern right now, though may be a tool a reach for later, and that reiki might be, too. One of my close friends recommended one in Portland that I plan to see.

· **Walking Buddies:** As I heal during my chemo and radiation, I want to have walking dates in beautiful places around town. See flowers, water and friends (current or new ones who have only "met" me here). For some reason, my heart tells me that Discovery Park is an important space for me coming up.

· **Gardening:** I mentioned it before, but I am very excited to have a garden. I am a nurturing person, but people and animals are the only beings I have done well with so far. (Other than with my parents' collection of parrots growing up. Those guys were assholes.) My dad will teach me how to care for the plants once we get to that point (he's very talented), but we are light years away from that point and time and the season is upon us to get moving with this project. If friends want to participate in the transformation of our dirt pile backyard—Garth has some dates set up—that would be truly transformative for my spring and summer of healing.

- **Diet:** This one is the biggest, most shocking change to me right now because my cooking and eating is both so personal to me as well as causes implications for my work. I also have spent so many years silently judging people who follow intense, restricted diets for seemingly minor reasons. But now I am in a place of trying to give my body every extra boost, real or imagined, to get through my treatment in not only the most successful way possible, but also in a way where I could have enough energy leftover to remain "Mommy" and "Caroline" (in that order) throughout. So, I am going (stifling a shudder) gluten-free. And following a diet formulated to reduce inflammation for my blood type, which is really specific and restrictive, too. Soup is still my ticket to wellness, I still really believe. Tasting all of your food so far has been incredibly restorative. Really. Thank you.

I like, too, that the word "terminal" feels a little like going home, or like a part of the airport where you wait for your plane. With your help, let's see what I can do to make the wait as beautiful and healing as it can be.

My Food Crazy Right Now | Caroline Wright

Ugh this *couldn't* feel more annoying or reluctant to me than it does, but here goes. Luckily I really love all food, so I know it will just be a matter of finding some new recipes that inspire me. My food choices right now:

Beneficial (as in has a kind of "superfood" status for my situation right now):

Beans: black-eyed peas, adzuki

Fish: Bass (sea or stripe), Atlantic cod, Halibut, Perch (ocean, silver, yellow, walleye), red snapper, American shad, Tilefish, Trout (rainbow), Sole

Grains: sorghum, teff, millet, quinoa, buckwheat, chia, brown rices that haven't been processed. No gluten.

Fruits: banana, blueberry, cherry, mango, guava, plums, prunes

Herbs: Curries, Fresh Herbs, Parsley, Turmeric

Seeds: Pumpkin, Flax

Oils: Olive oil (and no others, really)

Meat: beef, buffalo, lamb, venison

Vegetables: artichoke, beet greens, broccoli, chicory, collards, dandelion, escarole, ginger, turnip, Swiss chard, spinach, seaweed, pumpkin, sweet potato, red pepper,

parsnip, horseradish, kale, kelp, kohlrabi, romaine, okra, onion
Dairy: Hemp, sheep and goat's milk. (I'm mostly into goat and sheep cheese, not "alternative" cheeses.) Nothing else, really.

Avoid (these are foods that apparently react negatively to my blood type and cause inflammation):
Beans: kidney, lentils, navy beans, pinto, tamarind
Fruits: Asian pear, avocado (*Ack!*), blackberries, cantaloupe, coconut, kiwi, lychee, oranges (and OJ), tangerines (and tangerine juice)
Meat: bacon, ham, pork and quail (*so many good ones...*)
Vegetables: cauliflower, cucumber, mushrooms, black olives (*so, so sad to me*), rhubarb (*boo*), regular potatoes
Etc: coffee, black tea and white wine, carrageenan (*I already avoid this*), MSG, mustard, nutmeg, pistachios, cashews, peanuts and peanut butter, sunflower seeds and sunflower seed butter

Again, a more pain-in-the-ass list has never existed. If you are on the list to make your favorite soup, I would love to serve it to my family and I will be thankful all the same (even if I "can't" eat it). I sincerely promise.

Also, I cannot believe it is one month since that fated phone call from my internist. What a wild month it has been, to say the least.

My Chemo Meds Have Arrived! | Caroline Wright

That is all. Back to quilting.

(...I will be taking chemo pills from home at a prescribed time of day during my treatment. My first day taking them will be March 26, the day before my first go of radiation. I have an MRI tomorrow morning to help develop the particular road map for my brain as it faces radiation. I immediately got worried because they had distinctly said that they don't do MRIs until after the treatment, but then Dr. Tseng explained that it had to do with how large my tumor was and that my brain had a big space to squish back to and that natural swelling occurs a little bit when that happens. This means that the immediate post-op MRI didn't reflect exactly where the brain has settled back to be. I will have Garth update about the exact timeline and other details tomorrow.)

Okay, really, back to quilting. My best friend from Dallas, Sasha, will be here in about an hour or so!

Side Effects of Cancer | Paul Markunas

Just to provide a broader perspective on what Caroline is going through, I thought I'd throw a little light on what those of us who support the cancer victim/patient go through as well.

I came home to Windermere, FL (just outside of Orlando) a week ago.

In this week, I have made arrangements to close up our house (we were in the process of making a move to Scottsdale, AZ, even before the diagnosis), sent 15 boxes of clothing, kitchen goods and other stuff to our new "cubby" in Seattle, to transport my SUV to AZ, filed our 2016 1040 returns (thanks to our accountant who went into overdrive for us) and have worked to rehome our five jack russell terriers which is coming down to the wire before I leave on Sunday morning at 5 am.

I love all of our dogs with all my heart and soul. I am an introvert and love the company and collusion of my pet friends when I am ruminating and recharging and restoring at home, by myself, without outside stimulation.

We are finding new, permanent homes for all of them this week.

I was reminded today that I will miss the youngest puppies the most. We got them as a pair the weekend after my all-time favorite Jack Russell was bitten by a rattlesnake in our backyard and died. She was, and is, one of the brightest lights in my life. But in order to incorporate the new puppies into the remaining three adult Jack Russells in our family "pack" I slept on the sofa in our TV room with them for six months, night after night, to make them a part of our family, and to make them a part of their new dog family, without fear or suffering. It worked.

I so love all of our dogs, but this is the right thing to do. But it is a side effect of cancer. It changes everything. And not just for today and tomorrow but for the rest of what we have left to experience in this life. And it even changes how you experience what you have remaining.

I'm not whining. I'm grateful.

I love our daughter to the ends of the world and back. And I love those two boys with every molecule of my being. And I so love and admire Garth with his grace and strength to support Caroline, the boys, while still researching, fighting, carrying on.

But, still, there are moments of despair and pain.

I'm coming back to Seattle on Sunday. As Caroline says, "coming home." It doesn't feel quite like that yet for me, but from the love and warmth we have experienced from all the family Caroline and Garth have created for themselves there, it may soon feel like home. I really hope so. It would lessen the pain.

I will miss my dogs.

My dearest friends—the same ones I wrote the night I was told of the MRI results—all came to visit as soon as I told them they could. Not knowing how radiation was going to affect me—I had been told to anticipate severe symptoms ranging from depression, total lack of energy, to extreme nausea—and I knew that their visits would help me find a way back to my true self if it was hiding behind symptoms. I knew I would need our laughter, our joy, our story built in a life that wasn't defined by cancer.

From Sarah After Her Visit | Paul Markunas

From Sarah:

I loved visiting our Sweet Caroline. I felt like I was one of many friends marching into battle when I arrived. Holding back tears, I was resolved to be strong and lift her up.

It was business as usual in a lot of ways at the Wright House. Henry furiously building Legos, Theodore wanting to crawl in Caroline's lap to read. A quilt out and hints of other projects in the making, and hand knit sweaters drying on the bed. Garth and I slipped fast into our big brother, little sister fodder, which kept all things littered with humor. Our short time together had begun.

Caroline and I have always had a physical closeness that's been dear to me, and funny for me. I'm a 'Samantha' (for lack of a better millennial reference) in more relationships than not, maintaining an arms length of reason and coolness and diffusing anything emotional with a hearty laugh. But it's never been that way with Caroline. I attribute this to meeting in the prime of our hormonal adolescent years, both dressed in corduroy knickers and long sleeved bright red sweaters at camp; if we were holding hands with any guys that summer, we would have needed different uniforms. And so we held each other's. I couldn't have been more thankful for that real closeness last week, when moments that might have otherwise been uncomfortable for either of us presented themselves regularly. A cry on the couch. A walk to take Henry to school. A walk into a radiation office. When you have cancer, you need the human touch, and we had that down. It was a not-so-gentle reminder to me that it's all about practicing in life, and how thankful you are when your preparation meets said opportunity.

Caroline's gone first between us in all the ways that count in life. She fell in love first, got a grown up good job first, got married first, had kids first, and I learned so much and am so grateful to have had her go and test the waters. And now she is sick first. And I'm still learning. I watched as she got up early to write, or put her writing down to do a race with Henry. I watched her stop racing Henry to sit and rest, just to get up again and show me how to cut an onion. And then stop and hug her husband (in the middle of the day for nothing, ladies!) It was beautiful priority, free of the "shoulds" of life. My hummingbird of a friend had transformed into a butterfly, and I was seeing all her beauty in slow motion as she fluttered gracefully (sorry, babe, but yes I said gracefully) from thing to thing.

I hugged each boy twice, and then made Caroline get back out of the car when my time there had come to an end. I sympathized with Henry the most, as I was struggling to compartmentalize my own feelings. The box that worry went in didn't have enough air holes. The box of gratitude, too small. Fairness seemed obsolete. My heart seemed to break and mend simultaneously, and my mind was telling me I was better off for it. I wanted to sit down in the airport

terminal, take off my shoes and refuse to move in complete protest,
much like Henry had done earlier that morning to prevent me
from leaving. I related entirely to his logic and his heart. I repeated
the dialogue I had heard Caroline use with Henry to myself, as I
boarded the plane:

Are you sad Aunt Sarah is leaving ?

Don't worry, she will be back again soon.

Treatment Schedule | Garth Wright

Caroline had her baseline MRI this morning which keeps us on track to have her dry-run of radiation on Friday. Because the tumor was so big (and had squished her brain to the side), the recent CT scan could not be reconciled with her post-op MRI.

Schedule puts us to start Caroline's photon radiation therapy the morning of March 27. She will begin her chemo by taking a pill the day before. She will be in radiation therapy Monday through Friday until May 5. She will then take her last chemo pill May 6.

Although radiation effects can continue for 1-2 weeks after her last treatment, Caroline will get a 4 week "break" between her last chemo pill and her next clinic appointment and MRI. For up to 3 months after radiation therapy there is a chance of tumor "pseudo-progression" in which the MRI will present swelling that could be mistaken for tumor growth.

I will let everyone know how the dry run goes in my next post.

The Shape of Compromise | Caroline Wright

I am a person with very definite ideas. I am terribly stubborn, but because I work diligently to create the standards I demand, not many people fault me for it. In this light, I am driven. Creative. Talented.

However, something I have long since sensed about myself is that I have absolutely no idea how to regulate this behavior. I do everything to its fullest conclusion because I don't know any other way. In one sense it has always felt efficient and reasonable in that I only take on projects that I am capable of, so I should give it my all and make something great. This is true of my work, my kids, my marriage, my friendships and recently renovating our family house. The positive side of this is finding beauty in everything and bringing it out to its fullest extent. The negative side of this is that I actually throw my soul into these endeavors—I invest my whole being into everything I do—so I think it is also deeply spiritually exhausting. (My energy supply has always been endless, as well as my creative drive. I am, in the very core of my being, a true artist with vision and motivation.)

I recognize that this is my personality. I love my openness and belief in the world and how I interact with it. It has helped me thrive and survive regardless of obstacles; it has brought me an incredibly full and beautiful life brimming with genuine and encompassing love since a very young age. I have a beautiful family that I have worked to shape and heal. The people I love are precious to me and I turn myself inside out to show them that as often as I can. This is the very shape of my understanding of myself since childhood and gives me the light that I feel makes me who I am. I am not willing to change this part.

However, the piece that I know needs to change is the "badass" in me (who I also love, too, I must say). The reckless part. The girl who needs to prove her talents to herself and push the boundaries of what is possible. I honestly think that this is the part of me that landed me here, the part that is incapable of self-care in the face of the things I so love in this world.

This is actually physically hard for me right now. I am totally lost. And the more I think about how to find a solution, the more I lose my grasp on how to be. It's clear that this is an incredibly important, total lifestyle change—to do less, though not necessarily to care less—but I honestly don't know how to go about it and still feel like myself. This is actually as scary to me as the brain tumor itself, if not scarier, which I realize makes me a total crazy person. I have had a good few days recently (sleeping, eating, my wound healing and still feeling like myself), so I know this isn't the meds talking.

This lesson, to me, feels like the purpose of my situation right now. Again, it is a deficit I have considered in myself but I've been too busy or distracted to make the necessary changes. Now, in this situation, I am out of excuses and I need to find balance in my life for the rest of it. I need to figure out how to be my version of a badass who doesn't give her soul away so easily. Thank you to all of my loved ones here who have seen this about me before I could and have tried to fill this role without my even knowing to ask.

This is my next chapter—I am going to need all the help I can get to figure out how to write it.

Another Moment with Henry | Caroline Wright

Today was Sasha's last day of her visit and it was a beautiful one: sunny, crisp and showing the first signs of spring. Buds blooming on trees in the foreground, the snowcapped mountains in the background against bright blue sky. I started a different post today but got caught up talking to my mom on the phone and a meandering walk to lunch with Sasha and a giant trip to Costco filled with gluten-free hunting and gathering, nostalgic Texas-style. We finished our day as a family, huddled around the kitchen table eating a Persian noodle soup made by one of Garth's work colleagues called *Asheh Reshteh* that is meant to be shared on the first day of spring. I had never tasted it before yet it felt like home, which feels like a pretty accurate description of everything I find comforting right now. It's all different and the same all at once.

This also happened today at the breakfast table that I wanted to share with you.

Henry: I had a nightmare. *[Insert story about Bunny who got lost and hurt herself that I forget the details of now, as it was divulged to me at 5 am.]*...Who is going to raise me?

Caroline: The same people are going to raise you whether or not Mama lives a long time. It takes a big group of people, my love. You have Daddy, Gampa and Gaba and Aunt Allison and a lot of people who love you very much. And Mama, for as long as I am lucky. Always Mama.

Henry: Oh, okay. Am I going to Anders' house this morning before school?

The season is changing. Slowly, but I see some comfort in the distance. Different but the same, too. I love you always, my sweet Henry.

Finding My Rituals | Caroline Wright

At the end of this week I have a "dry run" of my radiation treatment—I put on the mask, they match up the scans and roadmap they've created for my brain and they make sure that the technicians know precisely what to do and when to do it. This step brings me great comfort and makes me feel like a theater kid again approaching tech week, which I also like.

In this week leading up to my practice as the last of my scabs heal (my scar is incredible, by the way; also, is "scab" *really* the medical term?), I am taking care to come up with some rituals to do with my upcoming treatment. I am seeking out things that are comforting and redefine my experience, allowing me to feel present and focused on things that make me happy and calm.

I've done well with this so far in terms of my MRIs— the first was traumatic because I was having seizures and a migraine during it and didn't know that music or earplugs were an option to ask for, after which I was totally disoriented from the seizure and talking to a technician I now clearly see *knew* I had a giant tumor in my head and ushered me out the door. (It honestly has haunted me a little bit and I've been trying to shake it off, especially in light of the fact that I now have a substantial relationship to this machine as well as the technicians who run them.) My second experience was about a week later immediately pre-op for my brain surgery; my third was immediately post-op, during which my machine broke and I sat with headphones that were causing my locked jaw to be so painful that tears were streaming down my partially numb face. The post-op one, however, was the most pleasant even in spite of the pain because I discovered I could listen to Abigail Washburn (that I have already posted about), and having her there kept my best friend Jeff with me.

I had another MRI early Saturday morning, during which I again listened to Abigail Washburn and held Henry's cherished blanket buddy, Dido. I also meditated, filling up the machine's cavity with light and love. I imagined light and healing being absorbed into my head in the patterns of the incredibly loud noises of the machine, almost smiling when they swelled with drama. It all worked for me.

So, as I face radiation—which, apparently isn't painful at all, but possibly stranger still than an MRI because of being bolted to the table by a face mask and the treatment being about twenty nonstop minutes—I am interested in collecting these comforts that compartmentalize this experience for me. Here is what I have so far:

- Wearing a rotation of clothing that I am seeing like a type of armor. I have two cashmere sweaters of my beloved grandfather's that honestly recall the sense memory of hugging him every time I put them on my body. My mom gave me one of them from his closet when he died (when I was sixteen), and I have carried it with me and put it in my closet every where I've lived since, even to Paris in college. I've never worn it until now. (She gave me another one that she had in her closet and was keeping for the same reason.) I also have a RuPaul fangirl t-shirt from my dear Dan that reads "Shantay You Stay" that I intend to wear if cashmere sweaters become too warm as spring settles in.

· I have regularly started to wear a selection of rings and bracelets, which, as a professional cook and generally awkward woman, is a first. I have a beautiful prayer bead-style bracelet from my sweet Sarah that has a Labrador stone in it for strength (she wears a matching one now, too). The beads are made of sandalwood and smell a little like the dresser drawers I used when I stayed in my grandparents' cottage in Michigan almost every summer of my childhood. I also wear a copper bracelet that one of my mom's colleagues removed from his wrist and gave to her when she told him my news, a man who was told he was going to be a quadriplegic and survived and believed that this bracelet held some of that power for him. Mom and I wept together from gratitude, and it holds that meaning, too.

· I want to listen to music during treatment but I want Abigail hold tight to my MRIs. Right now I am deciding between Billie Holiday, one of my kindred artists though I am not sure I could manage to *not* sing along, which would be problematic; Fiona Apple's "The Idler the Wheel..." album, which I adore and still reminds me of Jeff and, in true Fiona form is about the duration of the treatment itself; some mix of Sia songs because she featured prominently during the playlist Garth and I listened to during Henry's birth. I am still thinking on it.

I plan to meditate, too. And create rituals outside of the actual treatment for calm—I am going to start yoga possibly tomorrow and am committed to finding a class and teacher I like. And I've been waking up in the morning before the kids get up and I've been reading my grandfather's self-published memoir, feeling him with me like I do very often. My dearest family of friends are still consistently coming to visit through the end of treatment, so I will have a lot of good conversations and silliness to look forward to, as well as people who can hold my spirit in silence and profound love.

I am really looking forward to starting my treatment on Monday. People keep telling me that I am going to be exhausted and worn out and possibly feel terrible and low, and I am ready for it. Hit me with this shit. I have an army behind me—from my head to my toes, beaming out of my soul and running through my mind—and am much tougher than my smile may suggest. I got this, I just know it.

Calendar Notes | Glad Markunas

On Thursday April 6th there are two notes on my calendar...
'Caroline and the boys arrive' and 'Trip to Seattle' with my
itinerary attached. The first is what was going to happen and
the second is what will.

Caroline had planned to bring the boys for a visit over
Henry's spring break which we always enjoy! Now I am
heading up to be with her during her third week of treatment
and to see all her boys on their turf. Plus give Paul some extra
help and hopefully a bit of a break.

April 6th just happened to be the first day following a
quarterly Board meeting when I felt I could comfortably
leave. My boss and my bosses' boss have been beyond terrific.
They are allowing me to work remotely and determine when
I need to be in my Seattle 'office' and when I need to be in
Orlando. The only requirement is to keep them informed
which I do by noting it as an event on my calendar and
'inviting' them so it also shows up on their calendars.

Somehow I can't bring myself to delete the first note on
April 6th. It remains in hopes of moving it to a new date in
the near future.

Fuck You, Tumor | Caroline Wright

We received a call today that the MRI I had on Saturday morning showed tumor growth. I went in today for a last-minute meeting to jumpstart the chemo today and begin radiation tomorrow.

I am processing this—right now, I am feeling a thousand things, including sadness, fear and discouragement. Reality. And ready to fight.

I am going to go out for a walk now with my dad because it's sunny so I can pick Henry up from school. Garth will post tonight about the medical details of where we are now. More soon. Must walk.

5   RADIATION AND "THE DIAGNOSIS PERIOD"

The journey between what you once were and who you are now becoming is where the dance of life really takes place.

—Barbara De Angelis

Acceleration... | Garth Wright

Today the radiation-oncologist told us that Caroline's
MRI from Saturday showed marked tumor growth (in the
1 month since surgery). This is normal, an expected behavior
of a glioblastoma.

Because of the aggressive growth, she is starting her
treatment immediately. The first chemotherapy pill will
be taken tonight, and her first radiation treatment will be
tomorrow afternoon.

The hope is that the combination of chemo and radiation
will arrest tumor growth, but the tumor often does grow
back in the area that is irradiated. 10 weeks from tomorrow
will be her next MRI.

My Call with Sarah Jane | Caroline Wright

My childhood best friend—my BFF as we have said since the fourth grade—is an oncologist nurse practitioner. (Weird, right? One of the many coincidences of this crazy story of mine that makes me feel cared for and hopeful despite a string of bad luck.)

My walk with my dad yesterday was wonderful and restorative; the act of getting outside in the Seattle sun and moving my body around changed the subject a little and made me feel decidedly alive. Bouts of anger and sadness were crashing in on me like waves since the news of the change in plans in the late morning yesterday. (I suppose this is part of the "oncology rollercoaster" that Dr. Kane warned me about. I don't remember buying a ticket!)

At the end of our walk, Sarah Jane called. I haven't been picking up my phone lately—I've been a little creeped out by holding the phone to my right ear because of the tumor—but I was thankful to hear from SJ at that perfect moment. She reminded me that she sees this stuff every day and that, even though it seems scary now, it is still possible to eradicate a tumor though chemo and radiation alone and face a remission like I had been hoping for. She also confirmed my attempt at hopeful logic: right now I am four weeks since my brain surgery with an otherwise untreated cancer in my head (whose personality is to grow), and that it could have been much worse if they hadn't removed the full mass (which was actually a possibility given its location) and the four untreated weeks fed an actual mass that was there. She reminded me that she sees 80-year-olds beat their odds at GBM tumors all the time and I have no reason to believe now that I can't be someone who does the same.

I still cried to Garth last night. And worried about my boys and how long I'll have with them. And let my dad hold me and hear me tell him how fucking unfair all of this is and how this weak part of me is scared and sad. Sarah Jane gave me the hope that I needed to get it out and move on.

And then I took my chemo pill before bed last night. And so begins The Big Fight.

To: Caroline
From: Sarah Jane
Date: March 23, 2017
Subject: Good morning

Happy first day of radiation! Only 29 fractions to go :)

It was so great to talk with you yesterday. I have had a hard time knowing my "place" with this whole thing as I have never been on this side of cancer before...But you are still you and I am still me and a freaking dumb-ass tumor can't change that.

Love you BFF!

SJ

To: Caroline
From: Sarah
Date: March 23, 2017
Subject: Time on the mat

Hey love,

I moved my yoga mat from behind the door this morning, and spent a good hour there sending you lots of prayers and love. I'm going to leave it in the living room, and try and do at least a sun salutation a day while you are going through this 6 week treatment. I want so badly to be with you every day physically, but in spirit will have to do. Things like this will get ME through this hard time and help to make a habit of praying daily for you extra. Xoxox

Love you. Today will be fine.
S

Sent from my iPhone

A Few Random Thoughts Right Now | Caroline Wright

Right now I am eating a slice of toast after having been up most of the night throwing up. Not the first time I've done this, sadly to say, so I am pretending it's morning sickness or an aggressive hangover. In between bouts of purging I have been working through the night on the boys' blogs, uploading the backlog of blurry photos of my perfect boys to their websites. It brings me normalcy and comfort as I gear up for my first day of radiation today, hopefully after a nap.

A few random things that occurred to me in the middle of the night:

- This "low dose" chemo still sucks. It's hardly polite. It woke me up at 3 am, bolting me upright and gagging for the bathroom. Not cool, meds. Not cool. I'm choosing to hope that the anti-nausea companion meds I'm on take a little while to build up in my system. (I remember something about that from my week pre-op and, further, from the maternity ward where I vomited with every contraction with both boys, which was also decidedly not cool.)
- I am going to build a meditation shrine somewhere in my house. I don't know where yet because I can't readily think of a space where the boys won't steal and

subsequently hide anything I set out, but I'm trying to figure it out. I've been putting together all of the beautiful and meaningful tokens my loved ones have been sending—paintings, crystals charged with good energy, beautifully written letters, photos—and want to use them to create a physical space that brings me calm and spiritual integration.

· I officially pulled myself off of my beloved Spanish cookbook project last night in favor of the book being finished by a ghostwriter. It is sad and absolutely not something I could have imagined, but neither is a stage 4 GBM brain tumor. I love my work but I need rest more. It is a book I love deeply, but—as my sympathetic and wonderful agent reminded me—it is still just a book, even if an amazing one. It isn't worth sacrificing my energy for, nor do I feel responsible having people rely on me in case I have days where I just can't produce any work. Any energy I have left throughout this next process after taking care of myself needs to be focused on being present for Henry and Theodore. Period.

· I haven't mentioned it much, but I wanted to reiterate how much your letters *[to a PO Box I set up for the purpose]* mean to me. I actually think about that all the time, not just now. I read them in bed before going to sleep and they bring me a lot of joy and a feeling of being connected to a greater purpose. I have been deeply touched by you telling me your stories, or ways that our lives have crossed. It's so beautiful to read something written by hand that took effort to write and find a stamp and put in the mail. Thank you so much.

Attached is the commemorative (if unflattering!) photo my dad took of me last night as I took my first chemo pill as my dad, Garth and I toasted to our fight ahead.

First Radiation Treatment Done! | Caroline Wright

I want to take tonight to quilt and hang out with Garth and my dad, but I wanted to share a few impressions of my first radiation treatment before I do.

- It is actually the least traumatic of the machines that I have been introduced to in the last month or so. It's completely open and it is, relatively speaking, quiet. The radiation itself is delivered in short buzzes and the technicians do a pretty good job telling you where you are in the process.
- The technicians are really lovely. Today it was Mitch and Erin and tomorrow I am to expect Chris. I liked all of their energies; Mitch said "right on" and "fantastic" a lot. Erin said she managed to get away from her kids to put two small curls in her hair, which I appreciated, too, even though that sentence would never leave my mouth. (Certainly not now!) These technicians wanted to know more about me, not less, as if I was a human and not a patient.
- The mask itself made me feel exactly like a *luchador* (a Mexican wrestler made famous by Nacho Libre), which I consider a good sign. A fighter who is also still somehow

campy. I'll take it! After the 45 minutes or so (it was the "dry run" with a treatment immediately following, back-to-back, so it will never be that long again), I had a mask imprint on my face that made me feel a kinship with a trawled fish who didn't want to be caught.

- Fiona Apple was a weird choice I realized when I was on the table. I am encouraged to bring in my own playlist, so I will figure out one that is a bit more cerebral and relaxing. Meditating helped, too, and I look forward to getting better at it as the weeks pass.
- I'll be there tomorrow and all weekdays for six weeks, usually at 9:30 am. Mondays are my "doctor days" in which I meet with my radiologist, Dr. Tseng. Wednesdays are my blood-draw days in which they track my white blood count.

I mean it when I say it wasn't that big of a deal. It feels positive to be treating the cavity.

Send me all your love and light, folks. Let's do this thing. Together.

What Dreams Look Like From Here | Caroline Wright

I think anyone who knows me well can say with confidence that I am a very focused person. This is why I am thirty-three and have written three cookbooks, written countless articles for national magazines and started my career at a prestigious creative institution in New York for which 7,000 people applied for my starter job. (I am not "cutthroat," however, which is an important distinction because my drive comes from inside of me, a challenge to my personal best and not anyone else's. I don't see myself as a "winner" or any such bullshit. I still identify as a "New Yorker" but that stereotype isn't it; the driven, open, creative person in a land of opportunity is.) I generally succeed doing anything I dream to do because I will and make it so. It's there for someone, so why not take it with pride and gratitude.

I had a lot of plans. Many books to write, some in other people's voices, recipes to cook. A reputation to develop as the go-to writer with great taste and an even better work ethic. I saw myself has having ten or so books published by the time I was forty, mixed with personal, soulful projects like my upcoming self-published children's book. More importantly, however, I saw myself walking my kids to school every day and being there when they came home. Celebrating their friendships as joyfully as their birthdays. Meeting the people that they picked to love. Baking cookies and painting pictures together, figuring out how to understand the sports they play. Eating at nice restaurants in Seattle and around the world with my beloved husband as we met anniversaries and promotions and book deals, and drinking bourbon at home under grey skies.

My current situation obviously changes everything. Not only can I not will or make changes to the health of the tissues in my brain, but I also cannot even know what I am going to be physically capable of on a daily basis. I just wake up and am excited that I can move all my limbs and still write. The comfort (and luck, frankly, given my state) of this is inexplicable and I am beyond thankful for every moment.

In favor of hope, which is as an important mechanism for me right now as it is has always been, I am trying to find the shape of my dreams. For what's next. What I will do with various timelines that present themselves: one year, two years or twenty. The reply is very simple. My family will come first in ways I don't think I always juggled well because my timeline felt infinite and the challenges of my career felt pressing the way that they do when you're running out of the gate early in your career. Being present for my kids, Garth and my parents is my sole purpose in life from now on, this much is clear. I will continue to want to "work," because writing and cooking comes from who I am and I really have never seen it as such. (And being sick like this is expensive!) Going forward, however, I will be very conscious of the projects I take on and I am going to learn to protect myself, to push myself less in the ways that cause me deep emotional stress. To let my talents speak and my drive listen, as opposed to the other way around.

Otherwise, the shape of my future is exactly the life I had "before" in my past: to see and do beautiful things, to create, to spend time with beautiful people, and to live holding that bliss close to me. Nothing else matters. This is the shape of my dreams today.

Bapa | Caroline Wright

My grandfather and I were very close. In fact, before our recent connection, this was one of the only things my mom and I had in common. I think of him often—all the time, really—but especially so now because he already lived in this space I occupy now. He had a quadruple bypass at age 58 and he lived 22 more years, thankful for every day. He called it his "second birth date," the meaning of which I understand well from here. That is actually the space in which I met him, the changed and open grandfather who hugged his many grandchildren with gratitude and really listened to what people had to say to him. Here are some of the many thoughts I have about him right now.

....

I remember sitting in the dressing room of his summer cottage and watching him get dressed for church, usually in something like a tweed jacket over a yellow cashmere sweater or an occasional bolo tie when he was feeling jaunty. I remember that when he would wear his thin yellow swim trunks, I would stare at the shiny scars on his chest that looked a little like the path a snail would leave behind. I would watch him file his nails using the metal emery stick turned underneath a standard pair of clippers—something I haven't known anyone to do before or since—into peculiar triangular shapes that came to a point. He preferred fishing jackets and filled the pockets with things like thick black pencils and little notepads in case he had a good idea on the go. I see his big smile when he was sailing, even now. For breakfast, he would eat a Bays English muffin with margarine alongside an egg or a bowl of Cracklin' Oat Bran, which still reminds me of him, and I would steal a chocolate Carnation instant breakfast from his stash as an excuse for a morning glass of chocolate milk; we would sit in the morning sun together and eat as the other grandkids woke up and ran for things like swim lessons. We—my brother and I and whatever collection of cousins who were there at the time—would play Monopoly games that would last for days, in which he would pull some sort of negotiation and inevitably win; he always wanted to collect all of the pieces and cash and pile them in front of him to take a congratulatory picture of himself shaking the hands of the other players with a cheesy grin. He preferred to only buy products of brands that he either had written accounts for during his days as head of Leo Burnett advertising agency in Chicago, which meant that he kept Juicy Fruit gum in his desk at all times and had a fake Wheaties box with his face on it. He gave me my love of Frank Sinatra. He liked all gadgets and I taught him how to use the Internet, back in the days of dial-up. He wrote me an email the week he died.

Bapa died on June 11, 2001. I was sixteen and it was the summer in between my junior and senior year and I was working as a nanny in Chicago. I was the only grandchild to go to both of his funerals—the one in Chicago at his beloved church and the other in Northport at the chapel our family founded and where he is interred in a columbarium today. At his Chicago funeral among his community, I read aloud a heartbreaking journal entry I wrote during my flight about the man I knew, who was truly so different than the powerful businessman that everyone else did.

My family and I live in a house in Seattle that Bapa left money for us to buy, like he did all thirteen of his grandchildren. It was built in 1906 and every decision I made during its careful renovation last year I considered the respect he would want me to give such an old house with its own history. Our architect and now dear friend, Herschel, and all the contractors kept saying it had an old soul, probably like me. I like to think that it does: his. I had the house painted yellow because it was his favorite color and it looks cheery against the Seattle sky in winter. It remains the color of his summer home in Michigan, which will always be the original "Yellow House" to me.

I never liked my grandmother, his wife, who my brother and I called Muna. To me, she was bitter and mean, beautiful and terribly cold. I don't think she liked me, either; I always wondered if it was because of how close I was to Bapa. I wrote angsty essays about her as a teenager in creative writing classes inspired by the cruel things she would say to me. I was told by everyone around me that, even despite her fits of anger in which she banged her fists on the dinner table if someone said something she didn't like (usually me or my brother) or didn't sit up straight (and received an aggressive prod to the ribs with her manicured finger), she was older than me so therefore she was always right. That is Muna's legacy: she gave me a complicated, critical look at humanity from a young age. Bapa stood as her softer counterpart in my mind. Sometimes he was similarly determined and demanding of some view of excellence, but he took the individual into account in ways that Muna didn't.

As a young teen I lost my temper and yelled violently at Muna one morning after Bapa and I shared breakfast. I was on the computer in Bapa's office on AOL Instant Messenger and I overheard her criticize my two-year-old cousin at the time for being a brat, the kind of thing I knew her to say about me as a kid. Kids can sense that kind of venom—at least I knew I could. I ran out of the room and screamed at her, how dare she make character judgments of a little kid like that, that she has no idea how thoughts and feelings like that affect someone who is learning their place in the world. How she had affected me and how much I hated her for it. How toxic she was and how she hated my father, the only person who saw me clearly and would book the tickets to send me to their home every summer even despite her poor treatment of him and how my mom, also then silent and cold, would get all the credit. I watched her shake and put down her needlepoint, speechless and reddening at my display. Bapa walked in and put his arms around me and cried, saying he had no idea how I had felt and how sorry he was. Muna didn't speak to me for the rest of my trip. A few days after I left, she fell down some stairs and went into a coma. She never really recovered. After that, Bapa emailed me every week until he died.

Muna stayed in this transitional space—in and out of speech, in and out of consciousness, in and out of wheelchairs and colostomy bags—for the next decade. No one understood why and how she was holding on. My parents saw a clairvoyant—the very one that I spoke to last week and have not yet written about, Dorothea, to find out why. Dorothea said that the reason why Muna hadn't passed is that she thought she already had because Bapa came to sit with her every day. She was confused about which world she was living in, here or beyond. I visited her in her nursing home to apologize and read her some of Bapa's favorite Bible passages in January of 2011. She died three weeks later.

....

I had a vision of Bapa coming to sit with me in the ICU after my brain surgery. I held my mom's hand and he sat on the bed with me, I saw clearly behind my closed eyes that were being shielded by a washcloth for light sensitivity. After he left about thirty minutes later, my mom told me stories about him. I held them and Dido and cried.

....

I have been reading his memoir every morning for the past week or so when I wake up early before the kids rise. He self-published a memoir of his own as his legacy to his family that he handed out for his 80th birthday, a collection of stories and musings and quotes that offer a glimmer of who he was. In those pages was the Bapa I didn't know: the man who went to World War II as a reconnaissance photographer and pilot (whereas, for example, I remember the pictures of clouds that he took from that point of view). The boss whose secretaries (and their parents) wrote kind letters of thanks to. The man who survived a quadruple bypass and enclosed a picture of himself smiling gratefully at his nurse.

I learned two things that surprised me. After the war, he took a career aptitude test—something that my mom had always touted as being an extremely useful metric that made me roll my eyes as a teenager—on which he scored in the 99th percentile for creativity. I only knew his reputation as a fierce businessman. (My mom has some proof that my grandfather was actually one of the few men that the creators of Mad Men used as a model for Don Draper. Watching the show creeps her out because of how accurate it is to her memory of his work in those days and her childhood, a metaphor which speaks so many volumes.)

The second was that during this same period—before he had chosen to go into advertising and set his sights on Leo Burnett—he had the idea of self-publishing a travel guide of Southern California called "Let's Go." He had one of his war buddies mock up a cover and he produced a prototype that he used largely as a vehicle for interviews. This almost exactly matches my experience of how I got my first cookbook published and launched this beloved career of mine. My mom didn't even know this about him. It helps me know he would have been proud of who I am today and we share a lot more than I even knew.

I hope this memoir gives my Henry and Theodore a glimmer of this kind of connection some day, a long time from now.

....

Bapa came to talk to me through Dorothea, the clairvoyant and medium, last week. I will write more about it when I finish processing all that she said, but he talked about my writing this book, how much he loved Henry and Theodore and how he saw them so clearly as the amazing children they are. He described them perfectly with such love, as if they were his own grandchildren. As clearly as he saw and loved me.

....

Even today Bapa continues to teach me about the shape of love and death and how they really are transcendental. Just because I don't spend summers with him anymore doesn't mean I don't hold him in my heart the same way I did when he was alive. He is still teaching me things. In many ways, he is showing me that I don't believe in death at all. I miss him every day, but know he is fighting in his way alongside me. I like that idea and use it for strength, as part of the silent army that marches with me now.

Dreaming with Henry | Caroline Wright

For the past six months or so, Henry and I have been doing this sweet thing before bed that I love with my whole heart. Usually it is as I attempt to corral him into pajamas or after I've convinced him not to swallow all the toothpaste on his brush—some time when the calm begins to peek its head in through the blinds—and I ask the same question, "Henry, where are we meeting tonight?" We then proceed to have a meandering conversation about any variety of fantasy locations, which, depending on his mood, can settle easily into meeting at a Lego factory and looking for the biggest construction vehicle we can find. Other popular locations include chocolate factories, doughnut factories and racetracks.

Tonight, as we were cuddling and reading a book and Theodore was having his teeth brushed, I asked him where we were meeting. This was our conversation...

Caroline: So then, Henry, where are we meeting tonight?

Henry: I don't know, mama. I can't decide. You pick.

Caroline: I have always wanted to go whale-watching. You know, get on a big boat and see the whales swim through the water and follow their families. Does that sound like fun to you?

Henry: Yes! Let's do that.

Caroline: What will you be wearing so I can spot you right away in the crowd? *(This is always my final question.)*

Henry: *[With a sprawled grin and a twinkle in his eye]* I'll be naked!

Caroline: *[Laughs.]* Okay, that will make it easy to spot you! I'll be wearing what I always do, my yellow hat. You'll find me right away.

I am so thankful for this ritual of ours. Henry, I will always be there to meet you in your dreams. That is something I am able to promise right now and forever, which feels so good to me as your loving and hurting-yet-hopeful mother. Keep an eye out for that yellow hat. I'll be there no matter what.

Dorothea | Caroline Wright

I've alluded to the fact that Garth and I spoke to a clairvoyant. My parents gifted the session to me for my birthday; my dad got on the phone the very day that he arrived in Seattle from Hawaii, knowing how rarely she has openings from having his own session alongside my mom with her before. Their experience with her was uncanny—even according to my mom, who is the skeptic between them—filled with personal details that she would have had no way of knowing. She prefers to do the readings over the phone—something about your in- person energy being distracting to her ability to experience your inner self—and she sends you a recording of the session after. I love this kind of thing and had never done a reading like this before. Besides, I thought that the recording could be a healing memento for my family, too, in yet another light of my trying to find answers and solutions to fight my cancer.

My in-laws had the session transcribed, which was an incredible (and helpful) gesture. I'm thrilled to be able to share some excerpts here, even though it pales in comparison to the experience of speaking with her and even the recording itself. I've listened to it three times since with loved ones and pick up on different things each time.

The session began with her acknowledging that she had heard from my dad about my diagnosis and that she wanted to go inside my system and take a look. She asked me to close my eyes and focus my energy around me—to the left, right, front and back on her command—and she read my aura. She also spent time meditating on me before our session and channeled a medical guide on my behalf, the notes from which she also brings to the meeting.

A lot of what she had to say was shockingly medical, which I have been scrambling since to follow as leads to my healing. There were really profound personal insights and also communication with Bapa, both of which were obviously very empowering.

I've included here a shortened version of the transcript that includes the most fascinating parts to me and have provided me with a lot of comfort.

On the subject of what her (dead) medical guide, who she channeled during our conversation via her work as a medium, said to her about my cancer:

She said to me this particular cancer is definitely certainly a DNA imprint-related cancer. She told me that there would always have been the possibility that when there's a dysfunction, or a malfunction, or an imbalance in the system, that this could be generated. That this could be activated or triggered. Having said that, she said to me obviously we're looking at a karmic situation with this, because when we have an imprint in the body that goes back to literally the moment of conception, when that imprint is already present at that time, then we do know that there's a link into the illness. There's a link into the experience...is really what I want to call it more than an illness, honestly...that you need to have in order for the soul to complete itself in this lifetime.

...There seems to be a connection between your mineral and your trace mineral content, and absorption, or lack thereof, in the system that has a triggering and activation, and aggravating, or inflammatory almost result on your brain cells. She told me that this has something to do with an intestinal dysfunction. She told me that this is in particular around the minerals of copper and manganese, so trace minerals obviously. She told me that magnesium and calcium play a role, but primarily we're looking at trace minerals of copper and manganese.

She told me that because of these minerals lack of absorption, or blocking of absorption somehow, we also have electrolytic imbalance in the system, that then is not necessarily the cause or the root for the cellular miscommunication that's created this cancer really, but it's also...a supportive factor of confusing the cells even more. It appears that there is a sort of holistic or systemic issue in the intestinal cellular tissue, that doesn't allow for copper and manganese absorption and distribution in the system.

On the subject of my relationship to karma (in response to a question I had that referred back to her comment that this was a "karmic situation"):

Karma, not to be misunderstood as a reward or punishment, cause and effect sort of a process, but as a, "okay, what is important for me to learn in this lifetime? What's the intention of the soul?" Apparently with you, where you are right now, is a portion of that. I think that you are a seeker, very much so. I think that you have a very deep and profound desire to seek yourself in this lifetime. I think you have a very incredible, and true and genuine ability to love. I think that you have energetically everything you need in order to be able to balance the situation that's showing up in the physical body.

....

On the subject of my aura:

Let me talk a little bit about your aura. Let me talk a little bit about what's happening to you energetically and emotionally. When I look at the space around you, I go into the space in front of you, and the entire body, and the entire aura starts taking a very strong, very significant turn to the left. It's almost like 180 degrees, turns immediately, very strongly to the left. I know already that I now have a definite situation in the system that is soul, and emotional, and energetically related. Everything is moving into, and turning into what's the yin side of your being, the female side of the quality of your energy. The internal, the psychological, the spiritual, the intuitive being part of your system. Versus the right side of your body, the male, the active, the aggressive, the doing part. Right away I look at it turns 180 degrees right smack into my physical system. This was unusual with this, too: it's doing it from the back as well. This is very much related to your being.

About my cancer as it relates to my aura and what she can see of my being:

This is about your being. Of course you have to be active and do things in response to this experience. ... To not walk away from that, to allow yourself the grief, and allow yourself the anger, and allow yourself...Please don't try to be perfect in this process. Please stop protecting everybody else, and connect to the feelings you have about this. That mother part of you is so strong in your system that you're functioning from it. You're the nurturer, the communicator. You function so automatically organically from that part of you, that it's hard for you to get beyond that layer of yourself into the deeper authentic emotions sometimes, that come along with your experiences as Caroline.

...Like I said to you, you are so organically the yin, you are so organically nurturer, and you love to serve, and you love to...This is organic for you, I would not tell you change that, I would say to you keep that. There is so much healing for you in that, because you're one of these people that as you give, you receive, you love it. It's good for you, but I need you to be included.

...You do it in a very focused way that creates a direction, creates an awareness, creates a connection with yourself that makes you go oh my god, this is amazing. I really did not realize this about myself, and begin to balance. That tool, that emotional tool of opening and unfolding will create an energetic shift in the system. You are a deeply emotional person. We access your emotions in your meditation, in your breath, in your prana work, in your yoga postures, you're going to rebalance the body. Your body's first and foremost response is emotion, believe it or not. *(Duh. She obviously gets me.)*

...Then the space to the left [of my aura] is so good and strong and holding, so I think you can do this. Your space on the left side, the left side of the body and the left side of the aura, it's so good and strong and holding up. It's ready, it wants to go deeper, it's ready to do this, and it has the energetic radiance, and it has the resilience really, it's a very strong, powerful, very healthy energetic immune system that you have. That's the good news, honestly like, wow, you are strong, radiant in your colors. There's a density, a depth to it that makes me really happy to see it.

On the subject of Bapa, who came to her in the room to support me:

I haven't seen your grandfather. I know that your father mentioned it. I've picked up his energy prior to the session, and I have his energy a little bit over to my left, and a little further out. I'll try to make a good connection with him, but my sense with him, by the way, is that I get this very, very deeply loving personality. A very soft, very warm, but very present energy here. Moving a little bit closer, and having a sense of definitely someone that can bring guidance, can bring awareness. I see a lot of outdoor images now, like walking in the woods, getting out by the water, being outside, breathing deeply, going for long walks.

These are some of the sense and imagery that I have with your grandfather. Also I don't know if he liked books, but I see books with this person. Or he's laying a couple of books on a table in front of me, and he's pointing towards different books. *(I took this as a sign that he was supporting my work on this memoir, just like he chose to do, as his legacy.)*

I have a sense of like a smell almost of, I don't want to say food, but almost like earth. It smells like mint, smells like lavender, it could be somebody's garden. Could be talking about getting in the garden and using fresh herbs, and growing, or cooking mostly with fresh foods. *(I took this as a conflation of the energy my dad is giving me—cooking fresh foods for me daily, serving me eggs and wilted greens for breakfast, that sort of thing—and the fact that we are about to transform our front yard into a garden for my recovery.)*

...He showed me walking with her outside, and going for walks and being on the water, and loving that. That's very much a memory that he has of you, and with you, from the time you were little. Showed me you as a 10-year-old, 11-year-old little girl, and has just very much a sense of "I'm present, I'm present, I'm here and I'm present" [for you]. *(All true. And I like to think that this matches with my very strong instinct that places like Discovery Park and Golden Gardens will be key for my healing.)*

....

On Muna showing up:

I see an older female with him, I see this person very close to him. It's not his sister, I said, "Can you help me see who this person is?" He shows me, "Tell her it's M, it's M." A woman with the initial M, and then I see a big smile, and she's waving to you. *(That was very Muna. I can almost see her knobby hands in a queen's wave. I believe the smile would be genuine.)*

....

From Bapa on the subject of Henry and Theodore:

> **Dorothea:** ...He talks about your kids. "Oh my god, I love them."

Caroline: They're very special.

Dorothea: He's watching over them. Your father gave me the names and the ages of the little boys. So Henry is four and a half, Theodore is one and a half your father told me.

Caroline: Yes.

Dorothea: He shows me the kids and he goes, "I love the kids. I love them they're really...They're beautiful." He says to me, "Henry is quite an engineer." Your grandfather shows me he loves to fix, and he likes to figure everything out.

Caroline: Yes, he does.

Dorothea: The two boys have quite different energies, Theodore is very strongly in his heart, in his emotions. Henry is very...he likes to look at everything, take everything apart, understand everything, analyze everything. His mind is very quick, and his body is very quick to respond to what he sees. There's excitement about the world and how I can fix it, and how I can do this. Definitely an energy that came here to get things done.

Then she talked a lot about foods, she knew from my aura I was blood type O, and really specific things about my organs and thyroid and how I had the immune system to do well through treatment.

On the subject of terminal illness:

Dorothea: ... I don't accept that diagnosis of terminal cancer personally.

Caroline: Yeah, I don't either.

Dorothea: I don't, I'm so glad to hear you say that...Of course there's a severity, of course, and there's no denying that, it's obvious. This is something to take very, very serious, yes. I'm going to call this an experience, not an illness, I'm going to say that this is a challenge...I don't say this lightly, I really, really don't. If I felt that your soul is meant to leave this body and go on its journey home because of this experience, I would be...I've done this a long time, I don't believe in death, so I would tell you. I would tell you, Caroline. I understand you're a mother of young children, you have an incredible, beautiful husband, I understand all that. I'm not going to pacify you. I'm going to tell you this is a challenge, I'm not going to tell you this is terminal.

In response to the question I asked her, "Is there anything else I can be doing to ensure peace for my children?":

They're amazing, just be yourself. Let them experience that. That's okay, they're strong enough, they're loved enough, you have so much family support. Let them be a part of it. Don't over-protect them. ... Be intuitive with what they can handle and cannot handle, situation awareness and situation dependent, be intuitive with them. [The age] One and a half is very different from four and a half, but Henry is very curious, the more he understands the easier it is for him. Theodore just needs a lot of physical closeness and love with it, but I think you're doing everything right with that. I don't see a great deal to change anything in your approach there.

That was easily one of the craziest experiences of my life, speaking with Dorothea. Said by someone who has lived a very crazy month and a half.

Caroline's First Radiation Doctor Visit | Garth Wright

On Monday we had the first in-treatment visit with Caroline's radiation-oncologist. It was a short visit, but she made sure Caroline was feeling ok (it was day 3 of radiation) and proceeded to discuss:

- The expected permanent hair loss from radiation - the radiation field for Caroline's treatment is expansive. The entire right hemisphere will receive radiation and there will be spillover (at a lower dose) to the entire brain. It is possible (even probable) that the hair on the right side of Caroline's head will never grow back.
- The tumor cavity—it's huge! She showed us some images to explain how much brain and tumor they took out during the surgery. I would describe it as a "generous wedge of cake" that Caroline is missing on the right side of her brain.
- Reducing Caroline's steroids by another 50% to 1mg/day

There was positivity from the doctor, mixed with a healthy dose of realism. Above all, however, the doctor was encouraging Caroline to focus on staying active for the next 6 weeks of treatment and the 4 weeks after treatment. The next MRI (around 10 weeks) will determine our next steps.

Until then, Caroline is eating well, taking her medicines, and continuing to be a mother who chases her boys around the dining room table.

Regrets and Luck | Caroline Wright

In this place, it is strange to think about the shape of life. I know I keep saying that, but it doesn't cease to be true, day after day. Life as I knew it before the tumor is over, changed forever, without warning. That isn't necessarily a bad thing, just different.

I have been thinking about regrets, about how the idea of regret is important to those facing death. Would I would have wanted to do something differently had I known that I would end up with terminal brain cancer at the age of thirty-three? Would I have wanted to kiss more boys, do reckless drugs? Smoke cigarettes as a regular habit, which I loved to do on occasion? Use a microwave? Eat junk food?

My answer, genuinely, is no. I wouldn't have changed one thing. I am thankful I had Henry two years before I was "ready" because it made me the mom I am today, and gave us space to have Theodore with enough timing between them to give them their own identities. For us as parents, it also gave us the chance to enjoy parenthood to it's fullest, which I honestly do each day.

If it was just me, without the kids, I wouldn't need to turn myself inside out like I am willing to do now because I have lived a wonderful privileged life, even at thirty-three.

I have lived in love with one man for my entire adulthood (we will round the corner soon of being together longer than being apart in our lives, and married ten years next year); I have truly soulful friendships that give me the structure of the understanding of myself; I've fought for and protected the love of my family, and participated in stopping the cycles of dysfunction that have plagued our family's history for generations (as was my earnest goal from the time I was very young, around eight I remember now). I've lived abroad and thrown dinner parties in my non-native language; I have never wanted for anything; I have made a career and a way of life off of the talents that I was born with (and don't have to work too hard to access), and have set a life up where I am seen in the light of these talents. I'm not bragging. I am very, very fortunate and I have always been thankful for these privileges. (I don't believe in apologizing for them—I didn't ask for my lot in life, whether that is my emotional capacity, my access to education or this brain tumor.) I have always been honest and clear, however, with myself and deeply thankful for my good fortune, just like I am today.

Most importantly, however, I have lived every single day of my life as myself. I mean it. I have never pretended to be someone else or tried to assimilate. Not even for a minute. (I mean, in middle school I lamented the fact that I was different than everyone else and I wished I was "cool," but I didn't make changes to do so. To be even more honest, it was because I didn't know how and I did weird things like wear vests that I handmade, buttons included.) The person I am has changed slightly over the years—I've become louder and more outspoken about things I believe in, I've focused my life to tune out bullshit in the way that I think "grownups" do in my view—but it's all come from an authentic place. Always. I doubt there are many people at the end of their lives (if that's what this is) who can say that with true, deep acceptance.

My family, but especially Henry and Theodore, are the breakdown of this logic in a way. I am now Mama as well as Caroline, and while I think I would have been satisfied with Caroline's life if it was cut short, I will forever be sad that the Mama in me would be. Both for them and for me. Dorothea (the clairvoyant) told me that fear is a great catalyst for change, and that is how it's functioned for me—I am using this fear of leaving my boys to do *everything* I can to enact any changes to my story. I will fight, turn myself inside out, go through anything I have to in order to find any extra minute I can to be with them. Forever, as long as I live, they have my word. But if my time is up, I honestly hope they will know that I would never have chosen this for them and am so sorry they were born to a mother who left early, but that they were loved in the biggest, realest way by someone who is capable of a whole lot of love. I really hope they will know this for their whole lives, whether or not I am here.

My Theodore. | Caroline Wright

I have been writing a lot about my Henry, who is incredibly special and a cornerstone of the dream home I will forever live in. Garth is another and Theodore, too. They are the foundation for the very life I love and am fighting for now.

I may write about Theodore less, but only because we don't have conversations...with words, anyway. (He is 1 1/2 and doesn't speak; not surprising in our house as I'm not sure that Henry and I give him the chance!) Theodore and I have a very deep connection, too, and always have.

Theodore, Henry and I moved here in October of 2015, two weeks after he was born. Garth had moved a week prior to start his job as a lawyer for the EPA. I still had stitches in my body when I boarded the plane with my little frog-like newborn, legs still bowed from being inside my womb. His disoriented and newly 3-year-old brother clung to Gampa (my forever superhero dad) as he battled the flu. We now know that this was the true beginning of this wild ride— when I began growing my tumor, but also an insane set of life circumstances.

Theodore was buckled into a carrier for the first many months of his life in Seattle, held close to me as we ran towards this new life of ours at full speed. We threw blankets over him and dragged him to open houses as we battled our way into the Seattle housing market and we found our future home. He was buckled to me as we toured Henry's beloved preschool for the first time (on the same day as our home in Fremont, actually!). He nursed silently during coffee dates with new friends who are profound friends to me now. He, alongside his brother, would run endless errands to source materials for our house renovation. (Henry knows which vendors in the design district have the best play areas for kids and have the best trucks. Theodore only knows the inside of their bathrooms as his experiences had more to do with diaper changes.)

Henry suffered through these changes of our move to Seattle. He grew as he suffered, but it was traumatic for him because of his beautiful sensitivity and his life changed overnight (a feeling I am deeply sympathetic to in my current state). Theodore grew with grace and resilience, because his crazy life was the only one he knew. I cannot relay how thankful I am to have him as my second son. As a working mother with far too much on her plate (including a tumor in my brain), Theodore was my solid ground. He made me sit in a chair and nurse. He made me stop and look at his beauty. He rooted my overwhelming, swirling life and marriage in celebrating growth and love.

Theodore is truly the most joyful, kind person, even at only 1½ years old. He has been since he was tiny. To throw a few adjectives his way is reductive because he has so many. He is every bit as smart and nuanced as his brother, just silent and unassuming. Supportive. Present. Thoughtful. He is also in his body in a different way than I am or Henry is—he shows his love freely through nonstop hugs and the occasional butting of heads. He can already throw and dribble a ball well. He wants to make you happy, to make you laugh. He gives his love away naturally, effortlessly, to those around him.

I am so thankful to have this pair of brothers, so perfectly matched for one another. They radiate love in different ways, blending together like the most surreal sunrise.

I have been thinking a lot lately about how Theodore is never going to know a mother that is not terminally ill, if I am lucky as I hope to be. This makes a part of me so sad for him and his story, because he deserves to feel the comfort of time and his mother without a pressing negotiation with mortality as he grows. He deserves blissful ignorance and a selfish childhood, just like every other child.

But then I think of my sweet Theodore in specific, his graceful and loving nature, and I know that he will love a sick Mommy all the same because he doesn't know any other. And being seen by him is one place where I am not sick at all– he throws his arms around me and brings me his favorite toys and books the same as he did before my diagnosis. I realize, in his profound light, that part of me *is* not sick at all and that is the well from which I draw my strength: being their mom. Being their mom allows me to save every bit of energy I have to be the "me" I love and recognize for them, and in so doing *makes* me the me I recognize and love. Both boys bring me this, but Theodore—in part because he doesn't know differently and grows in his consciousness every minute—brings it effortlessly and without the pain of memory or comparison, like Henry.

I am so grateful today and always for my sweet, wonderful Theodore.

Done with Week 1! | Caroline Wright

Today marks the finish of my first real "week" of treatment. (The timing is off a bit because of our jumpstart, and now this is our second Friday in treatment.) Here are my wins for this week:

- The last of my scab finally fell off yesterday. I am a bit bald in its place, but I genuinely don't care. That is going to get worse before it gets better (or stay worse), so oh well. I may keep my hair shorn, I don't mind it now! It feels good to have the surgery officially behind me.
- I began homeopathic treatment this week to repair my gut as per Dorothea's recommendation. So far it's been a lot of tinctures in water and handfuls of supplements. I will write about this more, I'm sure, as the treatment progresses.
- I began to practice yoga this week, specifically in a class and also a private restorative yoga session. This is huge for those of you who know me well, as I am literally the least flexible person on the planet. (Officially. No joke.) I have locked up hamstrings from years of standing in a kitchen and, before now, I didn't have the instinct to fix it. So I'm in an old lady yoga class and loving every second. It's me and a bunch of fierce septuagenarians, and in that

crowd I am capable and strong and *even a little fit*. Fierce by association, I say. I slept like a rock that night and was sore the next day.

- I am still loving soup in a serious way. I have been eating it for lunch and dinner without boredom—you folks keep me very well fed with great variety, thank you—and it feels nice to be cooked for!
- I am still feeling fine. Not tired yet, though I admit I can see it on the horizon. I don't have any symptoms shining through the meds they are giving me to keep them at bay, so that's great!
- Walks. Daily walks are everything.

One of my best friends from high school, Leah, arrived yesterday with her baby boy and dear mom who I have known and loved as long as I've loved Leah. She was a bridesmaid in Garth's and my wedding and she's an all-around amazing woman. The energy and love is flowing my way, for sure. xo

On Privileges and Uncertainty | Caroline Wright

My best friend Jeff is a therapist in New York, as I've mentioned before. When he was getting his Masters from NYU, talking about what he was learning as a social worker was a weekly conversation of ours, usually from the comfort of the gay dive bar that we frequented between our two apartments. We were totally enthralled by these keys to better understanding society and people.

I remember our conversations about "privileges" clearly, something I hadn't really thought about before Jeff brought it up because that's the very definition of someone who is privileged. If you don't think about your lot in life, then you have it pretty good. And that isn't something to apologize for at all, in my opinion—it is just something to be aware of if you are going to attempt to connect with someone who doesn't share your same circumstances.

I've been thinking about my privileges a lot lately because I have had a really fortunate life so far, even including the circumstances of my diagnosis and prognosis. I could be *alone* and dealing with all that I am and have nothing worth fighting for. I could not have insurance. I found my team because of personal connections and favors through friends. These particular "what-ifs" are the space of my fortune, and

I am very thankful for my particular circumstances that include all of you here.

However, an edge of something that *many* people are saying to me is also making me realize that health is a privilege, too. One that I lack at the moment (in some very specific ways, though not entirely, especially my age and otherwise general health).

People keep telling me to "stay positive." I understand the sentiment behind this statement, I really do, but it burns a little. It implies that I am *not* being positive, which I genuinely and authentically am. Also, from where I stand, it seems as though someone is telling me how to *feel*, which can come across as condescending or unsupportive depending on the day. Furthermore, I am a mom. Not acknowledging that I *could die* in this situation feels not only cowardly, but it also feels like I would be doing my family a disservice by not preparing them or myself for that possibility.

I think that the people who tell me to "be positive" are coming from a place of the silent privilege of health—I don't have the luxury of not being realistic, unfortunately. I am doing it with strength and honesty and love, but I am having to think about all possibilities for the future all the same. It is how I have managed all other trauma in my life—with open eyes.

For the record, I am very hopeful and positive and I am spiritually running full speed ahead at this tumor. I believe with my whole being that if my DNA responds to the treatment I'm in, I will have many years ahead. I don't happen to believe that I can control my DNA or the science component of this just by willing it to be so. Whatever is going to happen to me has already been written in my genes and I am doing everything I can to maximize my strengths.

So, this is to say that I am both positive and a realist, and I don't think they are mutually exclusive. It is also to say that I deeply appreciate all of the love coming my way, I really do. I hope you'll continue to meet me here in my space of marching forward together, eyes open and charging on, believing that I have positivity and hope in my heart even though I occasionally talk about my funeral or what school I would want my kids to go to if I died. I think it takes both sides. For me it takes both, with a smile and a full heart.

I'm doing this thing. It's weird and unknown but I'm doing it and I'm hugging my family every day.

APRIL 2, 2017

Bali | Caroline Wright

Bali is a place that has presented itself as a theme of my
healing with this tumor. My cousin, Baxter, came to me first
because he is living there and saw a healer on my behalf as
soon as he heard the news of my tumor. His findings with his
guru have been really helpful, especially because it's what
started me on the path of really listening to my body in terms
of food choices. And breathing well.

Another love-of-my-life friend, Gillian (married to yet
another, Teddy), reached out to a former acting coach of
hers from college, a man named Per who lives in Bali now.
He sounds like exactly my kinda guy—a man who crafts
beautiful things from a spiritual place, who also has taught
acting classes. He makes these healing masks and amulets and
Gilly reached out to him to make one for me. Here I offer her
words of explanation, as well as the "masks" that Per made for
me (included after this entry). I plan to print them out and
start using them today. (Thank you endlessly, Gilly. I love you
more than words.) Here is her explanation:

*I met Per at 18 as a freshman at NYU. He's a big, loud,
jolly Danish man (I had a friend refer to him as, "Satanic
Santa Claus"). He's internationally known for his work with*

*Balinese Masks and has taught at NYU and Yale, among
other schools.*

*Talking about Per and his work is hard, because it's so
internal. We spent a lot of time running around the room,
pretending to be seaweed (yes, really), and sweating and
crying. Now, none of that is necessarily unique to acting school,
but with Per, everything felt freer. He was truly genuinely
interested in who you were and unblocking all of the shame and
neuroses we all had as (mostly) middle class kids trying to be the
"best," whatever that means.*

*Per's very big on imagery. He creates his own masks by
creating drawings, then traveling to Bali and working with
a mask maker he's known for years. The masks are made
completely traditionally, with the mask maker carving the piece
while holding it between his feet. The wood comes from the
knots of trees, so the trees aren't cut down. You ask the tree for
permission before cutting the knot out. Once they are finished,
Per wraps each of the masks in cloth and then packs them in a
huge suitcase, which he rolls around.*

*In class, every day would basically work the same: Per
would say, "Move, assholes!" and we'd jump around and
pretend to be seaweed for about an hour, until we were pretty
much complete sweaty messes. Then, we'd get to sit, and Per
would open up his suitcase. Some days, we'd get to look at
the mask before putting it on, other days he'd put it on us
completely blind. Then, we'd explore breathing in sandalwood*

and following impulses from the mask down our spines to our bodies. It was surprising work. I consider myself a somewhat skeptic, but the work I witnessed (people singing like opera singers when they usually couldn't hit a note or moving in ways I'd never seen them move) made me a believer in the power of imagery and what we can achieve when we remove inner blocks and allow ourselves to be inspired.

Since I've met Per, he's left the US. He spends most of his time in Bali (where he teaches) or in Denmark. He also has taken his drawings away from traditional masks and into pendants of his own design.

Also, from Per specifically about these drawings:

The first one is about the tumor the second one is about healing after chemo therapy...they are quite big but see if you can send them and that she can print them out...chemo must be around the liver and the tumor around the neck...the tumor drawing has two hearts inside the pendant...love to the tumor and love to your friend...

I have this fantasy that I will go to Bali as soon as I can manage it to meet Baxter's healer and have him pray with me over my head. And walk on a beautiful beach with my beautiful husband. It's a good dream for today. Until then, I have Per's masks and the love of beautiful people who are bringing me to Bali from the comfort of my home, which is really almost better than a walk on a beautiful beach to me. I am really in love with this part of my story right now.

To: Caroline
From: Sarah
Date: April 2, 2017
Subject: Random

_____

I had some pretty righteous gas yesterday and I thought I hope Caroline's not holding in farts. If you have terminal brain cancer you get to fart in front of the pope.

Xox

Sent from my iPhone

A Note from Sasha | Garth Wright

The Shafers, great friends from Dallas, lent us Sasha for a few days. This is her note about her visit:

I arrived Friday evening straight from the airport and into the always bustling Wright home. It was amazing to see the beauty of the new house they've put so much effort and love into over the past year. It felt strange as I walked through their door because it felt just like I was walking into their home in Dallas. It was filled with the same furniture (albeit with some lovely new additions) and the same warm, thick haze of love. With the hectic schedules of two families, each with two small children, it's rare to see even your closest friends. All of it combined to make it feel like they still lived a two-minute walk away.

Garth and Theodore greeted me at the door and by the time I reached the kitchen Caroline was already figuring out what she could cook me. Despite my protests, within 10 minutes dinner was before me.

I have always been in awe of Caroline's energy, both her aura and how she can fill each day with creativity. Honestly, when we first met, both of us bleary-eyed, first-time moms of 4 month olds, her endless energy really stressed me out. I couldn't imagine myself EVER accomplishing half the things she somehow did, each and every day. But as our friendship grew, Caroline gave me a gift. A tender, delicate gift. Somehow in my deep, dark secret of feeling like I would never be enough, I saw myself in the mirror of my new favorite person that my soul was desperately drawn to, and I remembered that I loved myself. I saw this amazing, glorious person caring for me and LIKING me. Me. The new, very lonely, constantly sick, confused and flailing mommy of a precious baby girl. Me. The woman married to the most charming, dedicated, wise man in all of existence who clung to that relationship because she was so terrified to make friends with women. But Caroline and I worked. In the fertile space of young motherhood, Caroline and I found each other and we became friends. And a part of me healed.

Because isn't that just what Caroline is? A healer. A bridge. Her uncanny wisdom. Her ability to love and be loved. Her genuine ability to know herself. Her connection with you connects you to yourself and in turn to others.

Saturday we met up with a few of Caroline's new friends at a clothes-optional lady spa. This is a fun way to meet new people I highly recommend! Naked! Her friends are disarmingly genuine, and I quickly realized how lucky Caroline is to have such authentic people surrounding her.

Later that night, with three of Caroline's new Seattle friends, we listened to the recording of the medical clairvoyant, Dorothea. Afterwards, we shared our thoughts. At one point, Caroline was saying how grateful she was for all the love and help being given to her and her family, and that she wanted to be able to give back in some way. One of the her friends said, "You are connecting people to meaning. That's what you're giving them."

It struck me so deeply then, and only now do I really understand why. Because Caroline's very existence does that and always has. Tumor or no tumor.

Cleaning Up My Brain | Caroline Wright

Yesterday we were standing outside of my parents' rental "cubby" building and I was watching the kids flirt with a gnome in the neighbor's garden. My eyes drifted to an old man cleaning up his the street in front of us, mostly because I was wondering if he was the owner of The Gnome. He was a classic Seattle elder, looking the part of a seafaring man who could also climb a mountain and stay cool despite his impressive beard. He was wearing overalls and looked a little like what I would imagine a very trim, very fit Santa might.

I watched this man for probably ten minutes, taking buckets of dirt and muck from one corner of the street, possibly near his house, to another. I watched him begin to methodically scrape the fallen seedpods and blossom petals, slowly like he does so all the time with great care and pride, from the edge of the curb using the flat side of a shovel. *Scraaaape, tap, tap. Scraaaape, tap, tap.* Over and over until it was pristine. It reminded me of watching someone build a mandala, or how I feel when I fold biscuits to make them flaky. Love and precision blended to make something clean and beautiful.

Today during my radiation treatment, as the machine buzzed in its powerful purpose, I imagined this man in my brain. I really did. I imagined him at the midline of my hemispheres of my brain, just where the muck of the tumor regrowth is located, as though it was his curb; I imagined him scraping it clean and tapping it into a bucket nearby. Slowly, methodically, and with great pride.

I am so thankful for this man, this moment, and my treatment. Clearing the muck away with pride.

Coming Out As Terminal | Caroline Wright

Yesterday we deemed Blood Draw Day, just like every other Wednesday during my treatment. (They have to monitor my white blood cells throughout the chemo and radiation in order to modify my medication if needed.) My beloved regular gal, Annie, has left for Taiwan where she will be for the rest of the month, so yesterday I had a random phlebotomist. This was our exchange as I settled in and offered my requisite explanation about my awkward, shy veins:

> *"Oh, look at your tattoo! What does that say?"*
> *"It says 'not today.'"*
> *"Oh, that's funny. Huh. Why would you have that written on your wrist?"*
> *"Um... Because I have terminal brain cancer and it means that I am not going to die today."*
> *"Oh. Well...* [Blinks and shifts awkwardly.] *Well, that's true of all of us, isn't it?"*

I realize through this exchange and many others that happen to me daily that this prognosis, even though I genuinely don't feel its depths on a regular basis, will be something I have to relive with strangers day after day. At least for now, while I still look like a patient, anyway.

It made me think about what I am going to look like, or how I am going to manage what I am going to look like, as I experience stages of treatment, which may include hair loss and regrowth (or not) and even possibly a loss of an eyebrow. Personally, I don't care about what I look like *at all*. Any time I am given in exchange for hair is not even a thought. Not even a breath of a thought.

Instead, the idea of future Caroline with many years ahead, whether because of my tattoos or because of my hair or whatever else, makes me realize that I will be "coming out" as terminal for the rest of my life.

I don't care, actually. Many of my dearest friends happen to be gay and I've always wholly empathized with their individual stories. Having terminal cancer has nothing to do with being gay, nor are they similar at all, but this is the closest simile that I will ever have. And I am thankful for it, as it helps me better understand my beautiful friends and a small part of their struggle. I hope they will help me understand how to get good at telling strangers oddly personal things about myself if I need to.

...And slay while doing it.

360 Healing | Caroline Wright

My mom is a brilliant woman who comes up with catch phrases really well. I like to think that it is a product of her occupation as an expert of Consumer Insights for restaurant chains. She is insightful indeed and great at coming up with distilled ideas that are marketable and memorable. Her most recent one to do with my healing has been "360 Healing" that she says a lot. It is rooted in the idea that I am approaching my circumstances with a fully realized view, like a pool filled by many different cups of water. I wanted to outline the sources of healing here to give them the light and gratitude they deserve, though I am sure I will focus on each of them more as I continue on my path.

- **Chemo and radiation / Western medicine:** This is a very important cornerstone to my healing, I have full confidence. I take chemo pills nightly and have radiation appointments daily, Monday through Friday, at the hospital. Today marked my second day of my third week of radiation. I take handfuls of pills every day and am very carefully tracking my symptoms.
- **Homeopathy:** I am having appointments with a naturopath in Portland who is approaching the healing of

my gut (inspired by the issues of mineral absorption that Dorothea suggested, reinforced by the recommendation from a dear friend) and the obvious internal imbalances that exist in order for my body to have been so out of whack to enact a tumor. I am seeing a second homeopath that my aunt found for me, a cancer-specific practitioner, who supports the force of the chemo and radiation. (I haven't yet seen him for a session, though he mentioned really interesting things like a virus that aggravates glioblastomas and causes them to grow, so taking specific anti-viral supplements in order to combat it.) I will write more on these guys as I continue down this road.

- **Yoga:** A friend found the perfect studio for me; being a part of it has been amazing and a huge part of my care. I have been going once a week to a private Restorative Yoga session with an amazing yogi (and for lack of a better descriptor, healer) there. Her soft voice and spirit lifts me each time and literally makes me weep with gratitude for her help. I also have been going to "gentle yoga" twice weekly to keep moving and breathing well, and it makes me sleep incredibly well. (I took my mom to class yesterday and she seemed bored.)

- **Walking:** My daily walks have been incredibly helpful in reinforcing my connection to nature, my community and my body. I have been walking to drop off and/or pick up Henry from school. Seeing the faces of loved ones there and saying hello is wonderful, as is getting out in the fresh air and breaking a sweat. And talking with Henry as we walk is always the favorite part of my day.

· **Nutrition / New Way of Eating:** I no longer eat gluten, sugar, chocolate or drink coffee. These are huge changes to my "foodie" lifestyle—especially one who has worked as basically a professional baker for the past few years and has never felt in control of my food choices, whether dictated by my job or unhealthy cravings. But I feel incredible and will never go back. I feel solid, even-keeled and never wavering in my body. I don't feel bloated (not to say that I "felt" bloated before, but I am just noticing that I was in its absence now) and I never rise or fall at the mercy of what I eat. I didn't realize the unsettling of my person by what I put on my plate before, possibly due to the distraction of the *idea* of what I was eating (and paying less attention to the *value* of what I was eating). Now my food purpose is clear—to root my body in foods that only help its healing. It is still tasty, as Jonas noted this week during his visit; this fact doesn't surprise me as my food choices don't change my love of cooking or my capacity to create interesting flavors and textures from fresh ingredients.

· **Meditation:** I set up my shrine downstairs to my friends, before which I have a blanket and lie down with Gilly's Balinese masks (really, with a piece of paper draped over one body part or another as I vacate and breathe). I have not yet been able to make this a daily practice, though I plan to. I have also been meditating during my radiation treatments, controlling my breath with each buzz of the machine.

- **Sleep:** I am sleeping well these days, especially since I am being tapered off of steroids right now. I go to bed at 10 pm every night, just after taking my chemo pill. It feels important right now.

- **Creativity:** This part is likely very clear to you as it is to me. Writing is how I process things and a space I make for myself to hug a part of me that I love so much. Quilting, which I try to do for a few hours each day, is an active form of meditation for me. I am still passively working on the *Charlie the Cook* book and making design choices for this one, the *Caring Bridge Project* memoir.

- **No Screens:** I am transitioning away from using screens *at all.* I have initiated the process of downgrading from my smart phone to getting one that only makes and receives texts and calls. We are getting a landline and a corded kitchen phone. Basically I am returning to the 90s and I love it (as Jeff has always prophesized to be my fate, anyway, given my love for Doc Martens, bob haircuts and now Seattle). I am transitioning into hand-writing these journal posts and then typing them, so I am not spending a lot of passive time at my computer as I write and edit.

These decisions, along with my general commitment to truly *live*, present in my life and with my family, are the shape of my positivity right now. The shape of my fighting. It feels really good.

I smile a big smile at myself in the mirror every time I catch my eye, rather than stare at my now balding head, as if to say: "Hey, stranger. I'm proud of you."

Jonas | Caroline Wright

Today I said a tearful, bittersweet goodbye to my beautiful Swiss brother, Jonas, on his 39th birthday (one he coincidentally and eerily shares with my biological brother).

We met forever ago now, but it is as if he has always been a part of me. He and I are very similar in my view: very sensitive and principled people, loyal to our cores and endlessly devoted to those we love; stubborn and unlike many we meet, so we can feel like outsiders on lonely days; we are endlessly but realistically positive. I am proud that he is my "we."

I was talking with my mom today, as we sat in front of the candle that Jonas found for me that flickers in "hope" and that he vowed he would light its twin each morning as I prepared for radiation and beyond during my continued healing, about how Jonas is distinctly family rather than one of my dearest family of friends.

It is very simple. I did not choose Jonas.

We met before either of us were formed as people, as if born into our siblinghood because our futures would knock us around a little and we needed each other. We have lived through life's challenges of the past two decades in an intricate but beautiful dance, either energetically meeting in unison or in compliment, depending on the need; it was always "we" and always crucial for the survival of that moment.

There has been no more crucial moment than now to dance together. His love and brotherhood, his reflection and energetic compliment, is a major key to my survival, I see very clearly. He breathes beauty and wholeness to my family, to my parents, to Garth.

I did not choose Jonas, no. He is the greatest gift I have ever been given in this lucky life of mine. He holds my healing on so many beautiful, complicated levels. Thank you, Jo, for being my "we."

....

Here is a note that Jonas wrote about his visit during his flight home, despite my hopes that he would catch up on a little bit of the sleep that Henry stole from him throughout his week's visit. It is written in his native tongue, French, as well as mine, as a signature of his generosity and humility:

> *La nouvelle vie qui est la nôtre depuis quelques semaines, celle qui a remplacé la vie "normale" que nous vivions avant, m'a donné la chance de partager quelques jours avec Caroline et de lui apporter un petit peu d'aide dans cette nouvelle vie, mais également de découvrir la magnifique maison de la famille Wright.*

Le plus important qui ressort de cette semaine, c'est que malgré la situation, Caroline est toujours Caroline :-) Toujours aussi bavarde pour notre plus grand plaisir. Les journées bien chargées, entre les traitements, les séances de yoga et la gestion des enfants passent à une vitesse folle. Grâce à l'aide immense de Paul et Glad, ces journées semblent presque normales.

Je me rends encore plus compte de la chance que j'ai d'avoir rencontrer la famille Markunas/Wright il y a 21 ans. Mon cœur est rempli d'espoir et je me réjouis de passer nos vacances d'été ensemble dans le sud de la France.

Après le déchirement de la séparation, il y a quelques heures, étant donné le fait que je serai à nouveau de l'autre côté de la planète, la bougie hope (achetée à Seattle) sera allumée chez moi tous les soirs pour Caroline, afin de transporter mon amour et mes pensées positives jusqu'à elle.

Merci Caroline pour ces quelques jours si importants que nous avons partagés et merci d'être présente dans ma vie et dans mon cœur.

Ton frère qui t'aime très fort.

For most of you who don't speak French, I also would like to add a few words in English, even if Google will translate it pretty well:

Life has changed for ever for all the people in Caroline's close circle, but the most important thing is that Caroline didn't change. She is still the welcoming, warm, awesome woman that I am so proud of. I have had the chance to meet her 21 years ago and am so lucky to still have her in my life and heart. I wish we were not living so far away from each other, however I feel so close to her everyday as I have her with me in my heart.

The week I have had the chance to spend with her has been very healing and even if I am happy to fly back to see my beloved wife and kids, I would have love to be able to stay longer to be able to help more.

The days at the Wright's house are very busy. Between the treatments, the yoga classes and the children, there isn't much time to rest. Caroline is very lucky to have Paul and Glad with her. They are doing so much !

I will light my hope candle (bought in Seattle) every evening to send all my love and my best thoughts to Caroline and her team.

Thank you so much for being in my life. I love you.
Your Swiss brother

Things. And Sleep. | Caroline Wright

I have been writing, writing, writing—I have switched to a notebook, as I told you I had, but it is slower than I thought and my writing has not become less verbose to compensate—but I must sleep because Teddy and Gillian and Phoebe are coming from Brooklyn tomorrow and I am going to explode. Before I head to bed, I wanted to leave you with a few thoughts.

I am going to lean into this bald thing and do "real" hats. I am feeling that knit hats and scarves, no matter their beauty because I really do have some lovely ones, make me feel a little cancer-y. So I am going to bring back the brimmed-hat-on-a-daily-basis look. Watch me. Hat shopping is ahead.

Oh and shaving my head is totally necessary. I re-shaved my head again this weekend with my dad's help and not only do I look fierce again (the scars and bald patches don't bug me at this length), but it helps with the aloe-based goo I am supposed to rub on the burned spots. The growing-out look made me feel like a very patchy, somewhat sad-looking Chia Pet.

I accidentally ate outside of my eating habits today at lunch and it was bad news for my body. I could feel my brain get angry, I got super tired and my stomach became upset. I would prefer to skip a meal (shocking, I know) rather than feel cornered into eating something that makes me feel like garbage. It took a nap, a walk and a few alkalizing drinks to get me back to feeling somewhat normal. Never again.

Diving right back into Week 3 of treatment tomorrow only to hug my loved ones a few hours later! What a good Monday it will be!

Post from Leah Sellers Simpson | Paul Markunas

From Leah:

I've never known someone who is sick, like really sick, save my grandparents and a close family friend when I was young. I struggle with what to say to people during difficult times and circumstances I can't possibly understand. And I have an unhealthy need for control and certainty in situations.

So to say I was a bit nervous as I approached the Wright house last Thursday is an understatement. I kept wondering, "How should I act? What do I say? Is it okay to laugh? What if I cry?" As I rang the doorbell and saw Caroline round the corner with her signature smile, I immediately felt at ease and realized this very obvious and simple truth—she is still just Caroline. Only sick.

We spent the afternoon alone in her house and talked as she quilted and we both drank hot tea. Our conversation ebbed and flowed as we laughed about distant high school memories, reminisced about our years together in New York, and cried as we talked about our children, her prognosis, and the future. It was raw yet filled with laughter and hope, the way that conversations with Caroline tend to be.

Over the next four days, we ran errands, went to treatment, picked Henry up from school, read stories, baked cookies, went to the farmer's market, and even on two 3-mile(!) hikes. I often found myself forgetting that Caroline was even sick and the impetus that had brought me there. I was amazed at her stamina (although not surprised) and in awe of the tender and honest way with which she cared for and talked to Henry and Theodore.

It was a beautiful visit. One I wish I had made sooner. And that wasn't prompted by a cancer diagnosis. It's easy as I get older and life gets more complicated to make excuses for why it's hard to set the time aside to see people. Even the people you love. I've already learned so many lessons from Caroline and the grace with which she handles things. Perhaps most importantly, she's taught me to make time for the important things, to focus on the joy of the present, and to be grateful for every single day in the future.

I will be back soon.

On Meals and the Company We Keep
Caroline Wright

On Saturday night, Garth and I went on a date proposed at the last minute by my dad. We wanted to take advantage of our still novel and often willing caregivers, but also celebrate the fact that I am halfway through my treatment and holding strong in terms of my energy level and health. Our truly wonderful dinner at our favorite Lebanese date night spot in Ballard inspired me to think about my favorite meals of memory. Here are few favorites that spring to mind; I hope you'll permit a bit of rose-colored reminiscing. I guess that's what memoirs are for, so here it goes.

....

Garth and I spent a weekend in Rome once and fell into the kind of love we have now. We grew up that weekend, holding hands together. We did so over plates of creamy *cacio e pepe* and slices of blistered pizza. Over negronis and artichokes. The restaurants had been recommended to me through my friend and former boss when I was working in food television production (before I wrote cookbooks), who told me that they were originally from Mario Batali! Eating like Mario Batali, it turns out, is pretty memorable. The *cacio e pepe*, tossed tableside as Garth and I held hands and acted like newlyweds, was the best dish I've ever tasted.

....

During the research period of my forthcoming cookbook in the Delta del Ebre region of Spain, our crew (Daniel, the chef whose stories I had the honor of writing, and my co-author; Johnny, the brilliant photographer; and I) met one of Daniel's chef friends from Barcelona, Quim Marques, at a cabin with Quim's family surrounded by rice fields. There were a few incredible meals that weekend—delicious, juicy *botifarra negre* sausages that tasted like the very best pâté I've ever had with a crackled olive oil "poached" egg and a glass of red wine from Priorat, all served at breakfast, for example—but the most memorable to me was one cooked by a fisherman. One of guides in the delta was the proprietor of the cabins and rice fields and a local fisherman; he took us on a meandering visit of the delta that made Johnny and I (the "Americans" in Daniel's posse, accompanied by whatever the Catalan equivalent of an eye roll would be) squirm with our mounting to-do lists running in our heads. At the end of our long day of adventuring, researching and shooting (photos) from the back of a reluctant Spanish van, our fisherman tour guide hopped out and threw his net—illegally and giddily, I might add—into a spot where the overflow from a dam was occurring. (It had an effect for the fish swimming there as if in a proverbial barrel, which didn't seem quite fair for them in the end). He pulled the writhing net out of the water full of many dozens of fish like a cartoon bear licking his lips. It was sunset and the light gleamed on the watery rice fields, I remember noticing as we drove back to our cabin. Our fisherman, with the help of Quim, cleaned and quickly fried the bounty of fish. We ate around midnight that night, which was my first exposure to an appropriate Catalan dinnertime. I sat next to the lovely Daniel and he showed me how to debone the whole fried fish as his friends laughed and he told me stories about how he became a chef.

....

My first friend in New York, Sonya, introduced me to Gillian and Marc, friends of hers from her conservatory acting program at NYU. Garth and I had just moved to Brooklyn, where Gillian still lives, so I invited them over for dinner along with a few others in their college crew. It was my first experience of many cooking for this pack of hungry, poor actors, but this was by far the most historic. We ate pot pie, roasted sunchokes from the Park Slope Food Co-op, and apple cobbler. None of the dishes were extraordinary. We talked of politics, the Spanish Civil War and Ira Glass. They were smarter than me and loved to stand in the kitchen as I cooked. I had found my tribe, unchanged almost a decade later. I had never belonged like that before and that is the night it all began.

The first Thanksgiving I hosted for my parents while my Sarah happened to be visiting was at "40 Berkeley," our final Brooklyn apartment that still feels like home to a really big part of me. I loved that place—the parlor floor of a brownstone in the oldest part of Park Slope—desperately. It was the setting of where I found myself over and over again, where friends gathered every weekend, a place filled with joy and life and heartache that only New York can inspire. It was the place of so many of these meals I'll write about here, the inspiration for the kind of energy and beauty I have only begun to channel for our home here in Seattle. Anyway, I don't remember the precise Thanksgiving foods Sarah and I cooked that year; all I remember is cooking with my beautiful Sarah with the care of an overbearing mother because of her allergies. The glow of the candlelight on the tablecloth and feeding good food to my family. I think homemade green bean casserole was involved, as was a juniper berry-brined turkey.

It is really hard to choose the particular dinner parties at 40 Berkeley that were my favorites. I cooked in regular rotation for our closest friends, shouting over bad movies and eating perfect roast lamb off of paper plates, to refined and meticulously planned coursed and seated dinner parties. Ours was the home where friends announced engagements, pregnancies, promotions. We hosted an awesome New Year's Eve party our last in that apartment, because I became pregnant with Henry soon after. (I blame my uncharacteristically slinky dress and the 23 bottles of champagne that we chilled in our bathtub filled with ice; needless to say it was a surprise when I found out three months later about future Henry when I was moving Garth to Dallas for his first job out of law school. My process of leaving New York is another wild story for another day, but yet another installment in my profound belief in living the adventure of life with open eyes and a joyful heart.)

....

Another story within a story as uncanny as our New Year's in New York is one during which I was homeless in Paris during the summer that Garth was studying for the bar exam. It was an incredible experience and a story for another day, but it brought one of my best friends and fellow literature majors— and easily one of the very best and most engaging writers I know—back into my life. At the end of this unbelievable summer (after even our trip to Italy where the *cacio e pepe* moment happened), Amy and I concocted a plan over a few glasses of Sancerre with our handsome men around us (before Garth and I had babies and theirs were with a babysitter). We split up and ran down the street in different wobbly directions and grabbed what we could from whatever stores were still open (it was a Monday, I believe, which renders Paris a ghost town) in order to make a lovely pasta dish and, of course, drink a few more bottles of Sancerre. I saw Amy in the distance, lumbering toward me holding a few melons. I stumbled my way through making a spicy zucchini and mozzarella spaghetti dish (a favorite from *Twenty-Dollar, Twenty-Minute Meals* that began as fodder for a wobbly lot just like we were at that moment). Amy sliced the melons (of the Charentais variety, if I remember correctly, though Amy wasn't impressed) and removed their seeds, poured a few glugs of port in their wells and smiled her wicked grin as she exclaimed, "First course!" The port was from her wedding to her wonderful husband Phil that I am sad I missed while I was in culinary school because I know it was fabulous (both by the lore surrounding it as well as the very fact that Amy is a beyond talented director and visionary and her parties are a direct reflection of that beauty in her). Needless to say, it was a great, memorable night in our apartment perched atop Sacré-Coeur. (No port or pasta was left to waste).

....

Our wedding meal, seated among our very favorite people, was autobiographical. The first course was the meal that Garth proposed to me immediately following: stone crab claws, smoked salmon and caviar. The main course was meant as a nod to the famous (and somewhat local chain restaurant in Paris) Relais de l'Entrecôte that has a proprietary herbed sauce that Garth and I love. It was our last meal before we left after we graduated in 2005. The cake was one by an artist my dad and I fell in love with, Sylvia Weinstock, that held Garth's and my two favorite flavors (of anything really, not just buttercream), being a rich chocolate and a bright blood orange. That meal ended with my feeling the most elegant I have ever felt while eating cake.

....

Even though this doesn't count as a meal, one of my most memorable food cravings was for the chocolate milkshake I demanded of Garth after laboring without medication for twelve hours to give birth to Henry. Garth, in the manner of an eager first-time father, ran out and could only find a McDonald's open at that hour. I slurped my shake down greedily with a smile on my face.

I had chocolate ice cream my only night in the ICU after my brain surgery. Apparently hospitals make me crave chocolate ice-creamy things, which somehow make me think of Bapa because we used to eat chocolate frozen yogurt together from TCBY any chance we could sneak it. I will never forget that milkshake, though.

Possibly my favorite memory of any single party at 40
Berkeley was the pizza party I threw to celebrate the end
of Garth's first year of law school. It was in the middle of a
particularly sweltering May. Of course, I started cooking too
late and the oven, cranked to 500° F with a sizzling pizza
stone inside, was causing all of us to sweat profusely as we
huddled over our paper plates. The pizza was blistered and
crisp, so no one complained.

These memories, it became especially clear to me as I
was writing them just now, were intended to be about food
but, even with pressing my (still as yet unaffected) long-term
memory, all I could remember was the *feeling* I had while eating
rather than the details of the menu. These memories (and
actually possibly even my whole relationship to food, including
the motivation behind what and why I write) have more to
do with the people I was with rather than what I was eating.
The food is always some range between good and interestingly
good, but that is a product of grocery shopping and a few very
simple skills that I happen to believe that anyone can learn to
do well who wants to do so. The people, my people, are what
made these meals memorable. I want my boys to learn to cook
well—something I or someone in my army will ensure for their
futures. What I want even more for them is the belonging and
love I found around those plates I just mentioned. Love makes
everything taste better. It makes for a truly rich life.

Bapa and Sunsets | Caroline Wright

Bapa had a thing for photographing sunsets. (I think my uncle is sending a print of one to me right now as I write this.) I totally get why now, though I am more partial to sunrises, and especially to my husband who finds me in the morning when he comes back in from taking the dogs out and smiles excitedly as he says of our first-class view from our dilapidated front steps, "Hey, honey, Rainier's out."

I rush to our mudroom windows to catch the sky awash in pink, purple and orange, like the fire is rising from the Earth to begin again.

Bapa celebrated the end of his gift of a day and I celebrate the beginning of a new one. I'm wondering if I should start snapping photos.

Halfway Mark Reached! | Glad Markunas

After today's treatment Caroline has officially completed 3 out of 6 treatment weeks. Or as her doctors said, she's "at 30 gray" or half way to the goal of receiving a total dosage of 60 gray units of radiation by the end of her six weeks. The unit of measurement is named for Dr. Louis H Gray, an English physicist, who invented the field of radiobiology.

And as is standard practice at 3 weeks, she had a check-in appointment with a radiation oncologist. Her primary one is Dr. Yolanda Tseng who is attending a conference in Australia this week so she saw Dr. Lia Halasz who is equally impressive and sees patients from a 6 state area! Everything is going as expected and her "lab results were beautiful."

During the course of the meeting, Caroline learned the outcome of pathology that we all have been waiting for regarding a MGMT genetic biomarker of her tumor. When this marker is present, there is a correlation with increased efficacy of treatment. However, Caroline's was not present or in medical terms, *"not methylated."* What's interesting is that the medical professionals don't know what that means in Caroline's case for a couple of reasons. The one big and positive wildcard is her age at 33. As described by Dr. Halasz her young age is *"the trump factor and could aid responsiveness."*

Plus we learned that they don't have a lot of data on younger patients as 59 is the average age that people are typically diagnosed with a GBM.

A very clearly good development from today's meeting is that Caroline can stop steroids given all the positive progress! A real win for sleep in her future! The cessation of all steroids is also based on her excellent blood labs done weekly to assess her overall health in spite of the radiation and chemotherapy.

So consistent with Caroline charting her own path her whole life, she once again is defining her own, unique journey! Her way.

(Usually Garth handles the medical updates. I am writing on his behalf since he is attending a conference in Washington D.C. and will be back late tomorrow night. We miss him!)

The Many Faces of Cancer │ Paul Markunas

In these busy, busy days trying to help run a household with two small boys, two dogs, a husband who works 10 hours a day and a daughter who has terminal cancer, there isn't a lot of time to think or respond to the non-essential stuff.

Still, as I sit with Caroline morning after morning in the radiation oncology waiting room at University of Washington hospital, I am saddened, impressed, and sometimes amazed at the many faces of cancer.

This morning we saw a woman whose face had been completely reconstructed and who was still undergoing radiation. It was not pleasant to look at, but, by god, she was there to keep going, to carry on. Or the lovely older woman named Kathy from Whidbey Island who commuted to her radiation about two and a half hours each way to treat three tumors—one in her liver, one in her lung and one in her stomach and who wore a knitted hat with a panda's face and ears that Theodore couldn't take his eyes off of. Or Pam whose husband was given a year to live and was there with him for his fourth year of treatment who found the time and kindness to bring a hand-knitted finger puppet to Theodore and an artisan pencil from Bolivia for Henry, the brother she had never met.

Children in wheelchairs or on gurneys, prisoners accompanied by a police escort, old people with oxygen tanks, young people with shaved heads and scars as big as the stitching on a football. A woman who had to straighten all the magazines in the waiting room because she needed something to do. People who are afraid, sad, some alone, some with others who still seem very alone and lonely.

And your heart breaks and yet it is grateful at the same time.

How have I missed all these people my life? How have I not seen people for who they are really?

In this place we are all the same, those of us with and without cancer. We wear the same clothes, think the same thoughts, are scared and grateful for the same things.

We are all human.

I have never been in a place where humanity has been so reduced and yet so elevated at the same time.

I know I will never be the same again.

Blessings and gratitude from the depths of pain and sadness.

Somehow I know that, regardless of how this turns out, the world will be a better place because of it.

I just know it.

Believe | Caroline Wright

On Wednesday, again at a Blood Draw Day, I was sitting with my mom and dad in the waiting area. I clocked an older woman with a mid-thigh length black Cher wig and round wire-rimmed glasses like those made famous by John Lennon.

This woman walked over to me a few minutes later and initiated the following conversation:

The Dark Lady: Hey, I like your hair.

Me: I like yours, too.

The Dark Lady: I had a haircut like yours ten years ago. You look awesome! *[She gives me a high five.]* Good luck! You got this!

Guys, I have been blessed by Cher. Damn the odds.

The Diagnosis Period | Caroline Wright

It would be obvious to state that I was scared when I heard about the tumor growing back a few weeks ago, or that I was saddened a little by my lack of genetic marker that has been correlated to the body's receptiveness to the type of chemo I am on now (and hopefully will be on for a year to come). I was both of those things. I am not now. I have done a lot of thinking on it.

Other than its aggressive nature, we really don't know my tumor very well yet. I have come to think of this period—to include radiation and the four-week untreated break afterward—as the "diagnosis period." (After that, I get my first MRI and that is considered my new baseline.) In speaking with the doctors, a team I trust inherently and thoroughly, I realize for everything they know (about brains in general, but certainly statistically about patients like me in specific), there are many things they don't. It's a trial and error thing in a lot of ways.

They don't have very much data on a 33-year-old with a GBM, as it is not common. Even in the face of statistics, they can't know about the specific genes or behavior of *mine*, which is oddly comforting right now. We know now, too, that my age and tolerance to the treatment so far are both very positive according to the doctors.

The other thing I wonder about are all of the softer factors—these massive lifestyle changes I've made to the environment that the tumor knows from before in my body—and how they are changing things. *Nothing* about my choices are the same now, down to how I brush my teeth (with alkaline clay and oil pulling, if you're curious). I sleep more. Healing (and my family, one in the same) is my *only* focus. I'm making serious, permanent changes in these areas that prioritize joy and mindfulness and celebrate the kind of love I am so fortunate to have in my life.

If I was to be honest about my instincts—those crazy in-tune feelings I had that led me to my internist and also caused me to know that my tumor was re-growing based on my symptoms during my post-op healing—I am feeling very positive about my health. I can say that I don't have the sense that my tumor is growing now.

Remember those little men with the white gloves I talked about meeting in my body at the ICU? The ones that took note of everything being in its place? They are finding some differences lately, ones I am choosing to feel are relatively minor—like some difficulty with short-term memory on occasion and challenges with word recall in conversation on occasion, too—because they absolutely could be a product of the radiation from what my doctors told me before the treatment started. And, honestly, being slightly addled is fine by me in the long term because that implies there could be a *long term*. Besides, I am married to a hunky genius control freak who I would be happy to have boss me around for the rest of my life. The men with white gloves are very impressed right now and feel as though they are adrift in inner tubes on a lazy summer stream. I feel better than ever before and have to believe that this is a factor they can't see in any statistic.

There are things the doctors can know about me based on the statistics and then there are things that they don't because of the fact that I am an outlier. I am an outlier, indeed, and own it. I'm not placing bets or making guesses; I'm living in the moment, thankful to be here. This is still, like I say, the Diagnosis Period. Keep crossing those fingers and sending love. (I re-read my favorite letters in bed before I go to sleep. I meditate before a shrine to my friends with little objects that people have been giving me—crystals, tiny paintings, favored tokens like that—that I've arranged on a windowsill in my basement.) I am of the belief that the love from all of you is part of what skews these odds of mine.

My Dad, Paul, Gampa | Caroline Wright

I've wanted to write about my dad but I haven't known where
to start. He's taken care of me my whole life, but now at 33, he
is back to making me eggs in the morning. It is an unexpected
twist to say the least. I am more grateful for him now. We are
both far less angry, less trapped in our strong hold to each other,
than when I was a child and, later, a teenager. I think a lot about
my dad, all the time actually. Here are some of my thoughts
knowing full well that even these pale in comparison to him and
the very real and beautiful life he's helped to give me.

My dad is a young guy for raising a 33 (and a 35)—year-old.
In retrospect, that may have been a tough choice for him and
spared him of a few adventures, but it means I have a blonde
dad when most of my friends' dads are greyed. I remember
being in the third grade at recess telling a friend that my dad
was turning 35 and that I wanted to marry him or someone
just like him someday. (I didn't.)

My dad cries at *everything*. There was a period of time as a kid
when we watched movies in weekly succession and he cried

each time, whether or not the movie was sad. I would roll my eyes and make fun of him (even though it is a quality I share with him). I see him cry almost as often these days. I don't make fun of him now. Sometimes I cry, too.

....

My dad can't do anything a little bit, or even a normal human amount. (It's where I got it from and his is the voice inside me that I am now trying to occasionally get stoned and *chill out*.) This is why he had, until recently, five Jack Russell terriers, an affinity for collections (clocks, china sets, artwork, prints of birds and plants, cowboy hats) and an affinity for extreme fad diets. He wasn't planning on being a grandfather at the moment of my pregnancy with Henry (nor I a mother, but we found our footing quickly), though he ran headfirst at it and visited Henry every single month of his first year despite living a plane flight away.

....

One of my favorite "Dad" stories could have been so easily solved by Google, had it existed in the late 1980s. In Chicago, where I was born and lived until I was six, we had two big dogs—two beautiful English setters, one of whom was deaf. I remain confused by the next step of the story to this very day, but he had somehow fallen under the impression that Florida, where we were moving, was too hot for dogs. (*As if no dogs lived in the whole state?*) He found good homes for both Misty and Chamois, but I know how much it broke his heart. I hate that he had to do it again, too, especially in the face of his fervent vows to the contrary when he took in the most recent pack. I'm happy that it seems now that two of their Jack Russells, one of whom is also deaf, will join us in Seattle soon.

....

My family was taking a trip to Italy the summer before my sixth grade year, the summer before I joined my brother at his prep school. My dad was again under the false impression that Italy was as hot as the face of the sun and we humble Floridians would not be able to manage the heat. So he whispered into the hair stylist's ear (*I'm not kidding*) during an appointment just before our trip and she *cut my hair off.* (I started my new school year that fall and my brother's friends said to him that they thought his *sister* was coming to his school, not his *brother.*) My dad made us walk many miles across Rome—from the Pantheon to the Baths of Carcalla, to be exact, as he didn't believe in taking taxis on vacation for fear of missing any sights—and my brother and I got heat stroke anyway.

....

We drove from Florida to Canada once for "vacation," too. My dad insisted we drive through the night, but finally mercifully let us stop at a Radisson—I remember it clearly now—for a shower and a short nap at about 3 am.

....

My parents have owned something totally unbelievable like forty houses in their 35 years of marriage. A lot of moves and restlessness. My dad has left each one more beautiful than when he found them. I did one renovation and joke that it was the reason I grew this cancer. He is a madman, a genius, and an artist and remains unfazed.

....

I used to cry—as recently as a few months ago—at the idea of losing my dad. I honestly can't imagine my world without him. I hate that he has to imagine his without me.

....

I was thinking about Bapa the other day, about how much of my life is defined by our connection and the years we had together. How I've carried him with me, especially now, and that he's shaped so much of who I am.

My dad is that person to my beautiful boys, tailor-made for their sweet and sensitive hearts. A perfect and healing match for all. They will love him as much as, if not more than, I love Bapa because of Gampa's insane devotion to them, which they return in kind. Forever.

My dad is so much of me. He is my positivity and insecurity, fearlessness and sass. He is my funny story and quiet place. He is my embrace, my tears, my broad smile. He is my faith, my health, my future and past. He is my adventure and I his.

I will love you forever, Dad. Thank you for making my life so beautiful and worth fighting for. And for helping me fight, making me stronger and more beautiful in your light, like you do with so many things in your life. We're in this together, as you say. And thanks for the eggs along the way.

The Real Things | Paul Markunas

Thinking about life and love and important things today. The real things. Over my life (I'm turning 60 this summer),I remember the real things vividly.

As a child, playing piano and singing at 2 in the morning to calm myself and regroup after bad family moments with an alcoholic father and difficult mother.

As a young adult in college (and after) and then a young married father, finding moments of peace with meditation and long walks along Lake Shore Drive in Chicago. Finding a few good friends along the way.

And later, finding my loves in my dogs, my garden, my painting, my wife, my children.

And even later, finding my spiritual home in Santa Fe, a place that feeds and calms me still, even if only for a week a year.

Now I am grateful for the things that I am seeing as the most real and lasting of all:

My two grand-boys are everlasting. Worth every second of energy I can give them. They are pure, beautiful, triumphant, exhausting and deeply lovable.

My Jonas. The son I needed and wanted and got, albeit in a roundabout way.

My Garth. The son-in-law I treasure and, at this current moment, commiserate with. We are bound together for life and we will prosper in spite of what happens.

My darling Caroline. I never appreciated you fully until this raw and uninvited event. I see now the beauty of your vivid and giving soul, your energy and compassion for those you love and touch and your focus to get better, to heal, to continue, to surpass.

These are the real things for me. I don't want to focus on anything else.

Playlist | **Caroline Wright**

Today, in radiation, the music was blaring and I forgot to tell them to turn it off, as is my preference. The songs that played in succession (*not kidding*) were as follows:

"Only the Good Die Young" by Billy Joel
"Let it Be" by the Beatles
"Yesterday" by the Beatles

So, yeah. And there is nothing else to do but focus on them. Weird.

Talking to Henry about Radiation | Caroline Wright

On Monday, Henry stayed home from school because of
a fever and a cough. This meant that Garth and I had our
first opportunity to bring him along to the hospital. On our
way there, we brought up the topic of my treatment and the
expectations for how to keep his germs to himself, things
like that, and gave him the especially focused moment to
ask any questions. We asked him if he wanted to know about
Mommy's treatment and if he wanted to see the machine.
This is the conversation that followed:

> **Caroline:** Do you want to come see the machine that
> zaps the weed in my brain?

> **Henry:** Well, I don't like loud noises.

> **Caroline:** I know you don't. This machine doesn't make
> loud noises; it just makes a buzzing sound. It's a table that
> moves around with some lasers and a buzzing noise and
> that's it. But it wouldn't be on, anyway, if you wanted
> to take a look. The people who run the machine aren't
> even in the room when it's on. Do you have any other
> questions about it?

Henry: What do you think about when you are in the machine? Do you think about the whole world?

Caroline: I think about my world—you, Daddy, Theodore, Gampa and Gaba—and I usually just have quiet time.

Henry: My world is your world, actually. *[A long pause.]* Does the radiation make you scared?

Caroline: No, not at all. I'm really thankful for my treatment. It helps me fight the weed in my brain. It makes me happy to go to the hospital and see my doctors.

Henry: *[Another long pause.]* One time I made a really big ship. It was bigger than a caterpillar.

At the hospital, Henry did a really great job—he wore his mask, he sat quietly as I met my doctors and nurses as I have every Monday during treatment. He came with me to deliver cookies as I have also done every Monday during treatment (or "Cookie Day" as the receptionist team and my technicians have come to call it). He saw the tables and the lasers and one of the sweet technicians showed Henry my mask and how it all worked. I could almost see the wheels turning in that beautiful brain of Henry's, knowing how much this was for him to process. As we sat in the doctor's room with an out-of-place mural of a Hawaiian beach on the wall, he curled up on the chair and leaned on Garth's arm.

I see you there, sweet Henry. The overwhelm, the fear of the unknown. Your world is my world, actually, Henry, and I'll hold you in it forever.

After Teddy and Gillian's Visit
Posted by Paul Markunas

From Teddy and Gillian:

It feels so impossible to talk about our week, because nothing is easy to put in a simple box—the week was at once just a wonderful time with our dearest friends and a time of very specific challenges, a time of watching our children play (and fight) with one another, and connecting as individuals, away from all labels that we've collected over the past decade or so. So we've come up with a number of moments that stuck out to us as important in one way or another that we wanted to share:

- *Walking into the Wright house and being hit in the nose with the wonderful aroma of Caroline's meat sauce, which immediately transports me back to my early twenties as a hungry and struggling actor. I want to bottle this and wear it as a fragrance.*
- *The incredible and ferocious love of Paul and Glad for their daughter. Sitting in the waiting room at radiation with Paul and watching him going to bat for Caroline when her radiation appointment for the following day is changed to a completely different time. Seeing Glad working on her blog entry as we all*

get ready for dinner, making sure that it's perfect and that she hasn't forgotten any important detail before she's able to close the computer and join us.

- *Sitting at the table and brainstorming Charlie the Cook ideas (and oh are there many!) with Caroline, joyfully thinking of all the amazing recipes and rhymes she'll be writing soon enough.*
- *Going to yoga with Caroline, which she claims is easy, but I find myself emotional in the middle of it, and very sore the next day.*
- *Watching Phoebe (our daughter) and Theodore hide themselves in the closets and cabinets of Paul and Glad's new condo, playing hide and seek as only one and a half year olds can (joyfully and terribly).*
- *Having a dinner party at Herschel and Margaret's house (who also put us up during our stay—thank you!!!!), with our kids opening and slamming doors on a different floor and thinking, "I could do this forever," and hoping we can.*
- *Watching a section of Caroline's hair slowly fall out due to radiation*
- *Singing "Down by the Bay," to motivate me, Teddy, Phoebe, Caroline pushing Theodore in his stroller, and Henry up what we have dubbed, "Meltdown Mountain," by their house, due to the slow but constant uphill climb.*
- *How quickly and easily tears can flow, and how they can be swallowed up by laughter just as easily.*
- *As Phoebe battled with poor Theodore (she's learning the*

concept of sharing), Garth pouring us a glass of Caroline's vermouth. And as we left Seattle, Phoebe calling from the backseat, "I miss Henry. I miss Theodore. I miss Caroline. I miss Garth," which is how we all feel.

- *Essentially this. Life is happening in the Wright house. Wonderful, messy life. Yes, having terminal cancer seems like a full time job, but our beloved Caroline is who she's always been. She's surrounded by love and support. Another very vivid memory is Caroline reading out loud the letters she had received that week with great appreciation, so if you're reading this, keep writing!*
- *Final memory. In the kitchen (where I feel like I have all of my memories with Caroline) as "Let it Be," by the Beatles plays. I really hear the line:*

"And when the night is cloudy
There is still a light that shines on me Shine until tomorrow
Let it be"

Let that light keep shining on Caroline.

A Very Lovely Thought | Caroline Wright

I have no idea what happens after death. Since I am not religious—though speaking out loud to more people about my beliefs that makes me think I am actually agnostic over atheistic—I don't have a preconceived idea, which isn't helpful to me now.

I don't happen to believe the whole dinner party in the sky thing, the paradise thing. That seems logistically and spatially improbable. Crowded. And, after all, I am actually part skeptic and it just sounds too good to be true; and so far, I hate to admit, that when things sound so good they usually don't happen that way. They happen somehow unimagined and often ultimately better, but not the way one originally thinks to be "good."

I like the idea of reincarnation. My dad once told me in the car after seeing Cecilia Bartoli in concert when I was a kid in the second row, where we hung on every note and screamed "Brava!" after every aria, that he felt talents were carried through lifetimes. That one person would work on their talents and almost pass it along to another, which always felt like a beautiful idea in terms of having a "gift." It helps to explain how someone could be born capable of singing or drawing or dancing like the great artists that communicate beauty so clearly through their art.

Or is reincarnation like it is in the movies? Closing the eyes of one body and through a slow fade from black one wakes up as another character, starting over again? This makes sense to me in terms of relationships, offering one explanation for why and how I have known the people I love so intensely, like I knew them before because, indeed, I could have. It also means that leaving here wouldn't be goodbye to those I love, but rather the people I will find again on another path. That helps me with the idea of my boys—my Garth, my parents, my Jonas, and each of my deeply loved friends, too– but especially my boys. It means that no matter how long I have—which I believe still will be a while, by the way—I would search to the ends of the Earth or beyond to find their sweet souls again, to hold them again. This thought is comforting to me now.

Then, there is one part of me that considers what this beautiful healer in my life, my restorative yoga teacher, Jodi, says during my guided meditations and soothing poses: how there is this part of us that is never born and never dies. (She, I think, uses it as an access point for deep meditation.) With that sentiment, I do find a deep calm. Maybe there is just a quiet nothingness that releases all mortal ties and all we are left with is an essence of that person. And, as I happen to *know* (rather than just *believe*), the love that was created through them forever changes those it touches, too. My love lives in my Henry and my Theodore and family and closest friends and all of you here in some way already. This writing is the closest to Heaven I may ever get, who knows. It's beautiful to me that my boys will hold a book someday and know their mother, even if they can't remember me. That, honestly, is my view of Heaven right now. And, in terms of my mortal aspirations because *I very much am still here*, this beautiful thought is one of the many that help me fight, to earn every minute I get with them going forward.

I hope to live in this beautiful life of mine, holding my children here, for a long time. But, as Sarah Jane (who is sleeping downstairs as I write this) says, I didn't *do* anything to create this tumor, so I may not be able to *do* anything to stop it. (What I am saying is that I know it is largely out of my control, other than to maintain the otherwise good health of my young, strong body and organs.) This writing is as honest of a shot as any—to carry my very healthy soul beyond my body and bury it deep inside my loved ones, my children, my husband, my parents and have them know how very deeply they are loved by me and how that love continues forever, no matter how long I have to stay and where I go from here.

After Sarah Jane's Visit | Posted by Paul Markunas

From Sarah:

I am back home in Orlando and getting settled after my trip to Seattle and wanted to share some thoughts. First, I must warn you that I am not one of Caroline's articulate friends that studied literature and loves to write. I work in the medical field and I cannot even remember the last time I wrote a full paragraph. So I will share my thoughts with you the only way I know how which may or may not make sense, but I know Caroline is used to my random stream of consciousness so I guess it is fitting...

LOVE
Caroline has always been one of the most loving people I know so I am happy to see that she is completely surrounded by love and support right now. She has been blessed with parents who are willing to relocate 3,000 miles to be with her and the boys. She has been blessed with a husband who works all day and is still able to help maintain a busy house without complaining. She has been blessed with friends willing to travel from other countries to see her without hesitation. She is blessed with these things because she would do this for all of us. She has always loved her friends and family unconditionally and she deserves every bit of extra love and support she has been receiving recently.

STRENGTH

Caroline is scared and she is realistic about her prognosis, but she is not giving up. She has always been stubborn and now this is working in her favor as she fights every day to do any little thing she can to beat her cancer or at least slow it down. I truly believe she will have more time than her doctors have estimated because of this trait.

PERSPECTIVE

I have worked with cancer patients for more than a decade but I have never had someone so close to me diagnosed with cancer. This is new territory for me but Caroline and her family have been wonderful guides and I hope I can somehow translate this experience into being a better, more compassionate nurse practitioner.

HUMOR

Caroline is still Caroline, just sick (as Leah said). She is still the mom that hosts naked Lady Gaga dance parties for the boys after bath time. She is still the friend that will belly laugh with you when you look at old photos and read old emails from freshman year of college (we thought we were such big shots!).

TALENTS

Despite having a tumor the size of a tangerine in her brain, she is still able to write as beautifully and articulately as always. She is still baking cakes for neighbors and she cooked almost every meal while I was there last week. It makes me sad to think that she could lose these gifts so I will cherish every word she writes and enjoy every morsel of food she cooks.

COMMUNITY

One of the things that touched me this week was seeing the outpouring of love and support she is receiving from friends and neighbors in Seattle. I hate that she is thousands of miles away, but I feel so comforted knowing that she is surrounded but so many wonderful people. From neighbors like Page and Randy who mowed the lawn and cleaned the house while watching Theodore to friends dropping off soup or offering to take Henry to school. If the situation were reversed, I know for a fact she would be helping each of these people. That is just the kind of person she has been her whole life and it just makes sense that she is now getting the same in return. I thank all of you for taking care of her while many of us are so, so far away.

I am grateful that I was able to visit my BFF and I so happy she is surrounded by so much love and support up there. I cannot wait to visit again soon.

Three Cheers for Caroline! | Glad Markunas

It's nearly the end of Caroline's radiation and chemotherapy initial treatments. Five weeks of radiation and chemo are nearly over out of six.

For the last six radiation treatments, the beams will be more directly focused on the site of her initial tumor to maximize the impact on any remaining cancer cells at that site. This starts tomorrow.

The great news is that Caroline has taken all this radiation and chemotherapy amazingly well. She is not overly fatigued. Her weekly blood work has shown excellent results—no anemia and healthy counts all around. She has not had severe nausea and she has not lost weight.

These are all positive signs about her body's ability to accept the severity of the treatments and to fight against the cancer.

After the treatments end, there will be four weeks of no treatments and then an MRI and medical assessment around the first of June to determine her status and the success of the treatments.

But let's all take one moment to give three cheers to our lovely Caroline who has remained positive and cheerful throughout this tough process.

We all know that the love and support everyone has given her has made her attitude possible which may be the real key to her longer term success. Please join her Mom and Dad in...

THREE CHEERS FOR CAROLINE!!!

Garth | Caroline Wright

Today marks Garth's and my ninth wedding anniversary, though our fourteenth year together as a couple. Garth and I have been together for what feels like a few lifetimes. That is not said in a punchline-to-a-marriage-joke kind of way, but more of an acknowledgement that we have lived and love in each other's light for a long period of time for our young lives. We are a funny match in a lot of ways—we couldn't be more outwardly different—but we have given each other the parts of ourselves that balance out the other. He makes me whole. He grounds me and keeps me from flying away completely into the clouds. He gave me my two beautiful boys that both look like him depending on the day.

He supports me endlessly, examples as follows: we live in a house that he watched me spill money into and design and love and he loves it now, too (even though I think it turned out so cute and maybe a little girly and he wasn't allowed any input); my career at its highs and lows, never once losing faith in my talent or capability; being an incredible father and teammate for the challenges of parenting. The most baffling support yet, however, has been in the past two months since my diagnosis. He has been gracious and selfless and strong and organized in ways I am not sure I could have been if the roles were reversed. He emotionally meets me where I am on any given day, managing to be positive and hopeful with me despite being scared. This is the current iteration of our symbiosis, the way that we share the parts of ourselves to make each other whole, as this positivity and hopefulness are mine and the real and obvious fears are his. Together we are optimistically realistic (or realistically optimistic?). We are one, whole.

I couldn't be more thankful to share this messy and terrifying and beautiful life with you, Garth. I am here, present, for you and because of you. To close this open love note to you, I will leave you with the passage we heard at our friends' wedding, the lucky couple Derek and Dana, about a year ago now. It is from Captain Corelli's Mandolin by Louis de Bernieres; it spoke so directly to our long-lasting love and so I will share it now:

Love is a temporary madness, it erupts like volcanoes and then subsides. And when it subsides you have to make a decision. You have to work out whether your roots have so entwined together that it is inconceivable that you should ever part. Because this is what love is.

Love is not breathlessness, it is not excitement, it is not the promulgation of promises of eternal passion. That is just being in love, which any fool can do. Love itself is what is left over when being in love has burned away, and this is both an art and a fortunate accident.

Those that truly love have roots that grow towards each other underground, and, when all the pretty blossoms have fallen from their branches, they find that they are one tree and not two.

Henry's New Obsession | Caroline Wright

Henry has been fixated on Phoenixes lately. (I am not sure where this comes from, like any fixations of any four-year-old—excuse me, Henry would insist I point out that he is 4 and three-quarters—kiddo I know. Alas.) On our walk home from school yesterday, this was our conversation:

Henry: So when do Phoenixes die?

Paul/Gampa: They get old and die, and then are reborn from their ashes and start over.

Henry: No, no, I mean when do they *die*? When do they stop that? Stop starting over?

Paul/Gampa: That's a good question, Henry. I don't know.

Caroline: It's cool, the idea of people starting over when they die, right? I like it. But sometimes our bodies do stop, that is true.

Henry: Phoenixes are so *cool*. *[I take his hand.]* I love you, Mama.

Caroline: I love you, too. So much.

I wanted to stop walking, hold him and tell him that he didn't have to worry about me dying. I so wish that he didn't have to and I am doing all I can to fight and be me, a mom who loves him so intensely, even knowing that I can't protect him from this. What I wanted to say without leading him into naming the underpinning of this conversation (my death) was that I will always be reborn with every memory, either the ones he would hopefully hold dear, like treasures inside his heart, or ones that I have documented for him in all of the things I have made for him and Theodore, like his baby books, my cookbooks, quilts, knitted sweaters, and this very writing. I will always be there for you, my boys. All you have to do is think of me and I will be born again, just for you.

Lucie, The Cousins and Me | Caroline Wright

My mom's cousin Lucie has always been an interesting character in my life and my brain tumor has made her even more so. I remember hearing about her vaguely as a child, as we had never met, because she died from a brain tumor. I remember not knowing too much about her other than that, but my sensitivity as a young child caused me to be fascinated and deeply saddened by her death. Over the past few weeks, I have spoken to her two brothers and learned much more about her life and circumstances. I can say for sure that we would have gotten along well and had a lot in common, even aside from the fact that we were both diagnosed with aggressive brain tumors in our thirties as mothers of young children.

She was a musician. She was restless, full of life and lovably stubborn according to one of her brothers. Her diagnosis at age 38 came as a total surprise after a raucous family wedding weekend, one of the first times away from her kids with her siblings who were also liberated from their parenting responsibilities. Both brothers recounted that weekend with joy and palpable fondness for their sister. Especially in light of their beautiful weekend together, both brothers were shocked to learn that Lucie suffered a grand mal seizure the next day. The discovery of her tumor was shortly after, followed immediately by her emergency surgery. Hearing this part of her story made my heart break for her, knowing the panic I felt with my very little warning of my surgery and the pace of the discoveries during my diagnosis, surgery and prognosis. Imagining myself in her shoes, facing an immediate fight for life without any time to see it coming, feels scary to me by comparison. It's not like she had a choice, which is a feeling I am also familiar with.

She was diagnosed with a stage 3 astrocytoma, which is a different tumor to mine (both in terms of prognosis as well as just generally being different people, as I've written before). However, both are decidedly unfair. Both cruel.

Lucie apparently did as I did, immediately righting her life to a compass of accepting her tumor with a dedication to fight. I wish I could have asked her so many questions. She lived for 8 years after her first surgery—a fate and a fight I would be very thankful to share. (In eight years, the scientific world could be a different place. My world would be a different place: Theodore would be speaking and, of course, remember me by then; Henry and I would share many more conversations; my heart would be full of gratitude, the same as it is now in so many ways.)

Another important and unusual connection I share with Lucie is something that happened today. Both of Lucie's brothers told me that my aunts Elasah and Susie were so supportive of Lucie throughout her fight and especially later in her final weeks. Today my cousins—the daughters of Elasah and Susie—arrived at my house to take me to radiation and spend a weekend together that I have been so looking forward to. Tomorrow we are going to look at the tulips in the Skagit Valley. It is strange to me, this precedent of theirs to support me now, as if it was written in their DNA just as my tumor was written in mine.

I am thankful for them, their visits and their love. I am thankful to know Lucie a little bit through her memories and the lives she touched. That, all of this, is a beautiful thing from where I am now.

Radiation | Caroline Wright

Today started my final week of radiation. (My final three days, actually.) People keep congratulating me and, while it is surely an accomplishment to have fared so well health-wise (for which I am incredibly grateful), I am not excited to be done with it. I've been so grateful for it on a daily basis and enjoyed the company and care of my team. It is helping me fight my weed, as Henry still says.

I don't want to forget this experience so I am inspired to share it here as it is the only radiation of this kind I can have (the dose is the highest and strongest amount possible; any more causes necrosis of the tissues in the treated core area), and I want my boys to know what it was like. Here is a detailed account of a morning at my radiation appointment:

> My dad and I arrive at the radiation oncology floor, having been carried by the slowest elevator packed with people looking for the cafeteria. It's usually pretty easy to spot those going to the radiation oncology center, as they often appear very sick: in head wraps, on oxygen tanks, in wheelchairs. I don't, so sometimes get surprised looks from my fellow cancer patients.
>
> The glass doors of the lobby part to reveal two young receptionists with headsets on. Both look significantly

younger than I am, but I always appreciate their energy and smiles—they always talk about such normal things, like the weather or their weekends, as one of them hands me a buzzer (in the manner of a casual dining restaurant) and a ticket to validate our parking. My dad and I take empty seats, scanning the room for any of our friends we've made. (If it's a Monday like today, I use this waiting time to deliver boxes of my chocolate chip cookies to the receptionists, my radiology techs, my team of radiology doctors and nurses, and the receptionists—all pregnant— at the brain tumor center upstairs.) I wait for my buzzer to blink and beep and, as soon as it does, I march toward Room D and deposit my buzzer in a metal bin as I set off. The heels of my boots click as I walk purposefully and confidently down the hall on laminated wood flooring, following the salmon artwork as the nurse told me to do on my first day almost six weeks ago.

I arrive at my room, greeted by my radiation techs and my radiation mask resting on the table. The room is larger and colder than a typical exam room to accommodate the large machine that lives at the back wall. (I've since asked my techs what it's called; it's an Infinity radiation machine by Elekta, for those who might care or want to look it up.) It is a large suspended circle with metrics around its perimeter, almost like a lighted clock face. There is a table in the middle of the room; the sheet that is draped over the top accentuates how smooth, flat, and cold it is. The techs snap in a different head rest as I note that the one they are removing from the previous visitor is suited for a child. I slip my glasses off my face as I make a joke to my now friends; Ken usually tells me what he ate for dinner the night before.

I hoist myself onto the table, lifting my legs instinctually in the "tabletop" position I remember from Pilates class. Someone slips a molded pillow under my calves to hold them in place when they eventually adjust the angle of the table. Someone else from behind my head asks me my name and birthdate then snaps my mask into the table, largely immobilizing my face. I use my feet to scoot my body into a comfortable position for my face to rest in the mask. (I have learned the correct fit and can often predict my adjustments they suggest, a scoot upwards of a millimeter or so, so that my head sits comfortably in the well of the hard plastic head rest that now sticks to my bald head like thighs on car vinyl.)

I close my eyes, knowing we are about to start. The techs retreat to their viewing booth, their door clicks shut. An electronic arm revs and slowly passes by my head like the arm of a photocopier. I sit for a few seconds, presumably while the techs are figuring out how to adjust the table so that the scan they just received on their computer overlays onto to match the previous MRIs and radiation treatment map designed by my radiation oncologist and translated by the dosimetrist. The table keels like a boat to my left and stops, *click*. It adjust right in two short bursts, *click-click*. A few seconds pass.

The buzzing starts over my right ear. One long buzz that sounds exactly as if I was testing the sound of the game "Operation!" that I remember playing in the cafeteria during the after school program at my elementary school. *Buzzzzzz*, I breathe deeply and see white light—a reaction of the radiation on some ocular part of my brain, actually—filling my brain cavity, I exhale. Shallow breath before the next—*buzzzzz*, breathe in, out. Think of a mantra gifted to me through a letter I read the night before: *find love, find light*. Breathe out.

Table clicks again. The arm overhead—different to the scanner one, it looks more like the swinging light that the dentist shines in your face—moves to a new spot. I like to pretend it is controlled by a joystick that the techs handle but I never ask.

Two more sets of buzzing, one big sweeping pivot of the table (I think of it like a construction crane that Henry would point out if we had been driving downtown), another buzz; a pivot of the table, returning to center, a move of the arm underneath the table; table pivots back to its previous station. More buzzing; then after a few seconds' pause, footsteps. Voices chatting. "Now let's get you out of there," the more formal of the techs always says as he unclips my mask. He lifts the mask away from my face and I always rub it and shift my jaw as I resume talking and making jokes.

I hand back the foam ring I've been clutching and they remove this sort of bridge of sensors (that determine the angle of the table) that had been sitting as an arch over my waist. I sit up and slide down from the table. I replace my glasses on my now red and warm face. I thank my techs and beam, "See you tomorrow!," as I march back to my dad.

This whole process takes about twenty minutes. It is totally painless and not scary at all. It is routine now, and I find it almost charming that I was ever nervous about it. I love the excuse to wear Bapa's sweaters (I have two in rotation that I remove immediately upon returning home; I plan to take them to the cleaners on Wednesday) and spend time with my dad. Theodore is often with us, though not always if his social calendar is full; pushed-together chairs in the radiation lobby, however, have made a perfect impromptu daybed for our prince as he dozes.

As I have said before, I am deeply grateful for my radiation sessions and the experts (of all kinds) that meet me there. I find it to be a joyful experience, strange as it is to admit.

On Wednesday, I get to sound the gong that all those who finish their treatment have the privilege of doing. It will be bittersweet, but proud. And joyful. Very joyful.

Priorities and Reiki | Caroline Wright

A few days ago I was very fortunate to be at the center of a healing Reiki circle, suggested and organized by my friend, healer and restorative yoga teacher, Jodi. She emailed to say that she mentioned my story and our work together to two powerful Reiki masters she works with whenever possible and they offered to do a tandem session—Jodi and her colleague Heather led by their mentor, Michael—for me. I had very little idea of what Reiki is, but know that anything Jodi would suggest for me would be something my soul needs.

I may find the words to describe our session together, but I haven't since. Committing language to this energetic knowledge and transformation they handed to me that was so overwhelmingly powerful feels impossible. I am still in disbelief. And it is most certainly a healing tool I will continue to check in with as I move forward. As I always do in my sessions with Jodi, I wept with gratitude for the light of these healers. Light I hope to borrow and internalize and outshine my cancer. Light that reinforces the power of the unmedicated, clear mind that still very much lives inside me.

At the end of our session, during a moment in which each member of the trio spoke about what and how they experienced my being, Michael offered advice for how to clarify and prioritize one's lifestyle with the whole being and healing at the core. His points had to do with categorizing each task in one's life and analyzing each in order to weed out unproductive or toxic sources of energy. The categories were as follows: the things you *should and could* do, the things you *need* to do, the things you *don't want* to do, and the things you *want* to do.

He said the things that you *should and could* do are just your logical mind's way of convincing yourself to do something you don't actually want to do. That the *need* to do category is about basic human functions—things that are truly required to do in your life in order to stay alive. The *don't want* to-do's are obvious and should immediately fall away. That leaves you with the *want* to-do's, which are what feeds the soul. Focus on the needs and wants at the core of one's life and nothing else will matter.

I have been doing that a lot lately, looking critically at all of my life's choices and determining what needs to wash away. As usual, I have many ideas. They are rising up like beams of light in my soul. They aren't borrowed from anyone else, but rather belong to me. They point to the path of my healing and I am following with an open heart and mind. And so far, it's working.

The Garden | Caroline Wright

It is embarrassing that it has taken me so long to write about something so dear to me as how our garden came about, but it felt strange to announce my excitement for it without actually having demonstrated that yet. Today is the day.

When I was diagnosed, our front lawn was a byproduct (and reminder) of our year-long remodel to our old home. The remodel was particularly traumatic for me, with very deep emotional and physical demands that I eerily joked "broke my brain" in the months leading up to my diagnosis. I honestly thought that I was suffering from some form of PTSD from the year's work. It turned out that working alongside largely condescending contractors, while literally being the glue that kept the project together, was *not my thing* to say the very least. (Especially while raising my two beautiful boys full-time and writing the biggest cookbook of my career.) At the end of the work, we had a home we adore, but we also had insurmountable debt and the worry and heartache that came along with that (as well as dirt and rubbish piles in both our front and back yards as souvenirs). And then a month after being "finished," of course, I was diagnosed with my brain tumor and, well, you know the rest.

In the light of my diagnosis, which is a costly and permanent fixture of our new way of life, home improvement felt impossible. However, my vision for this beautiful place I've made has also felt more pressing to accomplish, too, because I had obviously hoped to enjoy the manifestation of my "next step" ideas before leaving it. And so we move forward.

My dad is truly an amazing gardener and we have both long held the fantasy of being able to garden together someday. My dad decided that the garden was going to be our first undertaking on the "next step" list because of how healing and active it is and how, too, it fulfills our "someday" dream. I mentioned it to a few neighbors, mostly in an attempt to hint that the eyesore of the lingering evidence of our remodel was going to finally go away.

Now, let me just mention that we don't have ordinary neighbors. We live on a storybook, child-filled street where our neighborhood kids trick-or-treat en masse (and offer the insider tips if you need to peel off and hit only one more house before bed), we are gifted bikes that someone grows out of, are brought cupcakes left over from a big sister's birthday sleepover. And all of those instances I just mentioned were from well before my diagnosis, so you can imagine the kind of support they all have shown since: last-minute babysitting drop- offs; cookies with kid-drawn notes (the best kind); stealthy surprise lawn mowing and kitchen cleaning. As a former New Yorker, I honestly never thought that neighbors like this could exist, at least in my story. I feel so incredibly lucky to live around such kind and generous people. Among the wonderful things our neighbors have done for us—most definitely the most touching of all—is orchestrate and complete the setup for our garden in our front yard.

See, one of these particularly generous neighbors happens to be a landscape architect. She and my dad shared ideas. Her wonderful husband stepped in to offer to be the organizer and muscle behind the project, and my parents its generous backers. And so, without my participation whatsoever (a rare relief for me, especially to do with improving our home), flowerbeds were built and plans were drafted.

A Saturday arrived almost a month ago now when this landscape power couple marched into our yard and began commanding the attention (and brawn) of all the neighbors on our street. They had the dirt pile loaded onto the back of the truck within what felt like minutes. Theodore and I watched in awe. All I did was deliver a plate of warm cookies and hang out with Leah in our living room as we watched the action from behind our bay windows. It felt amazing to relax and watch a plan come together miraculously as if sprung from my head but never communicated. I was humbled to witness a space come together in which such care was taken to imagine me (and my health) and my kids spending a lot of time together there. There is a bench nailed to the side of the largest flower box in case my medication made me tired. The boxes are especially high to save my bending over. There is space for the boys and their trucks when they inevitably grow tired of weeding and planting.

What I love most about this space is that it not only arose from a painful memory, an ugly place from the open sore of our remodel, but it is a place that was made out of love and community. It is in our front yard where I can garden and watch people I've grown to love pass by with their dogs of as they pick their kids up from school. It is a place I plan to spend many hours nurturing as well as allow it to nurture me, and one in which I learn alongside my boys as my dad teaches us how to make things grow. A place to share our shared dream with so many people.

It is moments like these that I can't believe I've built this life. I am overwhelmed with gratitude.

My dad and I picked out flowers this week—a few fragrant shrub roses and a mixture of annuals and perennials in warm, cheery colors. My best friend Sarah sent me a few of her strawberry plants from Nashville, the most perfect place for them to be. My dad and I will plant them later today after I return from the hospital.

I have decided that establishing and tending to our garden is going to be one of the replacement healing rituals for my radiation. I want to spend time in the garden every day and watch beauty grow there. Please feel free to come by—bring a cutting from your garden to add to ours, maybe, or share your gardening knowledge, or just say hi. It all adds to the beauty and, I think, my healing. I'll be there with my bald head tucked under my wide sunhat, smiling with my hands in the dirt or cutting flowers for my table.

Thank you to the generous and beautiful neighbors for creating such a healing space for me. And to my parents for giving me this space where family memories will grow. It is the first place I plan to go after I come home from radiation today on my last day. I hope the beauty of our garden offers some small bit of joy to our community as a reflection of the love and joy the community has brought to us.

6 _____ FOLLOWING

MY

INSTINCTS

Your soul knows the geography of your destiny.
Your soul alone has the map of your future, therefore you
can trust this indirect, oblique side of yourself. If you do,
it will take you where you need to go, but more important it
will teach you a kindness of rhythm in your journey.

—John O'Donohue

MAY 14, 2017

From Your Mom On Mother's Day | Glad Markunas

Sometimes being a pack rat has its benefits. Like when you rediscover real treasures that have continued to increase in value over time. Two wonderful and very recent rediscoveries are the attached Mother's Day cards that Caroline made which will always be priceless to me! They clearly show her creativity, writing talents and love of baking. And for Caroline, celebrations are always reasons to bake...even back then.

Who knew then that this would lead to her developing *Cake Magic*, a cookbook devoted to baking and a busy summer last year promoting her book, including being on QVC with host David Venable who if he wasn't a foodie could be a stand-up comic! As Caroline says in the book's introduction, "there is magic in baking someone a perfect cake...and that cake, even the promise of it brings people together."

As Caroline's mom, I have come to see her in recent years as one of the most caring, loving and positive people I have ever met. She continues to amaze and inspire me each and every day as she faces her new challenges with love, patience, warmth, dignity and always with a positive outlook. And she is an unbelievable Mom to our two beloved grand boys, of that there is no doubt.

From one mom to another, Caroline, I love you with my heart and soul, not just on Mother's Day, but on every day. You have helped me to become a better mom and a better person. Your life is an example to all of us moms out there, now more than ever. Thank you from the bottom of my heart.

Hope you and every mom who reads this has a special Mother's Day today and perhaps even enjoys a piece of homemade cake!

MAY 16, 2017

Prayer Warriors | Paul Markunas

I got up at 4 am today so I could fly to Phoenix to move into, stage, and then put our new home on the market there. It was to be our retirement home. We now will call our 600 square foot condo home in Seattle.

I got an Uber from the airport, a female driver from the Dominican Republic in a black Mercedes who had lived in Phoenix for 30 years. She went to the wrong terminal and was frustrated with me because she said she was on the west side of the terminal and where was I? I said there was no west side on my terminal. (Turns out she went to Terminal 4; I was outside Terminal 3.)

She told me she thought about canceling my ride because she sensed my frustration with the directions...

But she said the minute I got in her car she knew it would be ok.

We talked about things and ultimately she wondered if I lived in Phoenix or was visiting and why was I there.

I explained that we had purchased what was to be our retirement home with visits to our family in Seattle, including our special times with two busy grandboys.

Then I explained about Caroline's diagnosis and how it had changed our lives and how we couldn't do anything else.

She was so amazingly understanding and open and warm.

She told me her mother was in a group of "prayer warriors" in NYC and with others in Massachusetts, NJ, and Florida and that Caroline would be their focus while she waits for her first follow-up to her chemo and radiation. She was going to call her mother as soon as I left her car. I believed her.

She told me that she knew that Caroline would be OK. That I was not to overly worry. That it was going to be ok.

I told her I know how fierce island women can be and I accepted her words of encouragement and was grateful for the band of warriors being on our side. And I somehow knew they would be. And I loved that they called themselves "prayer warriors." That makes sense to me.

So that got me thinking a bit. Maybe that is what God is—the connection we feel and find and act upon between seemingly unrelated humans. Maybe when we feel a connection with another and hear that connection in their words and see it in their eyes and feel it in their souls, maybe that IS the divine that we can access while bound to this existence.

While I am not looking for it actively in my everyday life, I welcome it when I feel it, like I did today.

If that is what it means to believe in god, I believe. Thank you Prayer Warriors. Thank you.

Access to Love | Caroline Wright

Another topic Jeff and I discussed at length one evening awash in Campari was one he brought home from his training as a social worker. We discussed the concept that one's level of adjustment in their world was directly related to their "access to love." The adjustment—I don't even know if that's the word we used, but it was the essence of that, if not—encompasses a lot of aspects, like self-worth, confidence, one's own capacity to love, and a wide array of versions of "success" in life. The topic was more spoken of in terms of a commentary of socio-economic privilege, if I remember correctly, but I have been thinking a lot about it in my own life recently. It has been a source of great comfort.

If I am not around to raise my boys as I hope and am working to be, I know I will have left them with a rich legacy of love. I have been thinking about it a lot, especially as the parade of visitors of Henry and Theodore's chosen aunts and uncles are only just now dwindling since it began in mid-March. I like to imagine that I've stored my hugs and love in each of them, maybe bits of my voice and soul, too; over the years that come my boys will know the bespoke love of their mother as if transcending time and mortality through the arms of my friends and family when they need them most.

I know, deep in my heart, my two beautiful boys will grow into two beautiful, well-adjusted men. They are too good—just built that way, it is so clear—and they have profound access to love. It spans countries and time zones. It is in their front yard and in their school. It is at home with Gampa and Gaba and, of course, Daddy.

I am hopeful that I will be in their lives for a while to help shape and love them, I do. But if that chance is stolen away, I know that there is a lot of love out there buried in the souls of those I love, my particular brand of soul-bearing raw love that is funneled into their bodies and hearts every day since they were born. I hope they will feel me forever and pass my love onto their children who I may not be lucky enough to meet.

Their access to love, my love, is my comfort today. May it last forever in them.

After the Hellegers Family Visit
Posted by Paul Markunas

From the Hellegers:

It's no surprise that as soon as we entered the Wright home last week, we too (my husband Neil and four-year- old son Edgar) felt like we were at home. After cohabitating on Berkeley Place in Park Slope in our lovely but spatially-challenged brownstone apartments for five years, we consider them family. Back then that came with the benefits of fresh baked cakes and pizzas left over from cooking classes and recipe testings. While learning how to actually use a knife and make a proper risotto might have drawn us one flight downstairs, more often it was the long-standing hallway conversations that lead to bottles of wine and talks through the night, that rooted them to our lives. And when their friends adopted us for their Sunday nights bad movie nights, I'd say we were living our best childless years together.

So what strikes me as special now is to see our young boys together, or those humans we somehow made, as I often think of them. Edgar and Henry are a few months apart, and their magnetism was a wonderful surprise. Holding hands at the zoo and building forts they'd disappear in for hours couldn't have been sweeter. Of course, we could have done without their potty mouths or their makeshift slip-n-slide in the bathroom one afternoon, with those matching devilish grins. My mind automatically flashed to those two boys in college doing keg stands or whatever equivalent college stunt—egging each other on. Although because we raise our boys quite similarly with music, books, and theater prevailing over sports and pseudo-masculinity, that would probably equate to the two of them starting an Emo revival grunge band or taking an all night train to Monaco to gamble while studying abroad in Paris together. Oh, a mom can dream!

Our children's ages become like markers in our lives, and I will remember this time with Henry and Edgar being 4, Theodore nearly 2, as particularly special. Being around Caroline, Garth, Henry, Theodore, Paul, Glad, and four black and white loveable dogs, it was all about the small things. Watching Caroline quilt and our talks—truly being ourselves and catching up, no bullshit. Meeting the supportive ladies of her gentle yoga class. The hugs Garth gives her after work and watching the strength and resolve he has as a father. Paul's measuring out of her meds and pushing me to break a sweat while we walk. Having a heart-to-heart with Glad in the kitchen while she loads the dishwasher—the mundane things like cleaning being such a gift. Seeing how their lives have been turned inside out, just as Caroline's body has been turned inside out, all to be together for as long as possible. Theodore's expressive eyes, his big heart; he is her heart, which Caroline told me, and I can see that so clearly now.

The question of time and that screaming anger of WHEN WHEN WHAT HOW THE HOLY FUCK IS THIS HAPPENING? *is on everyone's minds, but it's not at all present in her home or in the way Caroline lives her life. Right now it's love and friends and food and laughter and tears. So much vulnerability but so much strength. I don't think many people would live their lives with the same courage, positivity and yearning for the present—while letting all of the other shit fall away.*

It's been a hard time for my family for different reasons and yet taking this time to catch up with friends and enjoy walks and time together has been so grounding for me, for all of us really. But what I learned most is that as grateful as I am to have Caroline as a friend and teaching me these life lessons, I just wish it wasn't her who was teaching them to me. I just wish for her to be here and to be healthy for a long time, beating those inane statistics. Because I believe that she can continue to teach us more about the world by staying firmly in it.

In Caroline's gentle yoga class, her teacher Sally had us all put our palms together and do tree pose in a circle. We are all connected in this life, we are all growing with our own roots and unique circumstances. But we are also all one.

The Threshold | Caroline Wright

As anyone who has ever spent time with me can attest, I am a "just one more" kind of gal. I so often lose myself in the joy of what I am doing or who I am spending time with or the conversation we are having that I completely disregard any other pressing factors of my reality. The cost of this quality in the past has made for things like hangovers, tardiness to a wide variety of things, missed movie times. (And frustration for Garth!)

When my best friend from Paris, Amy, came to town (she knows this quality best of all in me because she inspires it more than most people I know), I learned that this part of me no longer functions in the new world I've created. "Just one more" now serves a very different tame version of recklessness—one glass of red wine, staying up an hour later than usual like 10 pm—but it is a boundary that holds higher stakes.

This may seem obvious to state because, you know, it is obvious in the world of someone who is sick. I truly don't feel sick, so this is both a reminder as well as a surprise every time.

I'm figuring out that I have to put my body before my heart now. And that the former version of myself consistently would sacrifice physical well-being for a worthy source of true joy. My circumstances now have shown me that there literally is no reason worthy of pushing my body too far because of how carefully balanced my health is these days.

It isn't a change in the shape of my love for the people in my life, rather just including myself among that precious kin who need to be cared for carefully.

A side note, I am really proud of myself...Last night Garth and I had a date and went to the opera, which was beautiful and fun. I was carried away, as I tend to be in those rare displays of art and talent. But the rational part of me knew it was getting late and staying for the second half would let us out around 10:30 and I knew that would be much too late for me. So, despite my sincere desire to stay, we left in favor of getting to bed at my normal time. Turns out people can change!

MAY 19, 2017

In Between | Caroline Wright

Another strange thing about where I am now is negotiating the intentions of those who interact with me. I have to hold them and translate them. I keep the meaningful stuff and let the rest fall away with gratitude. I guess that's what I did before with things like parenting advice, but now it is much stranger and far more personal. You'd probably be surprised by some of the things people say, though now I am not.

I've been thinking about the difference between pity and support. They are very similar and often confused for one another in my interactions, but they are so very different to me. The space between them is judgment, whether intended or not. The space between them is the assumption that I am dying, which I very much am not right now. (*I'm not pretending I couldn't in the future, but isn't that true of literally everyone I meet?*) I am strong and healthy. I am living a life of my choosing and so full of love. I am present and capable. I am very much alive.

Pity has no place in my life.

Those who pity me don't know me well, which makes it okay somehow. To them I am a symbol of tragedy, only my brain tumor, only one tagline of an incredibly long, incredibly powerful story.

Support, on the other hand, stems from an active place, holding parts of my *life*. It has shown me that I am surrounded by some very brave and beautiful people. It is what you give me here through reading this writing. Thank you.

Wishes with Henry | Caroline Wright

The arrival of spring weather here in Seattle brought more of Henry and my walks together to and from his school. We spent the time talking and recounting his day, holding hands and pointing out our favorite flowers. This exchange happened recently, after talking about my radiation being over.

> **Henry:** You're getting better, though, right? *[He smiles and his eyes flash like on Christmas morning.]*

> **Caroline:** I'm feeling a lot better. I have a lot of energy to play with you now, just like I used to. But as far as the weed goes, we don't quite know yet. They will do more tests soon to tell its shape and size. I'm still fighting as hard as I can and doing everything the doctors say. We have to wait and see.

We hold hands. He plucks a particularly fluffy dandelion and blows it apart. The seeds flutter away and he promises to hold the wish in his heart as we walk home.

After Dan Plansky's Visit | Posted by Paul Markunas

From Dan:

When I visited Seattle, I never really thought that I was visiting a patient—someone diagnosed with a terminal cancer. I was visiting Caroline. In her core, Caroline's a powerful, stubborn fighter. Her determination to remain herself—whether that be as a wife, mother, friend, daughter, or member of the community—had been made clear to me through her writing. But seeing her in action was truly incredible.

Caroline is a connector—I've always known that. And her reputation in Fremont didn't disappoint. From the constant flow of homemade soups to the groundswell of positive energy of neighbors, I could see her metaphorical web at its strongest. I'm dumbfounded by her ability to make people feel more themselves and so special. I mean, she was in the habit of bringing fresh-baked cookies to her entire treatment team every Monday—WHO DOES THAT? It's inspiring to be friends with someone who looks beyond her own immediate situation to make others feel so welcome and good.

What I loved most about Seattle (aside from the coffee) was how natural Caroline and Garth are there. Visiting their charming home felt so familiar: it's as if their 40 Berkeley apartment had been carefully removed from its frame and dropped onto the streets of

Fremont. A home I already knew, just with more breathing room. And children. Another highlight was spending time with the boys. I loved getting to know their enormous personalities crammed into their tiny bodies and matching their quirks and features to either Caroline or Garth (or Paul—I'm convinced Theodore is a miniature version of him).

It's such a beautiful life they've built. And, despite the cancer, their days are filled with exactly what I'd imagined. The breakfast of ableskiver and bacon, the weekend trip to the farmer's market, and the outdoor classrooms of Henry's nursery school. I was so happy to be able to experience just a sliver of it with them and I'll cherish those moments of Caroline holding Henry and Theodore tight, reading them books, radiating love. Of Garth reassuringly touching on the small of Caroline's back.

My visit concluded with wig shopping, joined by Caroline's fabulous friend Adair. After scouring the outer neighborhoods of Seattle for nearly an hour, we finally found an adequate purveyor of synthetic delights. After sampling a few bobs and afros, I watched as Caroline donned the "winning" wig (a tri-colored Bieber-esque number). It was the ultimate declaration: I'm not hiding quietly with cancer, I'm living loudly. It's that exact attitude that will fuel this fight. A brain capable of such creativity, understanding, such logic, and love is deserving of a bold accessory to match.

Love To My Tumor | Caroline Wright

I know how crazy it sounds, I do. That I could love my tumor. In fact, these healers who have focused their energies my way have said that to me and, each time I heard it, I couldn't help to feel that the sentiment was a little glib, empty, New Age-y, and certainly impossible. But, now facing my life with cancer ahead, I totally get it.

We are in this together, my tumor and I. It has taught me a lot about the world, about people, about my body, about the shape of my love and my capacity to grow. It has brought truly incredible healing to my family. I have a healthy respect for what it needs (recalling a bit of how Bapa used to describe the respect for the water as a sailor to me, a kid clutching to a life vest) and have changed my life to find the balance it asks for. I am a better person because of it.

So many of my friends express the inverse. In their words, they hate my tumor for how nasty it is. They fear it because it will likely shorten my life expectancy, and are shocked when I say I don't. Anyway, in my life experience in the area—of choosing love versus hate—love is the only choice that brings beauty and opens up the world for change; hate, and its nourishment of fear, only blocks and stops healing. It halts progress entirely and locks everything in a negative, permanent energetic space that is impossible to alter. I have a lot of experience in this area, suffice it to say. I have always chosen love and continue to do so now.

I know it is unlikely that anyone else in my life could understand this idea because my tumor has changed so many people around me so suddenly and inconveniently. For me, being alone in this thought is okay, though—it's one of many surreal feelings in my life now that are truly personal and internal, almost incommunicable.

But, here, I will say it again anyway. I love my tumor.

A Symptom | Caroline Wright

Today I went to the hospital because of a new symptom: vertigo. Yesterday afternoon, while working on a project with Adair, I was flooded by a sense of spinning—I was sitting down, even, and the room twirled around me. I told myself it was a hunger response (that, strangely, since my diet about-face is no longer recognizable to me), or dehydration or tiredness. I went home, ate and drank well and went to bed at 7:30 pm, just after tucking the kids into their beds. I told myself I would call my doctor in the morning if my symptom persisted. It did and I did. My team told me that they couldn't order an MRI any earlier than Wednesday, which is my scheduled follow-up to my radiation treatment, but that I should go to the ER if I was worried because they would be able to make that call.

My sweet friend Katie arrived moments later as if descended from the heavens to take Henry to school and Theodore to her house for the day. Garth and I headed right to UW, just as if it was my follow-up, he continued to tell me.

I was quickly seen by doctors who performed all the same tests and asked the same questions and I continued to offer that I knew something was wrong, that my fear and nervousness were a symptom because of how rarely it finds me. A CAT scan, a bag of fluids, tests to my blood and urine and eventually an MRI later, I was assured that the vertigo I felt was a continued symptom of my radiation. (A little like the shedding of my right eyebrow, which only began about a week ago.)

The results from the MRI were very encouraging, suggesting that the radiation had done its job on my encroaching cancer cells. I am looking forward to hearing from my oncology care team next week during our scheduled follow-up appointments (and Garth or my dad's post at that point detailing our up-to-date knowledge), but I left feeling positive and renewed. I trust my body again—that apparently may suffer from vertigo on occasion due to lasting affects of the radiation—as a huge sigh of relief.

What started as panic and fear melted into calm and thankfulness. Thankfulness to my body for its diligence, to Garth for his unshakable calm and clarity and deep love in a scary place, and to my treatment that is still doing its job.

What a day.

Being A Parent From Here | Caroline Wright

Parenting, even under the best of circumstances, is hard. It shines a light onto your flaws, your fears, your insecurities.

My parents, I know, felt this space deeply in their own ways when I was young. I remember the shape of it well as their child. My brother probably does, too.

It caused me to read books on parenting, to feel indignant and protective when Henry was born. Rules and ideas change.

All I knew then and know now is that I would turn myself inside out for my boys. I've said it many times to illustrate my eternal devotion to them and their hearts, only now it has taken on a different meaning. I am asked to prove it daily. I fight every day for every minute I can spend with them, giving them my love in a way that is so deeply ingrained in my soul that the privilege of doing so is what makes me recognize myself.

And then I slip away with Garth for an overnight away, just like all the other exhausted parents of two young kids long to do. For an uninterrupted night's sleep, a wakeup *after* the sun has already risen.

Then we, The Parents, return to relieve the grand-parents. We come home to find it transformed, evidence

of my dad spending his weekend with grandkids not
just holding it together, but pulling together and healing
neglected parts of our home: a rearranged mudroom and
living room; my recent collection of hats (that would cause an
avalanche every morning) having been artfully arranged and
hung on hat hooks around the perimeter of the mudroom.
Vases of flowers, chosen because they reminded my dad of
a vacation we took somewhere or the bouquet I held at my
wedding, sat on every table. All of this magic was performed
in great part by my dad, then suffering from walking
pneumonia and severe bronchitis. This sort of generosity,
vision and drive is not unusual for my dad—it is his true spirit
and he spills it into everything he loves. (My mom beams
with pride and supports his creativity/loving madness, but it
is literally impossible to keep up with him.)

These singular, incredible parents of mine, those who
artfully rearranged and cleaned my house without my
asking while caring for my precious-but-tiring little boys so
Garth and I could rest, are standing in my house because
they sold theirs. They reluctantly left my side for only a
handful of days since my diagnosis (to accomplish matters
of deconstructing their well-rooted lives and plans for their
hard-earned retirement).

They've rearranged flights for me. They buy pants for the
boys when they see them on sale somewhere I would be too
cheap to shop in. They both fight tears when they look at my

pills on occasion or think of my surgery or my fight ahead. They have sold or given away almost every possession they carefully collected over their lifetimes, some from stories that started well before I was born. They gave away all but two of their precious dogs. They moved around the corner as soon as they possibly could so my dad can walk into my house every morning at 7 am to make me a giant healthy breakfast.

I get it now because I would do the same thing if either of my boys were sick. I would do everything in my power to *be there*. Sacrifice my heart, exposing my fears and insecurities, if it could lend them help or comfort for as long as I had breath in my lungs. It turns out that we are not different at all. I am proud—and very lucky—to be the same. A parent. With a smile on their face, love in their heart and tears in their eyes. I get it now, I do.

Parenting is hard, indeed, especially from here. But it moves mountains, too, and makes miracles happen. I believe that. Today and always.

MRI Results and Going Forward | Garth Wright

We spent all day at the hospital talking to Caroline's doctors and going through the MRI results (gathered a few days early due to a Friday spent in the ER).

First, and foremost, we were told the MRI was as clean as possible at this stage. The most that is usually hoped is that radiation and chemotherapy will arrest any tumor progress; this scan appeared to show the tumor slightly shrinking. Caroline's neuro-oncologist stated this good result was statistically only about 5% likely.

Next, we discussed the next wave of Caroline's chemotherapy. She will double her previous dose and take it 5 days out of every 28 (5 days of pills, 23 days off). This cycle will last 6 months. Caroline will start this next round of chemotherapy on June 14.

Finally, we were given a better idea of what the near future holds. There will be a doctor follow-up 1 month after the beginning of chemotherapy, a MRI in 3 months, and an appointment and MRI at the end of the total 6 month cycle. How Caroline's scan looks at that point will determine her next steps.

Keepsakes | Caroline Wright

I've surrounded myself with some pretty beautiful people lately. I honestly believe I always have, but my circumstances bring people to a place of deeper kindness much faster than ever before. People don't really shoot the shit with a bald lady with a scar, I've discovered. I find myself almost exclusively in profound conversation or discovering the edges of my deeper understanding at least once a day, which certainly is more often than before my diagnosis.

These exchanges—these transfers of humanity that fill me up and give me tools for finding hope every day—I carry with me. I save them like treasures, as they are incredibly precious and valuable indeed.

After a restorative yoga session the other day, my teacher Jodi sat across from me telling me of her work as a doula. We were discussing my powerful experience—opportunity, really—of giving birth to both of my boys. (Unmedicated, in a hospital in Dallas. Hard to believe now!) They were two of the greatest days of my life, without a doubt. Not only because they gave me my two beautiful, wonderful sons, but because I was given the gift of learning how strong and intuitive my body is. She lent me a quote she came across during her doula training, and now I've only held onto the gist of it. It was that "the secret of childbirth is not that childbirth is painful, but that women's bodies are powerful." I remember being shocked that my body—not my cerebral instincts— knew what to do to not only grow, but birth, my children. Jodi kept mentioning the "innate intelligence" of our bodies in her hushed voice that always holds the tone of discovery, gratitude or joy, and I couldn't agree more. That my body is so powerful is something I am overwhelmingly grateful for now, as is that I can hug my two boys each day as an ever-replenishing source of love and beauty born from my body, like how a waterfall feeds a flowing river. One that moves nimbly over rocks in its path, the way I can in their love.

The other keepsake I've collected lately also came out of a yoga class, one I go to at least once every week that focuses on the relationship between mind and body with a very thoughtful approach to listening to the shifting needs of one's inner voice. Our teacher—a very powerful and beautiful person I am so thankful to have brought into my life just by stumbling into a studio, which seems so wild and unlikely to me now—often begins our class with a gentle meditation. During these moments, a spiritual "settling in" of sorts, she tells us helpful things to set the tone for a mindful practice. A mantra she shared the other day really took hold, such a simple phrase but so useful to carry with me. It is intended for times of desperation, I think, but I've turned to it a few times since when the love and gratitude I am so conscious of holding in my heart every moment stumbles. Simply, it is: "I can see peace instead of this." It works when a change in perspective is needed, big or small.

These keepsakes are truly endless sources of comfort and encouragement, rooting ideas that align my focus on the beauty that lives so strongly and healthily at the core of my being. I really believe it's at the core of everyone if you know where (and, I'm learning, how) to look. It isn't always easy, no. I find, lose and re-find my kindness to myself and my circumstances every day. Some days are harder than others. But this is what the fight looks like for me on most days, and these are the resources (and loved ones) that make me stronger.

On Being A Survivor | Caroline Wright

I have been thinking about the term "cancer survivor" a lot lately. It's one that, no matter my timeline ahead, will never apply to me as glioblastomas are neither curative nor find the term of remission.

That's okay with me, honestly. The idea of owning being a "survivor" feels like an arrival to a resting spot, feeling comfortable with my cancer in a way that ignores it. (My cancer, like me, is stubborn and loud. The minute I would turn my attention away from her needs would be the moment she would demand my attention again, no doubt.) I strongly feel that I never get to be complacent about my health again. Not even for a meal.

My life now means that I pay careful attention to the way I eat, sleep, drink and breathe. I walk three to four miles every day and practice yoga two to three times a week to reinforce the connection between my body and mind. I take handfuls of supplements after each meal. I listen when people tell me to save my hugs when they are sick. My health requires a daily—down to the minute—calibration of my world and how it interacts with my being. My fight each minute negotiates my surroundings into feeding and supporting my body, rather than experiencing my world passively. It makes me present. It makes me thankful. It makes me more than a survivor: I am a cancer *warrior*.

I am hopeful that I will be around for a long time, but I know it will take staying strong in this fight.

Right now, for example, I am on vacation with my whole family in Colorado. It is restful and a change of pace, but I don't get a vacation from my routine. I still take my handfuls of pills after each meal, I still test the pH of my urine a few times a day to make sure I am eating and drinking what I need to in order to stay balanced. I still sleep sitting up, propped up by an awkward mass of hotel pillows.

My fight, even here on vacation, is in every moment and always shifting. It is in small places, like paying attention to the awareness in my fingers and toes, whether anything is going numb. Like wondering if the tiredness I feel is hunger or a call for a nap. It is remembering how much water I've had and keeping track of whether or not I've taken my seizure meds or my vials of electrolytes or the most recent round of my 5 or 6 immune system herbal support pills and tinctures. It's asking myself how many dark greens I've eaten that day and washing and sautéing up more if the answer isn't enough. This is all on top of the emotional component—to ignore strangers who my parents spot gawking at my head or engage them in conversation when I go to the bathroom at a restaurant to blindside us all with pity and a story of our waitress whose mother died of a brain tumor. I fend off doubt and fear in my own heart on a regular basis through breathing well, meditation, yoga, walking outside, and hugging and playing with my boys as much as they will allow me—but I also have to shield myself from it when it attacks unexpectedly.

On top of all this, I do genuinely find the "me" in my body—not just the patient—and actually manage to forget about being terminally ill for most of my day. I find myself genuinely happy, even overjoyed, with my life. This is what my being a warrior looks like. It means I'll never rest or settle, but that is true of my joy and love, too. I find it again every day and it, and I, am new again.

Hiking | Caroline Wright

I loathe sports. Most physical activity, actually. It's been a lifelong affliction. I have gone to great lengths to do next-to-nothing for a long time. For example, out of the combined interests of religious compassion and skipping P.E., I fasted with a friend for the month of Ramadan so I could claim to be too weak to play soccer. I was always picked last anyway, which I get because I was uncoordinated and I never cared one bit about running around to chase a *ball*. Or to win. It all felt very futile and silly, since one team wins and the other loses. Every. Single. Time. And besides, the people who played sports were generally insular, mean, condescending and a little too into their looks for me to think they were worth my friendship. (There have been outliers to this statement, including my jock husband, but you can imagine the turmoil of my youth raised in upper middle class conservative places where sports are treated like a kind of social currency.)

I have grown up to generally feel that sports on television glorify male aggression, violence and a shocking representation of corporate wealth. One loophole has been to host Superbowl parties, which gave me the excuse to invite my friends, other fellow misfits, over to eat dip and watch funny commercials whose humor is often most effectively conveyed through talking animals.

This is the level of sports hatred we are dealing with here. Garth doesn't get it. Luckily for him, our Theodore takes after him in the gross-motor-skill coordination department. (Also in the handsome department, which, by my life's calculation, seems to increase one's likelihood of fitting in; the track I know for sure decreases one's likelihood is to both wear one's headgear during the day and sport an unkempt perm. Purely conjecture, of course.) Henry, so far, appears to take after me, however. Thank goodness—I'll need someone to keep me company in the bleachers and help me find the concession stand at Theodore's games.

I could go on and on about my distain for sports and even expound upon the ways it's defined my life—my hobbies, my career—but I think it's sufficiently clear.

Knowing all of this, you can appreciate how unexpected it is to say that I've found a way of moving my body that I don't abhor: hiking. In fact, it's even more unexpected than that—I love it. I crave it. I love everything about it. In Seattle, I walk Henry to and from school daily over a long and hilly enough terrain to be considered an urban hike, which I need and love in my life for many reasons. But the kind that are the absolute best are out in the middle of nowhere, paths carved in the thick of trees or alongside a brook. Ten-year-old me would hardly believe this sentiment would spill from my mouth. (Nor would she have guessed current me would have undergone brain surgery and been diagnosed with brain cancer, either, so at least I've kept her on her toes.)

I love being in nature, feeling silent and like the caravan of people I'm a part of are the only people in the woods. Conversations in the woods, I've noticed, are always random. During a particularly beautiful recent hike on Bainbridge, Garth and I talked about everything from nineties music to our memories of prom. During hikes, we always plan our next adventures, too, which adds to the poetry of the nature and solitude and deep drinking-in of the mountain air.

Yesterday, my whole family and I went for a particularly beautiful hike here about fifteen minutes from our hotel. We hiked past a breathtaking waterfall, beyond the rushing water along a path less taken. It was well-trodden still, but many were discouraged by the near vertical rocky ascent. Luckily, none of us were discouraged—all but Theodore, then doubled over, asleep in the confines of the backpack that was carried by his sporty and willing dad—and marched along happily. My very favorite part was watching my sweet (slightly clumsy) Henry bound ahead over boulders and streams, pretending to be a jet yet stopping to pick up a favorite rock. He never complained and outlasted all of us with his dedication to the trail.

It was beautiful to see. The adventures Garth and I had planned felt fuller, more exciting to share with our whole family. Hiking blends the differences in athletic aptitude of our family members, while giving me the exercise and connection to the present that I need. The surrounding beauty of both the mountains and my adventurous boys is really the ultimate reward. Hiking, it turns out, makes me deeply happy.

Does that mean we are Pacific Northwesterners now?

Strangers | Caroline Wright

I have mixed feelings about interacting with strangers. On one hand, I have made beautiful meaningful friendships of strangers lately out of living in the open with my cancer. On the other hand, like today, I get smacked in the gut and have to go on with my day, finding my strength again.

I was at the farmer's market in the small town where we are on vacation. I was at a stall boasting collapsible, packable handmade cowboy hats and I was trying a few on while still wearing the headscarf I wear under my floppy sun hat. A woman walks up to me and the following exchange happened:

Woman: *[Hopeful, grinning.]* Are you going through chemotherapy?

Me: Yes.

Woman: I did too. You know, I saw your head scarf and I thought you might be. I just wanted to share with you that you can do it. I know you can. I did. Six years ago.

Me: Oh, good for you. What kind of cancer was it?

Woman: Breast cancer. You too?

Me: Actually, I have terminal brain cancer. *[Hopeful, smiling.]* So...you know. Living my life.

I know she meant well, that was clear. But I don't need her offer to pray for me or her tearful hug, especially on my Saturday morning at a Farmer's Market on my vacation. Maybe I should start lying.

And now back to regularly scheduled programming. With a punch in my gut. Off for a hike to find my breath and joy and clear mountain air, hopefully with a bounding Henry nearby.

Henry's Bomb | Caroline Wright

Today while my mom and I were hiking up the mountain nearby (that Henry politely declined in favor of playing in a creek and the promise of lemonade), Garth took Henry out of the hotel room. When he finds himself alone with Henry, he always asks him if he wants to talk about anything. (Reason 1 million why I love this man, obviously.)

Henry was walking around picking flowers for me, which is what he's been doing every day on our trip. (It has also caused me to think about how much I love this moment he's in—his sweet age combined with a level of expressiveness that shows his almost 5 year-old wisdom—and how lucky that sweet Theodore will have such a wonderful role model as he grows into a similar sweetness, no doubt.) As they were walking around the creek, he was talking about dreams he had been having recently. Garth just now relayed the sweet conversation that he and Henry shared while exploring:

> **Henry:** I had a dream where I grew up and made a bomb. The bomb made everyone nicer and better and also could bring nice people back from being dead.

> **Garth:** That's really nice, buddy. That is a sweet thought. Wouldn't that be nice for real life?

Henry knows where I am right now in my treatment, that I had an encouraging scan and that we're all thrilled but that the fight isn't over. He hugs my neck hard every day and talks about the foods I'm now "allergic" to. We still play chase, assemble puzzles, have dance parties and share stories about our feelings. I am so thankful for him as my firstborn, that he is the brother of my other wonderful sensitive boy and that he is present and aware of where I am now.

Between the hike with my mom and returning home to a Henry who wanted me to close my eyes as he presented me with a wildflower from the mountain, it was a perfect day. And having a husband who takes such good care of my boys' hearts is humbling and wonderful beyond words.

I am one lucky mama.

Where My Hope Comes From | Caroline Wright

I am not bragging when I say that I have had only a handful of truly hopeless days since my diagnosis. I'm not saying it's been easy, it is an active choice on my part and I spent effort and intention to nurture and protect my precious supply of hope. My hope is in part created by me, but it is largely given to me. I seek out and support its sources that I find and am incredibly grateful for them.

It comes first from my kids. Their open, bright faces looking into mine and seeing their Mommy is what makes it so. Just as the well of patience after a long day—the kind that replenishes as you dig deeper and push every boundary of reason and compromise in favor of bottomless, eternal love—so behaves my well of hope. And my energy to fight fear and doubt.

My parents are a huge source of hope for me. Their devotion, both to me and my boys (including Garth), is beautiful to witness. Their kindness and positivity, their hope, keeps me present. Their strength, too, gives me mine—they take on so many of the demands of my life that I can be strong and careful with my energy. To be with my parents as their child, believing the world as seen through their eyes.

My Garth. He finds me wherever I am, even if that's lost, and holds the most hopeful parts of me until they bloom again.

This space, this writing, brings me hope. Knowing that my boys will hear my voice here makes me feel hope for them and their understanding of me, both as a person and as a mother and the shape of my intense love for them. This space also sends my story out into my community in a way that brings encouragement and responsiveness to my experiences, making me feel seen and heard from a very strange place. This is an exceptional gift for someone who has to choose between love and fear every day.

The letters and words that reach me give me a similar sort of encouragement to here, but with a different sense of responsiveness. Those words are in a timeless place, on pages I discover in quiet, often while alone like first waking up or going to bed. Their autonomy is also their beauty, a communication of love and hope in a form that allows me to discover it but not necessarily have to respond to it, to hold it and feel its worth the way I choose.

My keepsakes, both held in my heart and the physical ones on my body and around my house, are another wonderful source of hope for me. These amulets and tokens—my collection of bracelets, for example, which have all been given to my parents by strangers and usually removed from their bodies immediately when they hear my story, and my "hope" candle to which Jonas lights its twin—send me beautiful and healing meaning each time I look at them. They are things that people have given me to help me fight or give me their love and strength. I have a shrine in the guest room of my house full of these objects and I love to sit before it and feel the collective glow of love.

I notice things I never did before. I see love and kindness—thanks to each of you—in so many places. I hold hugs longer, smile at strangers more often, make friends faster. I find hope in my soul because I choose to, but also because I feel it pouring into me wherever I go. I welcome it and hold it tightly.

Today's Thoughts | Caroline Wright

Here are a few things kicking around my brain right now—

- Yesterday, while washing my hands in the bathroom at the Denver airport, a woman rounded the corner from the stalls to the sinks and visibly startled at my presence, after which she offered, "Oh, I'm sorry, I saw you and thought I was in the men's bathroom." Neat. It brought back flashbacks of being called a boy by the substitute teacher in the sixth grade as I sat there in a dress. And how I came to think it was hilarious and a badge of honor.

- I just took my first two pills of my first "real" cycle of chemotherapy. (Yes, I take chemo pills at home. If all goes as well as we hope, this is the plan moving forward—five doses per month.) I'm trying out a different anti-nausea med tonight so let's hope I don't jolt out of bed puking like I did last time. Is this like some medical equivalent to a blind date?

- It feels so good to be home. It was great to be on vacation—Colorado with my family was a beautiful experience—but being home where I am capable of being high maintenance in a comfortable setting is really just easier. Also, there are other electively bald ladies here, which I also appreciate.

- Today I found out that my Catalan book project is coming out Fall 2018. It was so strange checking in with a project that I created from scratch that now has a fully functional and totally autonomous team that is working relentlessly without me. And I reinforced my decision for distance today, expressed pride and trust in their work, and fought the instinct to join them. All weird and good things that make me proud of myself today.
- I've missed yoga while I was away. I have become one of those people.
- I've been having dreams lately—really wild, vivid ones, the kind that upon waking you actually have to riddle out if it was real or not. They've been about my tumor, about this whole thing being a mistake. Like, *just kidding, you never had brain surgery* and that story that keeps coming out of my mouth isn't actually mine. *But then there were those MRIs, I remember that, the massive glowing white tennis ball squished in between the two hemispheres of my brain. Right, oh yeah.* Then my feet hit the floor and I shuffle to find my morning pills.

Off to bed with a bucket at my side, just in case...

Success! | Caroline Wright

No puking! Not a lot of sleep, either, thanks to sweet
Theodore. But no puking!

On Vanity | Caroline Wright

I have never considered myself beautiful. Or pretty. I have always had far more self-deprecating things to say about my looks and the shape of my body, which is so silly to me now, than kind ones.

I grew up in a Florida town filled with Florida girls, which was hard for a girl who doesn't tan and has *always* felt self-conscious in a bikini.

When I moved to Brooklyn many years later, I adopted the sort of hippy hipster, no-makeup vibe mostly because I'm lazy but also because makeup never made me feel beautiful. Makeup made feel like I was back in high school and I was trying too hard to hold a feminine form I didn't believe in. I liked the version of hip that celebrated truth and raw beauty in its own way. So I stopped wearing makeup entirely, except when I was promoting my work. With my long-lost dreams of being an actress from my adolescence that inspired me to take weird things like stage makeup classes, I had the skills to apply makeup like a pro (despite the fact they were rarely used). I saw those skills and makeup in general to be a tool, like an armor or uniform in which to be something slightly different than who I am at home, cooking in my yoga pants.

Occasionally I have the opportunity to be on television to promote my work, which is so many things including not nearly as fancy as the very bright lights make it look. On the very rare occasion that I would be paired with someone who could do my hair and makeup—nobody "talent" like me isn't usually afforded such a luxury!—I would feel at once fancy and incredibly out of place; this would cause me to awkwardly befriend the stylist because I didn't know what else to do. Through their eyes, I began to appreciate weird things about myself like my eyebrows. I did, I began to love my eyebrows—their expressive arch when I felt sassy, their entire lack of maintenance. They were, I realized eventually, one of the reasons why I never felt I needed makeup in the first place.

In fact, when I shaved my head before my surgery, I shrugged and thought to myself in the mirror, *eh, who cares, a girl's still got her eyebrows.*

This is all very silly, I realize—and I'm getting to that part. But permit me to talk about the face I recognize in the mirror a bit longer, as vain as it is.

So, about four weeks after my radiation was over, you can imagine my surprise when I proceeded to lose most of my right eyebrow. Just yesterday, Henry said to me, "Mama, why is one of your eyebrows grey?" I explained to him that it was because of my treatment that I now have much less hair in that brow. He moved on quickly.

Knowing that this was coming for a few weeks as I washed my face to find my hands scattered with hair, I had consulted my network of gay friends, who are either part-time amateur drag queens or wish they were, to find a solution for this mounting issue. Tattoos, elaborate stencil systems and even old-school filler pencils all seemed to circle back to the same issue I grappled with before moving to Brooklyn: fake and too much effort.

The hair loss, as Henry so astutely pointed out, seems to have stalled and now my right eyebrow appears the same shape and size as my left, just with an appearance of an even silver tone.

I've since decided that at the top of my list of "Things I Don't Give A Shit About Anymore," which I accrue sometimes (or often, compulsively, depending on the day) as I walk around, is Eyebrows. I don't give a shit about my eyebrows anymore. And having one grey one isn't a good enough reason to go back to makeup, back to the high schooler who wanted to fit in and awkwardly made her face look more like everyone else's.

I've earned this look of mine—bald head, mismatched eyebrows, tattoos and my genuinely carefree smile. Here I am. Fuck eyebrows.

A Place to Bloom | Caroline Wright

I moved to Dallas when I was about seven months pregnant
with Henry. I moved from one of two places I had considered
home, New York, because Garth had taken a job there.
This was not part of any vision I had for my life at all—kids,
absolutely, but Texas, not as much.

The challenges for me as a woman living in Dallas
were abundant, including living in a place that didn't have
an outlet for the kind of food media I was working in then
(magazines and television), living in a deeply religious place,
living in a place where the idea of a woman is very different
to my idea of me. More importantly than my internal and
personal challenges with our newfound surroundings was
what it meant for my son, a white, handsome little boy whose
life was already filled with innumerable privileges just upon
being born. I felt that it was going to be a huge struggle to
parent not only against the same cultural forces that marked
me as an outlier, but also that these forces created such
palpable expectation for boys especially. I didn't want that
for Henry (and, later, Theodore). I wanted them to be able to
make their own choices without the pressure to conform and
find nuance within their privileges. I wanted their childhood
to be authentic to them without the invisible pressures

influencing their inner voice. I wanted my boys to be able to be weird like I was because I honestly believe that those kids are the lucky ones.

I've considered other ways to bring a different perspective into our sheltered, privileged family, something that would reinforce our bond, love and connection first. I wanted to carry my best friend Jeff's future child. It would have physically brought more family into our very tiny one— we have few invested relatives and even those are far away. And it would have given our boys an extra special cousin, someone raised on a different coast but with similar values.

Then we moved to Seattle, which opened up the possibilities, in my view, for being weird kids, but privilege is still very much a familiar participant in daily life here. Our community is almost completely white and the wealth here is truly astounding.

Then I got cancer, which changed everything, including my capability for the whole cousin-birth thing. Grandparents moved here and our community swelled around us. A huge shift in my boys' world occurred. They both had no choice but to become truly open and flexible, which has been my dream for them all along.

Today, as my dad and I walked to pick Henry up from summer camp while Theodore played at a friend's house, I realized that this life right here turned out to be perfect. Their lives won't be boring or predictable at all, and they now have a bigger daily presence of family. It's beautiful and authentic, these forces in play in their childhood. I am proud of that and look forward to seeing the men they become.

Semantics | Caroline Wright

I, as a writer and a committed lover of language, know how important word choice is. I think about it a lot because small differences in things like verb tense can make for big differences in my perception. Of course it is jarring in terms of a narrative oversight, like saying that I "have" a brain tumor as opposed to "had." A small mistake, yes, but it tugs at the strength of my belief in my health—*do I have a tumor now, I wonder?*—that is an incredibly important pillar in my life right now.

Finding the right word to succinctly describe my current circumstances is another challenge. Describing myself as "sick" feels wrong because it is—I don't feel that way and, according to my blood work, I am actually quite strong. Another one brought up by a friend yesterday is actually the meaning of the word "terminal." Does that mean that the doctors haven't known anyone to live with a glioblastoma for seventy years? What happens if something else kills you first?

These words all appear to hold meaning that is universally agreed upon in order to constitute language and facilitate communication, I get it. The shape of living within this strange, new language is also strange and new. And slippery and inaccurate. The words have failed their ability to communicate my circumstances, despite being the only ones offered to me. I stand in an unknown place to me, made stranger still by the fact it is the very place where language dissolves.

A Rant | Caroline Wright

I am a very tolerant person, one of those bleeding heart liberal types who listen to and try to love everybody. My Dad makes fun of me for it. And while absolutely none of you here have ever offended me but rather show me the kind of support (not pity, as I've mentioned before) that I need, I find myself fighting being annoyed by strangers as it relates to my cancer on a fairly regular basis. In the moment, I smile and say thank you, but I have come to find a few words bubbling inside my brain and I need to get them out. Here are a few.

I know that meeting a very alive, friendly-looking woman with terminal brain cancer is likely (hopefully!) a rare opportunity for you and makes you feel a lot of things about your own life. Because I, however, live in this body and in these circumstances every day, it is a very common experience that every stranger who looks at my bald head wants to say something about it. That means that what feels like a rare opportunity for you happens to me at least once every time I leave the house. It bugs me and I actually like people. I feel really bad for those bald-headed cancer people out there who are having a tough time or, you know, don't like engaging about the most personal details of their lives without consent or warning, that kind of thing.

So, Person Who Does This, please consider how unusual this circumstance is for us. I mean, it has been generally accepted that individuals don't like to be used as a generalized representation of a whole, possibly unrelated, population, right? Like if you walked up to a black person and talked about the only other black person you knew, that would be offensive, right? What's worst of all with this is that, at the end of an unwanted exchange, I have to smile and offer (usually genuine) thanks because they meant well. It is so weird.

You should know that cancer comparing sucks in general, like mentioning that one experience you know to offer some sort of understanding to my circumstances (that you have no idea about because, you know, I'm shopping for vegetables and you just walked up to me). Firstly, there are innumerable cancers out there and rare few share characteristics. So offering your experience not only belittles mine (even though clearly unintentional), but the analogy you have may not even be relevant. Also on the subject of unique cancers and unique experiences, some cancers are curative. Others, like mine, are not. So when you mention that so-and-so cured their cancer by eating cabbage three times a day, that so-and-so likely had a cancer that could be cured. Your mentioning it only reminds me that I am in a tight spot and, watching tears fill your eyes as you realize this (if I have chosen to correct you) can ruin my day if I let it.

Listen, I know no one knows what to say to me. Of course I understand the impulse to want to help and encourage and communicate support. But walking up to me to talk about you is not the place to start. (I mean, walking up to me in general is already more about you than me—you have no idea the kind of day I've had or what is going on with me in that moment.) So start with eye contact and a smile. That says to me that I am seen and you're sending good energy my way. Along with sweet, comforting silence, the most respectful thing of all.

More Conversations with Henry | Caroline Wright

Yesterday Henry and I went on a date to see the new Cars movie. We both were so excited for the time together and to see a movie—only Henry's second ever in the theater and my first since my surgery.

Before getting dropped off at the theater by Daddy, we had a little time to do a few errands. Theodore had fallen asleep in his car seat, so Henry's choices were to stay in the car with Mommy or to go inside with Daddy. Henry said that he wanted to stay in the car. Only a few moments after the car door shut, Henry started asking questions.

Henry: Mama, why when you die is it forever?

Me: Are you talking about me, or just wondering in general?

Henry: I mean everybody.

Me: Well, death is a part of life. Every living thing has an amount of time that it is meant to live by its nature. Even seasons, they have their own life span. Summer flowers die by fall. They wear out. They've used up all they had to give based on the kind of flowers they were and how well they grew.

Henry: *[Long pause.]* Mama, why is life so short? I mean, why do we only get to live like 90 years or something?

Me: *[I laugh.]* You're right, ninety years isn't very long when you consider how long ago the dinosaurs lived. I don't think how long you live matters as much as the kind of life you make for yourself. The *life* part matters more than years. *[Pause.]* Can I ask you a question, sweetheart, about what you feel when you think about death? *[He nods.]* Does it make you sad?

Henry: *[Shifts, tight-lipped.]* No.

Me: Well dying doesn't have to be sad. It's about how you felt about that person that matters. You always hold them in your heart, and that lasts forever.

Then we went to the movies and held hands the whole time.

Timelines | Caroline Wright

At my last doctor's appointment, inspired by the apparent success of my recent results, the subject of my timeline resurfaced. My parents questioned my doctors, searching their faces for some relief, some new information. I actually plugged my ears as the doctor responded.

It's not a conversation I find useful. There is no way to know anything about my situation at all—if what I'm doing is effective, what part of what I've done already was the most effective and, ultimately, how long I'll live. All I can know is how my treatment makes me feel—in terms of my symptoms, yes, but also in terms of my perception of their efficacy and my participation in my treatment—and wait for testing. I also don't get the impression that they know very much about GBMs in general, and what they do know doesn't feel particularly relevant to me at my age. So, a doctor telling me a guess based on statistics without having the ability to know the individual efforts I am making (or how the people in the statistics lived *their* lives, for that matter), is what I mean when I say it doesn't feel useful. I am the expert of my own body in many ways. What I think and feel about it matters.

Also, it is a philosophical question: would you live differently if you were told you had a year to live? I don't have a bucket list. I love my life, right here and now. I am surrounded by the loves of my life and live in a home I built for them. I have no regrets.

I do feel like I will generally surpass the odds I was given. And if I don't, isn't living feeling surrounded by love and connection, the kind that fills me with a strength that seems endless, a beautiful way to go?

I'm here now and that's all I know. Just the same as anyone else, not questioning the reason why, rather how I can make it the most meaningful and true for as long as I get.

Finding Quiet on a Fault Line | Caroline Wright

When I was healthy—or oblivious to my tumor, I should say more accurately because I have no way to know how long I had it—I did what everyone else does and assumed that every gurgle and groan from my body was normal. I think moms are particularly good at this because of always being in the habit of taking care of someone else before themselves.

And now, knowing about my illness (both academically somewhat as well as how I have felt in terms of its symptoms), my struggle is the exact opposite—to *not* attribute every gurgle or groan in my body to my tumor. In fact, the dream of ever being obliviously healthy feels so far away now.

Standing in between these two places of consciousness, I see both ridges clearly. It feels as if the ground moves between my feet as I attempt to stand still. On some days I feel steadfast and confident in my body, but others I waver to either side. My moments of stability are quiet ones. And in these quiet moments I find strength and my own new version of normal.

In this place, attempting to stand still on this moving ground, I listen. I try to be kind to myself and ask for help when my instincts tell me to. It's a very new landscape for me.

Update | Caroline Wright

As I was just turning flats of berries into pies (gluten and sugar-free, of course), I was thinking about all of the random things that have made me smile lately and wanted to share.

- My eyebrow has inexplicably grown back. It's like it chickened out and decided that its brief retreat was a practical joke. I've enlisted a few people who will still tolerate my obsession over my eyebrows (bringing the conversation out of its retirement), including my dad, Garth and Adair, and none of us can figure it out. I'll take it as a gift from the eyebrow fairy, one of maybe my top five favorite fairies I know.
- My hair on my head is also returning—some of it, anyway. I don't hold high hopes for the very bald part—the part that appears pore-less and gleams in the sun, not unlike a polished bowling ball—so I will continue to shave it anyway.
- I have amassed quite the collection of heart-shaped rocks. I started to pick them up during our hikes in Colorado, but I've continued it on our hikes here, too. (The past two weekends! That's *right*, ten-year-old me!) I pick up these heart-shaped specimens and before I know it my

pockets are full of rocks like a crazy person. I see them everywhere now, in landscaped trenches occasionally or on a particularly gravely driveway, but I have to draw the line somewhere before it comes a problem. I wonder if this manifestation of hearts is a superpower unique to me as I traipse along the trails. I pretend it is, anyway. My collection is proudly displayed along the ledge above my kitchen sink.

- I'm working on the fourth children's book I've written since my diagnosis and it still very much qualifies as slowing down for me. Like I said, I'm a crazy person.
- On the note of slowing down, I told the backers in the Charlie the Cook Kickstarter that I will not be fulfilling the cookie incentive for those who purchased it and will be issuing gift cards that divides the food cost and shipping supplies associated with the cookie production. *Not* making thousands of cookies, as much as I would have truly—actually—loved to do that, is not a prudent decision for someone who is protecting their energy. I'm proud of myself, actually.

I'm feeling great. One of Theodore's first words (a very recent development!) was "happy" and I second that sentiment. We repeated it over and over tonight as cooly as identifying his nose or mouth.

Happy, indeed.

Unpacking Trauma | Caroline Wright

My life recently is finding a groove, settling into a new sense of normal. With that, the panicked urgency has slackened and a different kind of calm has taken its place. My health is something I monitor moment by moment, but I feel a general confidence in my routine and body that brings me comfort. In this less desperate, less shocked mode of living, it allows room for the trauma—the density at which the events of my diagnosis were paced—to breathe. To give my heart and mind time to examine the things my body was just surviving, practically speaking. I didn't have the space at the time to process my feelings about what was happening because the circumstances required one path: surgery. So facing it didn't feel like bravery but survival. And then the battery of news that followed was so scary, so complicated, for which I was completely unprepared, that I basically lived off of adrenaline until fairly recently. Now that I have found sleep and routine and the boys are relaxing, I am too.

I have been reliving the morning of my surgery, memories from the ICU. The moments I haven't written about because they were too bleak or scary and I didn't want to commit language to them.

I've been turning over other toxic things, too, like the fact that my brother has stated to my family that I am not his sister and overtly implied that he didn't care if I die. They nip at my heels. I keep walking forward and focusing on my loving family so they don't have space to take hold.

Then I remember what my sweet, wise friend Katy relayed to me about her own reckoning with the grief process of her husband's passing. The idea that she clung to recently was that the power behind a toxic thought is as easily taken away as it is given. I have been clinging to that recently, too, with these ideas that swirl around as if circling a drain.

The reality of processing my experience of my diagnosis, surgery and recovery is important, but accepting its positive role in my circumstances now is also very important. I'm finding my gratitude for it again. These things happened, it is true. But they also brought me here. Without them, I would probably be dead now or severely handicapped. I am deeply fortunate. Giving these thoughts power to scare me and relive the darkness over and over takes away from my day *today*. It doesn't serve me, it doesn't make me feel good or strong or capable. So as easily as I give them power, I can take it back. That's the beauty of a thought.

JULY 5, 2017

Hard Work as Virtue | Caroline Wright

My newer friends here would probably be surprised to learn that as at home and truly in love with Seattle I've found myself since our move—a deep belonging—I was almost as completely so in New York. The two places couldn't actually be more different in my mind, nor could the two versions of myself that experience those places.

The New Yorker in me thrives on chronic stress. This quality was probably nurtured by my parents and the state of my childhood in some way, but it was so embedded in me that I had no idea how different my inner narrative and drive was from other people's. I am incredibly stubborn, "single-minded" to borrow a mentor's phrase, and very creatively productive. I make, I do, I decide. I've been that way as long as I can remember. So that person in me was very satisfied by the speed and demands of The City. And to find a community of people who dreamed and produced as I did was singular and powerful, especially to me in my early career.

Jeff and I used to examine—again, over cocktails—where this comes from in me and the others we knew. Some of it was aptitude and luck, undoubtedly, but there was a tortured quality in there, too. We watched friends torture themselves to the point of leaving town, whereas I was making plans to stay forever and raise my future babies in Brooklyn. The payoff between the hard work and torture is success—without it, hard work can be very crippling. Especially to artists.

There is another element, too, Jeff and I postulated—a notion of hard work as a form of virtue. That someone who works to the bone and with passion is somehow doing better than someone else. There is ego involved. The person feels like they've earned something because they've bled for it.

I remember those days clearly because, until my diagnosis, I identified with being a New Yorker in this way who just didn't live in New York. I was on the hunt for the next thing, always. I was taking calculated steps to take what I wanted for my career. And I loved it because it generally worked for me, so I thought.

It's bizarre to look back now because I am not a shadow of that person. I walked away from that part of me, the idea of my career, the idea of what I wanted my life to look like. Hard work, the kind that I used to do in order to prove something, is stupid, not virtuous, from here. I am still busy and unstoppably creative, I still make and do and decide. The torture part has lifted. I belong here and now and nowhere else. The New Yorker in me has left the building.

What Cooking Is Like Now | Caroline Wright

A lot of people have been asking me what it feels like to cook now that my experience of food is so different, so restricted.

Now that, of course, I am actually turning back to cooking again—for many months my whole family and I devoured the meals brought to us by our community here, and then meals that friends cooked and stored for us when they came to visit. It was overwhelming to experience so much love and nurturing through food that way. It is something I've always written about, the power of food to convey that, but I hadn't experienced it firsthand like this before. It was so beautiful and humbling. And delicious! Friends, you all really know how to cook. Or if not, you had me happily fooled. I honestly couldn't have made better meals for myself, feasting off of the kindness and love and nutrition given to me by so many of you.

Now that our larder's stockpile (also known as our freezer!) is almost depleted, I have turned back to cooking, just in time for the farmer's market to burst. (Lucky us!) I can't help but grab flats of berries, brimming bags of greens, the last of the asparagus, young broccoli, and, and, and. I feel like I'm in France again with my shopping rituals and access to fresh produce. It is very inspiring.

Inspiring, too, are my restrictions in their way. I am determined to eat well without deficit of my favorite meals—like Saturday morning *abelskiver* made by Henry and me or the occasional pizza night with salad from our yard or homemade waffles in our freezer, pies from fresh berries at the market. These are the meals of our family, the cooking of my boys' childhoods. I am tinkering to bring them back and am almost there. Dinner parties—in which I eat the same as everyone else and no one is the wiser that it is gluten and sugar free and made up of anti-inflammatory ingredients—are ahead.

The actual act of cooking is as wonderful a presence in my life as always—the combination of thoughtful, joyful, quiet or dancing to music all at once—that results in joy and sustenance for those I love. Bliss.

Another unexpected angle of this is enjoying cooking from cookbooks. I have hundreds and used them all the time for inspiration, for pitches, for work. My job as always been to read recipes and see beyond the words to feel their flavor and style, so rarely I felt inspired to actually cook them. In a lot of ways, I felt less compelled to experience another cook's recipes because I was so focused on creating my own and finding my own voice.

Now that I can cook however I want. No measuring cups—ever—or wondering if what I am cooking could turn into the next pitch. In this way, too, it's like I'm back in

France before I went to culinary school, getting lost at the markets and trying and failing and figuring it out. It's so fun and beautiful and new again. I'm filling my recipe box with my new discoveries, building the repertoire for our future, for my boys and their childhood ahead that I hope will contain countless delicious meals made by me.

More Conversations with Henry | Caroline Wright

We recently drove by Green Lake's sports fields where Garth used to play soccer with friends on a team. He loved it, but he got hurt a few times and life just got busy so the playing lost momentum. Now that life feels really far away. Apparently, Henry felt that distance on this particular day, too.

Henry: Daddy, why don't you play soccer anymore?

Garth: Well, Mommy got sick and life changed a lot. Some things, like you guys watching me play soccer, would be too much for Mommy now.

Henry: When Mommy's cold goes away, can we watch you play soccer again?

Me: Honey, it's not a cold. It's not like Theodore's cough that just goes away and he's all better. I will always have cancer, sweetheart. It doesn't mean I won't feel good and play with you at a quieter place with less activity, like at home, right? It just means I can't necessarily do all the things I used to. A little like Daddy and his soccer playing in that way. *[I giggle.]*

My Brain │ Caroline Wright

"Yes, but how does your brain *feel*," one of my homeopaths always asks during our appointments. As I consider my answer, I equally consider how this is not a normal question for most people. It's like having to think earnestly about your awareness of your eyeballs—both the fact that they produce sight and how that looks, but also that these organs rest in your skull and how they feel while doing so. It's bizarre to attempt to consider a function that is so embedded in your understanding of what it means to be human and try to become not only aware of its behavior, but also attempt to be as objective about it as possible. All I know for sure is that before my diagnosis I never considered my brain *feeling* anything, rather I just took its capabilities for granted.

Now, finally, my brain is starting to feel like my own again. I never was particularly aware of its feeling strained or scrambled, but lately its been feeling like some version of normal, some version of the *feeling* of the brain I've always recognized myself to have. It generally retrieves what I ask it to. My vocabulary of feelings seem the same. I can still recite many songs from the nineties verbatim and I remember how to cook all of my favorite meals. I can still speak French.

Things that have changed about my brain are the pace at which it retrieves certain specific words and proper nouns, though that has never been my strength; my brain feels heavy and cloudy during the days I take my chemo pills. Occasionally I conflate things, like thinking we are on one walking route when in actuality we are on another, or thinking that someone just said something in yoga class when it was really at the last one. I forget people's names that I just met unless I try really hard to remember them. These little slips feel within the realm of normal for other people—now my being a little flighty or ditzy is credited to my brain tumor. The only real difference is that when people think you slip up because of a brain tumor, they correct you, whereas with a personality trait they silently forgive it. So that's new, too.

It makes me realize how powerful the brain really is— not just the assumed fact of that, but my *experience* of that, the *feeling* of that and the edges of that knowledge. How complicated taking care of the brain is and how much it is all wrapped up in one's sense of self without very much awareness of its actual function.

I don't care if this new brain of mine stays forgetful of details like appointment times, friends birthdays, groceries we need from the store. That's what lists are for. And if I make a mistake, the excuse of recent brain surgery combined with my bald head seems to do the trick every time.

I am just so thankful that I trust my brain again and continue to recognize my world the way I've always experienced it. I am endlessly thankful for these things, even though I've taken them for granted in the past. I know how precious they are now and I vow to myself to never lose sight of that awareness.

So, that's my answer—my brain feels like mine again. And I am incredibly grateful.

Things I Don't Give A Shit About Anymore | Caroline Wright

This list changes all the time. Things are often added, but nothing falls off. Here is my list as of today:

Eyebrows
Being thin
Working out
Personal drama, including gossip, ill will and
confrontation
Trump
Alcohol or weed (turns out loosening my brain is never
fun now)
Needing approval
The very existence of the Kardashians
Saying I love you to friends too soon
Being too cool for ugly, practical shoes
Being too cool for anything, really, especially talking
about how amazing my parents are even as a grown
woman
The size or shape of my butt or thighs
Wanderlust
Chocolate (!!!)

How tidy my house is when people show up
Hypochondriacs
The tan my Keens have given me
Trying to remember birthdays on their exact day
Operating a motor vehicle
The past

Henry's Sweet Song | Caroline Wright

Henry has been singing this song he learned at camp almost every day for weeks now. It is sung in a call-and- response style, line by line, and I love to sing it together with him. It often feels like a perfect summation of life right now, like it does today.

> *Forget your perfect offerings*
> *Just sing the song that you can sing*
> *There is a crack in everything*
> *That's how*
> *The light*
> *Gets in*
> *That's how the light gets in.*

Medical Update and Second Opinion | Paul Markunas

Caroline and I spent the entire day two days ago first having a routine medical exam at UW Alvord Brain Tumor Center and then following up with a second opinion from another Neuro-Oncologist at Swedish Neuroscience Institute at the Ivy Center for Advanced Brain Tumor Treatment, another of the several exceptional cancer treatment centers in Seattle.

First, the medical exam couldn't have been better. All vitals perfectly normal. All blood work within acceptable range. All motor skills and cognitive aspects functioning perfectly. The bottom line from a medical perspective is that Caroline is tolerating the increased dose of chemo therapy, now given 5 days every month for the next six months, without problem or damaging effects. Starting last night, her chemo dosage is now at the maximum amount permitted by her body mass (which is double the dosage it was originally) and will remain at these levels for the remainder of her treatment barring a recurrence or negative side effect yet to be observed.

As for the highlights of the second opinion at Swedish Neuroscience Institute:

—Caroline is now in a "stable" phase where the cancer does not appear to be growing at this time;

—Her prognosis remains unknown, the Neuro-Oncologist indicated that it is nearly 100% likely that this cancer will begin to grow again at some point (he had one patient that went 15 years without a recurrence to which Caroline replied "I'LL TAKE IT!"

—The indicators which bode well for her future prognosis are that the tumor was located in the right frontal lobe and was accessible, that she came out of the surgery and hospital with amazing speed and results—no loss of motor skills and a quick recovery (she went home 24 hours after surgery directly from the ICU) she tolerated all the radiation and chemotherapy extremely well—her blood work was normal throughout, she had little nausea and fatigue and she has remained active and alert ever since her diagnosis in late February.

—The biggest advantage Caroline has moving forward is her age. Her relative youth is unusual for a GBM patient and plays a large part in these successes we've mentioned above.

We discussed alternative therapies moving forward and possible ways to increase her chances of fending off a recurrence of this cancer, or at least delaying it as long as possible.

Possible treatments available (aside from continuing chemo-therapy which actually has little proven value for the type of "unmethylated" tumor Caroline has and possible pin-point radiation if necessary) are experimental and largely unproven.

The two "proven" therapies known to increase survival rates, even if only by a few months, are a device worn 18 hours a day on the head called Optune which sends electrical impulses through the brain and confuses the cancer cells so that they can not replicate (this treatment added, on average, four months to the survival rate of the patient) and the second being taking a daily dose of CBD, the non-halleucenogenic drug component of marijuana. It is known that CBD affects brain receptors directly and has been shown to slow the growth of brain cancer cells. (It has also worked wonders for epilepsy patients and is the main reason why medical marijuana has been approved for legal use now by many states, Florida and Washington among them.) Unfortunately, the dosage required is high and can result in some numbing of the experience of life, something Caroline is remiss to do.

The other treatments are bold, experimental, often risky, but all unproven to work on GBM cancers. Among these are cholesterol blocking drugs, anti-viral drugs of various sorts, injections of dangerous bacteria thought to attack cancer, and extreme diet regimes, all of which can be either expensive, damaging to overall health and organ function and inconvenient to say the least.

Bottom line: nothing is changing from here on out, at least significantly. Caroline has completely changed her lifestyle and diet—gluten-free, eating extremely well with healthy foods, naturopathic and homeopathic supplements for anti-cancer growth and overall health, routines of exercise (yoga, walking, hiking) and meditation (reiki treatments among them) and continues to show the same "you can't stop me" spirit which has brought her this far.

We are, all of us—friends and family alike—here to continue to support her as we all enjoy each and every day together in this uncharted place. An adventure for sure which has changed all of our lives in many ways for the good. Let's just carry on, shall we?

After Amy Wood's Visit | Posted by Paul Markunas

From Amy:

This blog post is a long time coming. I visited Caroline in the beginning of May during the weeklong absence of her parents, just a few days following the end of her radiation and chemo treatments. My dear friend asked me to write about my visit during this impossibly difficult time for her and her family. Although a simple enough request, it's been hard for me to find the words.

In many ways it would have been easier to write about one of the triumphant dinners that I had prepared thanks to Caroline's recipes or hands-on training. Or about our crazy-fun holidays together, pre and post enfants (e.g. strip poker in Normandy and how we attempted to protect Caroline's innocence with 5 hats and a few scarves, nevertheless exposing her to the genitalia of the losing party)... Or apropos our recent girl-weekend-out in Barcelona, where Caroline and the chef she'd been working with for her Catalan cookbook treated me to an epicurean night of sumptuous delights that terminated with me giving the Spanish taxi driver incoherent directions to my apartment in Paris! But I suppose now I have...)

I arrived on a beautiful spring afternoon with Seattle all a bloom. I was decidedly less fresh after a nervous, boozy flight in from Paris. My dream of visiting Caroline, Garth and their boys in their new home had come true although I had imagined different circumstances. Upon arriving in front of their brightly colored, hundred-year-old house in the hippest of neighborhoods, my disquiet abated. After some warm hugs and a cider or two, the mood was mirthful.

Caroline looked gorgeous bald! I think now of how tired she must have been after such heavy rounds of chemo and radiation but she didn't act so. What bliss to behold Theodore for the first time and to give little man Henry a big hug as he swung around in the tire swing at his school. On the walk home from picking him up, I listened to the delightful banter between mother and son and it goes without saying that their relationship is a remarkable one.

During my 4-day stay, Caroline and I did a lot of walking through tree-lined Fremont and the surrounding areas. She explained to me that this exercise had become a lifeline to her, helping her body to overcome the negative effects of medications and to stabilize her correlated mood swings. How grateful I was that we were able to walk together like this, stopping every now and then to take photos next to the flourishing fauna. Caroline spoke to me about the many facets of her illness: the reaction of acquaintances, friends and family members, the stigma of cancer as self-induced, the decline of her physical stamina after the treatments but also of her clarity of purpose, her heightened sensitivity to her surroundings, her exciting book projects, her deepened connection with Garth, her parents and of course her boys. We spoke often about Henry's keen and poetic observations and Theodore's sweetness; more beautiful children do not exist and Caroline is crazy dedicated to them.

I was pleased by the forthright nature of our conversations together. Garth was a gracious host to say the least and his selfless commitment to his wife and the kids is awe-inspiring. I loved seeing Caroline in all of her beautiful wigs (the feather one being my favorite!), she taught me how to make traditional Paella (a recipe that I've since inferiorly replicated, albeit with great pride), and my brother Tony and I had a blast making stepping-stones for the Wright's back garden. Our families' adventures together have been rich, joyous, and binding... and really, this last one was no different despite the pretext.

My young sister, my teacher, my mama partner, a woman who knows what it means to give life and yet to build oneself despite the children's coveted presence, my confidant, I am in perpetual admiration of her fortitude and grace. I know that this writing has been in large part conceived for Henry and Theodore's benefit, so that Caroline's incredible story will be told. Her bravery to face what's happening to her using such precise language is bewildering. Not all of us are so bold (or gifted at composition). The subject of her cancer stirs up in me a dark sadness and other such insufferable emotions that I'm frankly loath to face. Even though she is the one going through this journey, all those who love her are necessarily greatly affected and have felt anxiety about how to best vocalize our support.

Nothing could make me happier than to think of Paul's uplifting post yesterday detailing the current success of Caroline's treatments. Bravo darling! You are unimaginably strong!! Grateful for you every day.

Stable Choices | Caroline Wright

It was exciting to meet doctor Graber at Swedish hospital
the other day and hear from another revered, competent
source that I am in fact doing well. It was also especially nice
talking to him because he was forthcoming with alternative
treatments and discussing some theories that are floating
around across the various research hubs in the US, some of
which I could possibly consider for myself in the "can't hurt,
could help" category.

The trick is, in this place where my most recent scan
is clean, there aren't usually treatments that are actively
pursued by the doctors, which is both maddening and
wild to me. Most trials would only accept me if there was a
"recurrence," or evidence that a tumor was growing back.
That defensive tactic feels reactionary, like it puts me in a
position where I am waiting to fight this thing in my head
whose nature it is to grow until it has already taken hold again
and gained momentum.

I will not wait for that.

So with this in mind, there are few options for me.
One clinically proven option is this thing called Optune, a
collection of sticky pads that adhere to your shaved head like
a helmet and deliver low pulses of electric charge to your

brain that disrupts cancer cells from dividing. My radio-oncologist, Dr. Tseng, who I trust implicitly, implored me to consider it. Dr. Graber, too: he offered that I even meet people who had been using it through the hospital or through the Optune company, he begged me to "just try it for a day." There is data there, proof that is helps and it prolongs this stable period by a few months. But you have to wear it *eighteen* hours a day and you have to literally be plugged into an outlet for most of that time.

That is not a life for me. I fiercely protect my boys' experience of my motherhood from the place of this illness because it will be the mother they wake up to the world alongside. Telling them I am hopeful and not afraid while being plugged into an outlet feels like the worst possible way to live for me. Besides, it would largely prohibit the kind of activity I have found to be helpful so far—the walking, the yoga, the face time with our beautiful community, being the mother I recognize. And the doctors can't know how much *those* factors are affecting my life—there is no data *there*, no way to measure it. But I know that these are the factors that have played and continue to play a large role in my healing and "stability."

No, I will not become a robot.

The only other intriguing thing that Dr. Graber mentioned was the use of CBD, a component of marijuana like the more known THC, but without the "high."

Marijuana, because it obviously is received into the actual brain, is a very interesting therapy to me. Dr. Graber mentioned that it has just as much of a chance to diminish or impede my cancer cells—the particularly stubborn "unmethylated" sort that aren't even known to respond to the chemo I've been taking all that well.

It also feels really powerful, this CBD hope, because it feels destined—like, *of course* I was meant to be right here in this state where marijuana is embraced legally and socially and live with my cancer.

The CBD dose that Dr. Graber said was associated with the study feels very high—200 mg, three times a day—and I am still just as protective of my mothering and activity in this therapy as any other. So I am talking to friends with more experience with the health benefits of marijuana to find the right oil (one with as little THC in it as possible, because it doesn't agree with me) and the right way to take it (like fish oil, in a spoon? with food? I don't know). I am speaking to another naturopath on the subject this week and look forward to this lead with an open, hopeful heart.

I was talking to our friends about this on our recent getaway and said that I would literally try anything from this stable position. I joked that if there was a study that monkey poop killed my cancer I would be sourcing organic, sterilized monkey shit and eating *that* three times per day. I would, without hesitation.

That there is a viable option here in my proverbial back yard that could help—Dr. Graber said that CBD was even known to kill glioblastoma cells in a petri dish setting—is incredibly exciting to me. I know my mom will hate this idea and likely say things to both my dad and me that offer her discomfort in small but insistent hints, but that is a risk I am willing to take.

Robot with a power pack? No, thanks. Accidental sort-of stoner? A resounding yes.

I didn't think the idea of mothering from here could get even more strange or surreal, but it seems to be headed my way. I got this.

Old Lady Yoga | Caroline Wright

I am embarrassed to admit the nickname—given lovingly, I assure you—of the yoga class I am dedicated to twice weekly, but there it is. Among us regulars, we Sally (the teacher) devotees, I am the youngest by at least one generation, if not two. One of my favorite ladies told me last week she is 82; she can touch her toes better than I can. I like to ask her about her granddaughter who sounds only a few years younger than I.

I gravitated toward this group not only because of its classification of "Gentle," which it very much is, but also because of the women who frequent it. They range from quiet to brassy, but each classmate I speak to is kind and encouraging. And, before I came to know them as acquaintances, I appreciated that every person in the class has a body that shouts something at them—whether their shoulder or hip or fingers. That I don't put my head below my heart (and haven't since my diagnosis) doesn't stand out as odd.

And then there's Sally. She is the teacher, the sunny, goofy guru at the front of the class who seems to genuinely care about each of us. (I actually think she does.) She is quick to laugh as she is to acknowledge gratitude, to make a joke as easily as finding silence. She encourages each of us to listen intently to our bodies and carve our personal practice out of that transparency each time. With her help, I manage to. She has never made me feel anything but deeply strong because, as I've learned in part through our practice, I am.

Another of the gifts in this class is a spritely, smiley woman who assists the class registry named Shannon. She has always asked me questions about my illness with eye contact and a lack of pity. I admire her boldness and her preference for straight "real" talk, almost reminiscent of the New Yorkers I love, but smilier. I was surprised to learn a few weeks ago that she had plans to return to Canada, to Montreal, and even more so that her reason was that she "wanted to speak a second language before [she] die[s]." That was shocking to me—both her candor as well as the fact that she is making choices that hold both her life and death in them in a positive way, the way I have come to do so often.

And what little I learn of their lives—grandchildren, former careers, long-term hobbies—I can't help but wonder if I will be lucky enough as them to earn as many years as they have.

And I realized that another reason why I love this class— that I, at age 33, am in a very similar place to these women. Grateful for each healthy day. Thankful for our capabilities and gentle to our bodies. And living comfortably with the idea of death as a character in our days, regardless of how far off in the distance it arrives. And the beautiful part is that they are positive, living life fully. They are *out* in the community among friends. Just like me.

I am deeply humbled by these women and so appreciate their community. I am honored to belong among them.

Another Rant | Caroline Wright

Given my career background, I have often found myself on the subject of food and having a lot to say—it's a topic full of political, socio-economic and even religious triggers. I didn't know the healthcare side of it, but now that I do, I have a few things to say on the subject.

My new friend, Bob, and I were discussing our doctors' advice on food as it relates to our cancers—his, colorectal, and mine of the brain, both very serious. He told me that his doctors told him to avoid vegetables and eat refined, non-irritating foods like white bread. I was aghast, a doctor recommending that a cancer patient eat the least nutritious food when their body needs it most. The thought honestly made me mad and it still does. At the time of my diagnosis, my doctors just told me—*not kidding*—to eat whatever I want, whatever "felt good" to me. Luckily for me, I am a food professional and can take care of myself in that department, but if I wasn't, I would be completely adrift. (The only place in which I understand this advice is to those who really suffer during their chemo treatments—in that case, do eat whatever feels good, whatever stays.)

This just feels like the biggest pile of bullshit, honestly. Bob and I have had our immune systems attacked (with very good reason) and both of our doctors have not offered advice on how to use our bodies' first line of defense, its basic nourishment, to help give it repair or strength.

The thing that angers me most, though, is how arrogant it is. Why is it that on any other matter to do with my cancer, the doctors refuse, as if bound by a secret pact, to offer any information about things they don't know? It is abundantly clear that they don't know how foods relate to bodily wellness, so why the hell are they giving immunosuppressed people such stupid information?

As I see it, it begins with common sense stuff. Your body needs things that grow from the ground with as little interference as possible from pesticides or processing. Eat ingredients that your grandparents would recognize. If you eat foods where living things are involved, the happier and more honored they were in their lives, the more they will serve yours.

I really don't think I'm overreacting. Doctors are positioned as powerful, trustworthy characters and, essentially, deities within our care circles—which, to a person whose illnesses are as serious as mine and Bob's, rules our world.

They should do more research. They should consider that pills don't solve everything. They should recognize that the body is inherently powerful and smart if it's listened to and can do more than they know if supported well. And they should consider, too, that maybe white fucking bread isn't the way to go.

On Eating | Caroline Wright

I've recently shared my newfound perspective on cooking
and how my restrictions have actually inspired me as a
professional cook. Eating is a different story philosophically.
It is introverted and largely selfish. I listen intently to my
body and try to eat only what it asks for. It isn't stressful
at all because I make the nutrition available to myself by
carefully shopping and eating. I thought I'd share some of my
guidelines I think of when eating:

- I eat dark greens daily. Broccoli is key; I prefer fresh but
  I keep some of the organic frozen stuff in my freezer for
  use in a pinch.
- I try not to eat too many cold or raw foods—the
  occasional salad or smoothie on a particularly hot day,
  sure—because they don't feel gentle. It feels like a bit of
  a shock to my system to process cold foods in a way that
  doesn't happen with warm foods.
- My "restrictions" as Henry calls them are as follows:
  gluten free (corn and potato free, also, so that means
  few GF products), refined sugar free (only fruit and
  raw honey), no coffee, no chocolate, no citrus other
  than lemon. No fried foods. I exclusively drink alkaline,

oxygenated water throughout the day after my morning mug of green tea with honey and lemon. No alcohol.

- In terms of foods that come from animals—eggs, honey, dairy and, of course, the meat itself—I only eat from the farmer's market with rare exception. I've noticed a huge difference in quality, of course, but also in flavor and texture. I prefer to eat less of these foods but better quality.

- In terms of snacking or grab-and-go foods, this area is a struggle because necessarily this dedicated way of eating requires most often time and thought. However, times in which my routine and my capacity to cook is sacrificed (like traveling), I have found a few snack foods that fit the bill. There are the obvious ones, like raw almonds or whole fruits, homemade sugar free granola, things like that. I carry with me these packets of "green shake," this powder that you combine with water and I use to supplement even "healthy" restaurant eating or situations like being stuck in an airport. I look for products that do not contain any sort of preservative and have five recognizable ingredients or less.

- I don't "cheat." Ever. That idea isn't even in my head. When you think that there may be a way of eating that would give you more time with your kids, that chocolate bar is no longer appealing.

- What junk food looks like now: a carob chip and granola mix I use for sweet cravings, occasional roasted nuts (I

only eat raw), a seltzer water if Garth is having a cider
and I've already had my day's full amount of the alkaline
stuff. I've made frozen pops for the summer that are only
blended watermelon and strawberries.
· I eat nothing from the microwave. Not even melting
butter or coconut oil for an ingredient. (I never did
before, but now there are really no exceptions.)

It's really been working for me so far. I am proud that these
two sides of myself—the generous creative cook and the
picky, careful eater—find harmony from my kitchen.

The Unspeakable | Caroline Wright

There are things that I wouldn't say out loud from where I am now. But pretending I don't think them is silly and, even worse, makes my vibrant life sound like a song of a single note. Since this space is one I essentially see as a secret passageway to future me or future Henry and Theodore when they want to know more about this time in their mother's life, I don't feel ashamed in using this space as a receptacle for the thoughts I don't mutter. They are like snapshots of this place in time in my brain and body, nothing more, and are the narrative that I hear on occasion, acknowledge, and move forward. It is in the face of these fears that I wake with joy of what's real and live in what's here and now.

And now, out—

I worry that, if death does come for me, it takes a long time and the person and mother I am becomes unrecognizable to my boys and that would be the person they say goodbye to

I worry that another surgery down the line, with even less freedom of margins than the first surgery, could mean a change in my personality or capabilities and I am unable to connect with those I love so deeply

I worry that I could cause unthinkable pain to our boys and not be around to shield them from any of it

I worry that I could become a burden to my loved ones

I worry that I could lose my ability to write or express my feelings

I worry that, for the ones I love most, the sadness of my death would overshadow the memory of my beautiful life

I worry that if I don't survive my parents, my death would render them childless (biologically, anyway) and I wouldn't be there to tell them it wasn't their fault

These thoughts are ugly and terrifying and true. They live in my heart right next to the ones that make me feel shiny and powerful. I wanted to write them here for both a version of future, healthier me to read as well as my Henry and my Theodore when they are not quite so little as they are today. I wanted these future pieces of my heart to know that I have these fears and even sometimes see them wash over the faces of people I love as I talk to them. Right now, I am staring at them in silence and choose hope. My personal rebellion is to keep living, completely in love with my life, without being defined by fear.

And so I return to motherhood, to walking to take Henry to preschool and chasing Theodore around our playroom. These thoughts live here so I can live there.

Watching *America's Got Talent* | Paul Markunas

On *AGT* tonight, a lovely 13 year old girl sang like an angel. Her dad is dying of colon cancer.

I look back to our beautiful Caroline who sang (and still sings) like an angel and think, yes, it's unfair, but what's the bigger reason and purpose for all of this?

I've spent the last two weeks calling Duke University Glioblastoma Center (yes, it's the same cancer John McCain has) and finally, after several very nice and professional calls, was told that they have "nothing unique" to offer Caroline.

So, on to Stanford.

But, you know, it's a story. It may have already been written. But I am a player in it. Caroline's family and friends are players. And everyone who reads her blog is a player.

I believe in something bigger. I will not talk of terminal or think of timelines.

I only think of that voice of an angel I heard when she was young and still hear every day with her presence.

I'll let the angel decide the climax of this story. I'm there until the end. And beyond. And further than that.

Freedom | Caroline Wright

I've mentioned my brother a few times here, each met with sadness and pity, sometimes followed by emails offering suggestions. This will be the last one.

Well-meaning family and friends see a brother I used to idolize and adore. We look a little alike. I used to play baseball on a boy's team because he did and I endlessly wanted him to think I was cool. (And maybe pin me down and fart on my face a little less.) We stuck up for one another. He hated that I dated all of his friends in high school, but generally we were pretty close.

I missed this brother of mine for a long time after he decided to leave our family and cease all contact with us. I wrote him emails pleading for him to stay in touch, desperately trying to be close again. What made matters worse is that all while writing him and bending my perception and understanding to meet his, I was getting concerned but unintentionally condescending emails from my family members who he still kept in touch with pleading me to contact him or forgive him or whatever tune it took that day. My mom got it worse than I did and I know it tore her up as it did me.

I know why he left. I understand why he left and don't blame him, but I didn't choose the same path. Forgiveness and love of my parents is the reason why I not only have them in my life today, but in my home and at my table and as the devoted grandparents to my beautiful boys. He chose his path and I chose this one. I earned it and live in the light of its beauty every day, especially now.

Even after I got the sense that my efforts to reconnect were futile—a box of his belongings sent to a Googled address, returned unopened; dozens of emails over the years, including moves and my boys' births—I kept in touch with short reports of big news that I felt he should know. So, when I was told I had a tumor, his was *literally* the first email I wrote. It was short—it included the facts of the mass and my phone number with a request that he call, that this was bigger than our issues. Then I realized it was possible that he didn't even receive my emails after all of these years, that he had changed a setting within his account to divert the messages. So I asked my cousin Heather, who I love and know is in occasional touch with him, to text him with the facts. I felt strongly that he deserved to know my circumstances.

To be perfectly honest, the place I've arrived after many years is that I don't know if I would actually want to reconcile with him, whatever that means. He left our family at a very toxic point and so holds in time a very specific casting of our roles. He holds up the worst parts of each of us, met by the worst parts of him. And what, after twelve years, we would sit across from one another and attempt to catch up on countless milestones, an entire evolution of who we are as adults on the other side of essentially all of our growing up (including in many ways my parents)? And having to feel defensive of our growth and happiness because it didn't happen in close touch? I honestly don't know what I would say to him. We are both parents now, I've been told. I genuinely hope his parenthood has brought him the kind of love and healing it has to me.

Then I heard from a family member who contacted him directly about me (without my knowledge)—one who actually received a response. The response he received was that I am no longer Philip's sister, implying that he didn't care if I died.

Got it.

This bothered me for weeks. It would sneak in and stab me while I was bolted to the table for radiation. It would dive into the cool water of my mind during meditation. I finally called my therapist to talk through these feelings, a resurfacing of the anger and hurt that I hadn't found words to express.

She told me, very simply, that he wasn't the brother I remembered. That he had changed, so sending those emails and love to the void weren't reaching the boy I embarrassed during laser tag. They were reaching a stranger.

Yesterday I pulled out the contents of the box I'd tried to send him a few years ago. My parents had brought them to me during their move and I had them in my attic. I distilled the countless drawings my mom had diligently saved and stacked neatly, just like I've done for Henry, into another neat little pile containing the things that I could imagine the stranger, who I hear lives in upstate New York as a writer, would want. I tossed the other things, the artifacts of my Brother, in the recycling bin. May they come back as notepaper or an unknowing stack of paper plates. The rest I sent to my sweet aunt who always wanted healing for us. I asked her to forward the belongings to him without the encouragement to respond.

I will still love the brother I remember and hope he still lives inside that stranger in New York. There are framed photos of us as little kids hugging each other around my house and they will remain right where they are. I honestly do hope he has found love and healing, even though it hasn't looked like mine. I hope as a father his love of his children holds his inner child, too, in the ways I might not have been able to as his sister.

And so, Brother, just like that we are finally free.

After Jeff Barba's Visit | Posted by Paul Markunas

From Jeff:

Hello gorgeous Caring Bridge Community,

I'm Jeff—first time writer, long time friend of Caroline. I visited Caroline in the middle of June, and have put off the journey of being with and writing down my memories and feelings about my time in Seattle; Amy is right that it can be hard to find the words. But Caroline has been so generous with her mind and spirit on this blog, she inspires us to lean in, buck up, process, share.

....

So, some memories:

I arrive on the day of her neighborhood's Solstice Festival, and I barely put my bags down before I'm whisked away to watch naked people in body paint ride bicycles around the streets of Seattle. Am I in Heaven? I hold Henry on my shoulders (Theodore is asleep) while Caroline and Garth offer to answer any questions that all of these bodies might bring up for him; like a true Seattle kid, he is totally unfazed.

I go to Old Lady Yoga! I stretch and sweat and wonder at seeing Caroline working out and giving such caring attention to her body. When we lived in Brooklyn, we only ever exercised together

*when running the Park Slope Turkey Trot on Thanksgivings, and
more often we enjoyed connecting while treating our bodies like
garbage with booze and rich food. The kind, grown up, feminine
energy of the yoga group makes me feel safe and happy.*

*We take the bus to a farmer's market where Caroline buys fresh
food for that night's dinner. We meander home. We talk about her
diet, her developing understanding of her body and its healing. She
discusses learning to slow down and to focus on caring for herself
in a way she hadn't experienced before her diagnosis. We talk
about her children, her career, her legacy. These kind of rambling
conversations have always been the roots of friendship since we
decided we were besties in 2009. Her mind is expansive and vast,
and I never tire of wandering and getting lost in it.*

*I sit quietly in the living room while Caroline prepares some
food for dinner. She absent-mindedly sings "Summertime" from
Porgy and Bess, and leans into all the blue notes with a naked
melancholy that shakes me up. I feel in a new way the sadness that
lives alongside the love, hope and community she tirelessly cultivates.*

*On my last night, as Caroline and I settle in to watch a few
episodes of RuPaul's Drag Race, Garth yells down for us to come
see a Summer surprise. A double rainbow has stretched over their
neighborhood and anchored itself between hot pink clouds! The
moment feels profound and queer, like we have been anointed by the
PNW Gods. I know I'll never forget how magical it feels to be with
them in the pink light of a Solstice miracle.*

Since coming home, I've thought a lot about how familiar spending time with Caroline and Garth, Henry and Theodore, and Paul felt. (Glad was out of town; I'm sorry I missed you!) I think before I went I was nervous that somehow I wouldn't recognize the world she and her family have inhabited since her diagnosis, or wouldn't feel a part of it anymore. But what immediately struck me and felt like home was the love, energy, and commitment Caroline and her family pour into making life together something that is important and real, even when it's messy, difficult, and scary. I love this little family so much, and I feel really lucky to have shared that time and space with them.

And I feel lucky to share this space with you, her Caring Bridge Tribe! I'm happy to be connected to you though her, and that we can all bask in her pink light, double rainbow kind of magic together. Not today, B*tches!

Change of Plans │ Caroline Wright

I have been starting to weave together the writing from the early days of my diagnosis, to begin to build the manuscript for the memoir for the boys.

Going through these feelings again has been so surreal because reading my words from that time feels so different than the feelings that I've been processing lately about my survival of that time. Reading about the shape of my own survival, essentially. So strange and so postmodern. My favorite comparative literature professor from college and I would sit and talk about this experience for hours fueled by bitter espresso in a Parisian cafe, no doubt.

I've been trying to find the words to explain the space from which those early writings were penned, to state what's happened to me now that I can see it clearly: the process of being diagnosed. The transition from an individual to a patient. How your life—the patterns, the 'doing' and values of your days, not its existence—ends from one day to the next.

The last thing I remember from my life before my diagnosis is driving home from my MRI and sitting in my dining room sort of listening to a drainage contractor discuss solutions with Garth for fixing the newest leak we had just experienced in our basement a few days before. I remember feeling so confused, so cluttered in my brain and just unable to find more than a single sock for either of my boys. I would wander around our house, just holding one of them. I was already so compromised then. That was February 17 in the hours before I received the phone call that ended that life and began this one.

That was the last day I drove a car.

My parents were headed, at that very moment, on their last independent vacation, the last moment in which they didn't consider their fully grown daughter and her family's needs before their own.

This complete disorientation, this dissolution of a whole way of life and those of everyone who loves me, happened in the matter of three or so phone calls. The knowledge of my tumor put into course a completely unrecognizable life, as easily as changing the channels on television. My mom just kept saying it was like she was caught in one of those movies I made her watch at Christmastime, like it was someone else's life entirely. We would talk for hours on the phone every night on this subject, detailing the ways that, with every interaction we had with someone else about my tumor, our lives became incrementally more unrecognizable. More pity. More distance between the life we knew and the unknown.

It's a little like getting on a flight to a far away place. The passengers upon boarding are fresh-faced and tidy on a bright morning. You land, not just transported but entirely transformed, sweaty and confused. You arrive in the darkness in a land you don't recognize and don't understand the language. All you have is what you've packed in a battered suitcase; none of the clothes you have are appropriate for the weather. You find yourself slowly acclimating to your new setting through the kindness of strangers and the slightest metaphors you abstract from things that appear similar to those from home. Eventually you forget where home is.

I live here now, I imagine as I wait for my professor to pick up his coffee at the bar.

Random Thoughts from a Dad | Paul Markunas

Caroline writes so well about her life BT and AT (before tumor and after tumor).

I have been getting to know our daughter more and more these past months AT.

I'm sure every loving (key word: *loving*) parent can empathize with what we feel as parents living with our daughter and her family while she has a terminal diagnosis.

She wrote about the "unspeakable" the other day. Well, that exists for us, too, as parents.

Every little odd cough, skin color change, bags under her eyes, a memory lapse—they all remind us that she was diagnosed with fucking terminal brain cancer.

As her parents, we worry. We hope that cough is nothing. We wonder if there's something we can do.

But, you know, we're doing all and everything we can.

We are loving her, her children and her husband.

We are encouraging healthy changes in her life that we think (and what do we know?) will enhance her chances at survival.

So I get back to my post about the bigger picture.

A little background.

Glad and I had been ready for a change.

We tried with Scottsdale, but it never felt right. Too many old people walking around the grocery store with walkers and complaining about everything.

We didn't want to move to Seattle...the weather can be trying. But it seemed to be Caroline's dream. She got brain cancer. Took us all by surprise. But I immediately knew that my uncertainty about my life over the past two years was coming to a close. She was my purpose, our purpose, and those boys and Garth would be my life and my job.

Ok, she's lucky and we're lucky. They are lucky (the boys and Garth.)

But, there may not be a bigger picture. This may be (and I suspect it is) all that there is.

A wonderful loving life together with the family that we choose to embrace and hang with. What could be better? Could you envision a better day?

So, from now on, I'm going to do my best to accept what is and EMBRACE IT.

I think that's the secret to a happy life. Terminal cancer or not, we are ecstatic.

My Kind of Love | Caroline Wright

I have always been a person who falls in love easily, quickly and loyally. My sleeping-alongside kind of love was stolen years ago by this handsome husband of mine, but that doesn't stop me from falling in friend-love all the time. Or just acquaintance love. Or plane companion love. Being open and truly grateful and present to those who reflect those same qualities onto me. I fall hard every time, my step a little lighter from being embraced by the universe again and again.

This is why I—not kidding—have to tell the kind nurses whose names and faces I know not to talk to me when I am having my blood pressure taken. Because engaging with people actually makes me a little giddy, and so skews my results.

And it's not like I universally like "people." Some people aren't inherently nice or aware of their presence as a human and, to me, they just don't exist. I tend to see—and fall for— the kind ones. And there are plenty of those people around, I've learned. Even if our moment together is quick, it has changed my day. And I let it, because that's one beautiful thing that love does.

I've only met one other person who I've suspected to share this quality of mine: Heather, one of my few new friends in the "healer" category. She helps me to experience reiki energy and she has been my summer restorative yoga teacher while dear Jodi is away being beautiful and inspiring to other people. Heather is by no means an understudy; she is incredible and fascinating and I have a thousand things I could say about her. But the one most striking thing, I think, is that she is a beautiful, grounded soul who quite literally bounces and grins broadly every time I see her and has since the moment we met. And I don't feel special in this—I recognize our likeness in this way, this unbridled joy for the goodness of humanity and the beauty in a moment's ability to brush up against the exposed bits of being human with someone else.

So, after our last restorative session, I asked her how she can be a profoundly spiritual person, a grounded person, but also still so giving of herself, so effervescent. Mostly because everyone I've been close to since my diagnosis has talked about energy as being in a savings account or piggy bank or whatever chosen miserly metaphor, and that you have to, as this patient-person, protect your energy supply. I have taken this advice very seriously—in fact, I've even made myself feel as though it was my *fault* for getting cancer because of my lifelong disregard for my sacred love and energy "funds"—and made changes. I swear by restorative yoga, my meditations and gentle yoga class because they make me pause and refill my bank. And part of me felt a little repentant about it, like I was trying to repair a lifetime of damaging behavior.

Then Heather made it all make sense, so generously, so openly, so quickly with a love I recognize well. She said that, through her energy work and her practice of reiki in particular, she figured out that energy is everywhere. It flows through you and is given to someone else in the capacity that they give it to you. So the energy is not yours, it is not stuffed in a jar and parsed out in pennies. It is all around us, it connects us and shines like a light through us as beings.

The important component, she offered, is to give energy without being chaotic about it. To keep rooted in your sense of yourself while being giddy. To listen to your body and give it time to rest if it asks.

It all made sense through this gift of hers, and through her love I found a renewed gratitude for my own. My kind of love—big, boundless and *radiant*—is not in opposition to my health or energy. In fact, it is something that feeds me as a person. My kind of love emits and mirrors the love that is already around me; I am merely a channel for its reflection.

So, with feet firmly on the ground and with an open, silly heart, I am me. Not a patient-person with a piggy bank.

A New Era | Paul Markunas

I packed a 12' Budget Truck today at our new home in Scottsdale, AZ, which is now under contract and will close next week. We never slept a night in it after renovating it for the past six months. The last of our personal possessions we haven't sold are in that truck. It *all* fit in that truck.

The rest, all the artwork, the furniture, the antiques, the porcelain, the silver, all my clocks, have been purchased by our home buyers, gone to auction, or donated to good causes. Beautiful things that were fun to collect and see everyday to remind of travel, or research, or just a whim.

So it comes down to this one truck full of kitchen wares, dishes, our clothing, shoes, a few pair of cowboy boots for Santa Fe, and a few choice pieces of art.

And we know that this will be enough.

I told Caroline and Glad and Garth this morning, that this is the beginning of our final era—I turn sixty in two weeks—and that is the end of our collecting and acquiring so much stuff.

As hard as this year has been (and it has been our *annus horribilis* as our reigning Monarch coined several years ago after her home at Windsor Castle burned) it has also been filled with some of the best moments of our lives. Really.

We have had the joy of seeing our two grandboys nearly every day. Good days and bad ones.

We have gotten to know Garth in a truer, better, more accepting and ongoing way, like an old friend instead of a new one. And we have been there for Caroline in a way we never were able to be before. For the bad news, the little bits of good news, but more for the everyday help and care we can give to allow her to live more freely and focus on her health and recovery. We treasure her company and the loving space she always creates.

In a way, it's a first for Glad and me. We have never felt so fully loving and loved, engaged and exhausted at the same time by being a part of a bigger family on a day to day basis.

We welcome this new, and likely final, era with an open heart and open arms.

We are going to get through each day together and enjoy what this new era brings. Really enjoy.

Orcas | Caroline Wright

We left for a weekend away on Orcas not entirely sure how
we would get there. I was paranoid that my health was
deteriorating because I had been a little foggy for days and
was nauseated the day before we left.

Upon boarding the ferry, I was bundled in fleece and
clutching my paper cup of green tea, silent with worry. We
board and, after the boat's launch, assume a spot along the
rail of the boat's bow. The boat crawls into a thick, soupy fog
and I stare out into the mist. I feel bad for myself, which I
never allow myself to do.

With Garth's arms wrapped around me and staring
into a blanket of cloud, words (mostly clichés) fill my head.
An awareness of being me right now, held by Garth and
motoring steadily into the unknown, while also wondering all
the things I wonder when I feel a new symptom, sweeps over
me. My tea gets cold and very bitter as we stand there, but I
drink it anyway.

And then I look down at the water softly crashing into the
body of the boat. Because of the mist and thick fog, a rainbow
has formed in an arc around the bow, encircling the front of
the boat like a shield. It feels beautiful and protective and
hopeful all at once. I point it out to Garth and he sees it, too.

This breaks our silence and my worry in a way and Garth gets me talking about the books I'm working on right now. I wake up, chatting about new ideas and collaboration. I talk through my laughter the way I do when I really get going.

Then I am interrupted by the parting of the fog (and so our rainbow force field, too) to reveal what I can only describe as paradise. A collection of islands floating in bright blue glacial waters, as if the rocky coasts thick with evergreens are anxious to meet the crystal blue pool below by the way they stand directly out of the sea. It feels fantastic, like I've finally arrived in Neverland.

The boat paused at its first stop and we spot our nearby neighbor in Fremont, a connection that felt lifetimes away at that moment but with the loving, familiar grasp of home. He came to the ferry dock just wave hello as our boat passes. I am struck by this welcome then as I am still.

We arrive at our dock as a pair of wild-eyed explorers, the roles we reserve only for foreign countries. We take a bus to a meeting spot where our enthusiastic neighbor-ambassador from the previous dock has told his mother to meet us. And so we find Marie, an artist with grey hair and a frazzled, friendly demeanor that reminds me, once again, of a version of myself I hope to meet someday. She recommends that we buy some peaches at the store before we drive up the mountain. (I do, and they were the best I've ever had. I spent the weekend slurping each tender bite.)

We wind our way to her home, a place whose beauty is both humble and grandiose as if it has existed there since the towering trees were only saplings but coyly shows its age through its modern design. It was a place she dreamed of and communicated—simply, she insisted—to her architect son who had it built for her.

Again, I was struck with the poetry of this stranger's life and fortune of her age and her dear family and we had only just met. I kept thinking of her other son, the one I was still just getting to know as my neighbor and the father of a beautiful family of two boys just a few blocks away from mine, and how this beauty and fortune of theirs seems to be in their blood. *I hope it is in mine*, I thought. Actually, I know it is, I see it every day in my boys' dirty fingernails or their kisses that sometimes taste like peanut butter or on each breakfast plate my dad hands me in the morning or on a walk with my mom. *It's in my cozy yellow house, too,* I think as I wander around the house on top of a mountain on an island in Neverland.

My life, this life, is so astoundingly breathtaking. The love, the beauty, the fortune, the connection. Other than a truly memorable weekend with the finest adventure companions, Orcas gifted me the reminder of the immeasurable beauty I live amongst every day. Grand and humble, like Marie's house. Filled with awe and gratitude, like the hopeful adventurers with love by their side. And venturing into a foggy unknown, like the ferry, protected by a rainbow that cuts through the mist.

Love for Henry | Caroline Wright

One night recently, Henry, bundled and damp after a bath, joins me on our couch in the basement. He stops jumping on the couch to cuddle like he always has with me, nestled in the crook of my arm. He is gangly now and overflows his sacred nook.

Me: I love you so much. Did you know that? You are so much of my heart.

Henry: *[He grins, raises his eyebrows and widens his eyes.]* That's silly! I'm not inside your body!

Me: Nope, my love for you is so much bigger than my body.

Henry: Bigger than this house? Bigger than the whole world?

Me: Yes. Bigger than infinity. *[I smile and hug him.]*

Henry: It lasts forever. *[He nods confidently.]*

Me: Yep. Forever. Now give me a kiss. *[He does.]*

Henry: *[He pauses.]* My extra special secret kiss for you is in my heart.

Me: Mine, too. Always.

Then Theodore enters, wearing only a diaper, playing a kaleidoscope like a trombone. I love these boys infinity and will keep kisses in my heart for them forever. I will wrangle them for gangly cuddles as long as I am able, hopefully for well after they outgrow their precious cozy nooks.

Getting Ready | Caroline Wright

I Google brain cancer—makes sense, *la cancer du cerveau*.
Cerveau, oh right, and I am reminded of peeling membranes
from tiny veals' brains as a stream of cold water runs over
my fingers in the kitchen of my culinary school in *Bourgogne*.
How could I forget?, the then vegetarian who still lives inside
me asks with a smile.

Next, "anti-inflammatory," also easy. *Anti-inflammatoire*.
Then "gluten-free," the obvious *sans gluten*. "Glioblastoma," the
clincher, is the softer *glioblastome*. Someone inside me rolls her
eyes with Jonas, who has always reveled in the fact that so many
words between our languages are the same, especially those
that seem like they would be the most intimidating.

And so I am readying myself for our big trip, the trip
to France for my dad's 60th birthday, the meeting of uncle
Jonas and aunt Eglantine and the cousins in Nice for our
family visit. I have been working off of lists, both on paper
and in my head, of things I hoped not to forget for the boys
as I've always done for them. Now I do the same for me, too—
mentally packing all of these extra bags of pills and predicting
logistical solutions for differences to my finely tuned routine.

We are resting in Paris for a few days on either side of our
stay in Nice. The trip has been planned for over a year, and

the idea was always (as is always the idea when I am lucky enough to be anywhere near Paris) to visit old friends and familiar haunts from college. My parents have since changed their plans once again to join me in Paris so they can help me travel with the kids and see a bit of the fair city, too. I have plans to spend time with Amy, my college professor, and a few other friends who are living abroad.

I have been imagining what it will be like, going to the place where my love of food and cooking really began and not being able to eat my memories this time. Without gluten, sugar, pork or potatoes, Paris is going to become a very different place to me now. I am preparing to have to befriend the wait staff to explain my dietary restrictions as best as I can. I am also preparing myself to have to look at their sad faces and have the same strange conversations I have been having for months now, just in a different language and in a place that used to be home.

Present in Paris | Caroline Wright

Ah, Theodore. The living stereotype of the second child in so many ways. Henry didn't eat chocolate until he was almost two (his first was in Paris, actually). He didn't watch TV at all until after the age of two, either. We read French books to him every night and at the equivalent age to Theodore right now he had a handful of French words with a perfect accent. Theodore doesn't speak at all yet, only succeeding in making his thoughts known by an adroit use of grunts, pointing, nodding and the occasional "word" that lacks consonants. His relationship to sugar is so banal that he had a *chausson aux pommes* the other day that he actually didn't prefer, as evidenced by his single bite. Henry would have gobbled it up, starved of its sweetness.

Their differences of their first trips to Paris are probably the most striking example of this commentary on birth order. Henry was catered to endlessly—he napped only in cribs or beds—so we didn't manage to do very much exploring during that trip as not to disrupt him. Theodore has been passing out gratefully in a stroller, mid-bite into a hunk of baguette. Henry's trip was documented by a very expensive photographer that I arranged six months in advance. Theodore's moments are being captured by the quick-draw of an iPhone.

I contemplated guilt over these differences, especially because, as a second child myself, I make a very concerted effort to document their lives similarly so they each have their own childhood souvenirs. But then I realized, while passing a scene where Garth, Henry and I paused for photos, that this time I get to spend time and energy with Theodore in those places. He's experienced five or so rides at the carnival at the Tuileries, while Henry only posed for photos nearby to it. And he gets to wear a shirt stained with the day's food while doing so. I am pretty sure that this makes his Paris better for him so far. No posing for the future or an image on a Christmas card. Being here and now with nothing to prove, just the joy of the experience.

This same shift—presence over posing—has occurred in me, too. I find myself fighting the instinct to compose square-shaped photos for display on Instagram, even though I haven't had (or missed) an active account since shortly after my diagnosis. Now I just eat the *mirabelles* straight from the sack without pause for proof—the prettiest ones taste the same as the blemished ones. I see beauty everywhere and get to hold it inside me, let it churn and fuel the cogs of my creativity in my mind without the attempt to ask for permission from strangers first. I don't care what it means to be a food professional, if that's what I still am, in Paris anymore. I like being a writer here, though. Experiencing, eating and thinking but not processing or producing what it symbolizes—to me or anyone else—at the forefront.

It brings me to Paris, truly, possibly for the first time since I moved here for college. It not only brings me to be here alongside my boys, but also to be like them in a way. To experience Paris and its joy and beauty with an open mind. Being surprised by new things I've never seen before because I was always in search of a symbol.

I am so happy to be here right now, being changed and, in turn, letting Paris change me.

My Birthday | Paul Markunas

Today I begin my seventh decade of life.

The lovely dinner we all had together last night in a small outdoor cafe in Nice—four children under 5, two married couples all in their thirties, and Glad and me as the elders in the group—gave me the best gift I could ever ask for: a loving family together, happy, grateful, and for the moment, healthy.

We are among the lucky ones, to be sure. To be able to be together and know what that family love looks and feels like is truly a gift. We are all grateful for this day and for the moments we all have together.

My wish for my birthday is that those moments go on for a very long time. I have a feeling they will. *Bonne anniversaire vraiment.*

Thoughts in Nice | Caroline Wright

I've taken a few days to spend time with my family, to celebrate my dad and brother Jonas and his family, to vacate. We leave tomorrow for Paris. I am sad to say goodbye to brother Jonas and his beautiful family. Our family.

My mind is good at floating around. Here are a few places my thoughts have landed while in Nice—

....

Every night since we arrived here, we have eaten in the same restaurant in favor of its sequestered location (to contain our four little boys, including the cousins) and general understanding of my diet (though I was truly shocked to learn that their sauces were thickened by a bit of flour, instead of just butter, *comme il faut*). We have reservations there tonight and I am growing tired of sautéed carrots.

....

My boys are obsessed with *mirabelles* and *fraises des bois*, my two favorite indicators of summer in France. They will always have that like I do.

....

For the short time I was in Paris, I had in-depth conversations about the writings of William Blake and Marguerite Duras. I realized how much I miss that, and how literature and art is so intertwined with my life in Paris. It gives me a part of me that I love very much.

....

Zero French people have approached me to discuss my bald head. Over an exceptional dinner, Amy explained that the French would absolutely not imagine approaching a stranger about their illness as an effort to fiercely protect their privacy, that it would be very rude to do so. So far, she has been correct. The only two mentions of it have been by an American tourist who leaned over from the table next to ours at dinner, and from the stewardess on our flight over in the enforced darkness of a fake night's sleep. It has been all smiles and averted stares over here and, as a result, a true vacation for me.

....

I have been thinking a lot on the idea of a *bon vivant*, the romantic ideal of a person who lives well, mostly as it relates to food. A person who drinks the finest wine and eats only properly prepared, delicious meals. In my mind, it describes maybe someone like Gertrude Stein. The descriptor has nothing to do with health or my life right now, even though I feel like I am living a beautiful, full life. My terms just involve quinoa and a little less Sancerre, I think. I wonder what Gertrude would have to say about that.

....

I have been reading Hemingway's "A Moveable Feast" as I like to when I visit Paris for a short trip. Hemingway is contagious for me, however, and a bit dangerous to read when I plan to write, as my writing style can change in favor of being choppy and overly plain with Hemingway's phrasing kicking about in my head.

But I especially like his portrait of being a writer in bygone Paris and his idea of starting his writing with one true sentence. I try to do that in my own (verbose, rambling, poorly punctuated) way. I like having things in common with Hemingway while I'm in Paris, I guess. So there's that.

My Narrative of Paris | Caroline Wright

Tomorrow is our last day in Paris. Garth has already left, needing to return to work tomorrow as I cling to every last moment I can in this city.

Paris has always been a place of "becoming" for me, a growth-into, a transition-through-transformation setting. In Paris, I have found and rewritten myself over and over—

It is where I moved at the age of eighteen, my first home outside of the one I was raised in.

It's where I began to learn to read and write the truth. It's where I learned to think for myself.

It's where I met Garth and fell in love. More than once.

It's where I began to taste food starting with their ingredients and collect my vocabulary of flavors.

I've come here to write. To cry. To walk and think. To drink wine, to read, to hug loved ones. To find comfort, or find it or I changed instead.

I always had a dream of living here as a grown woman having become the version of myself that Paris had started. I wanted to live here for years with my children to help them see the world Paris had given me, and hoped that Paris would show them more of their world, too. In Paris, there is a healthy version of me without cancer and without the tether of hospital or doctors.

It makes sense, this craving to stay in the place where I was first found in so many ways.

I recently had lunch with my thesis advisor, whose brilliance is unparalleled in my life. Swimming in his waters for a moment again reminded me of being twenty-one and surprisingly the same as I am now. He said the same without prompting, which felt good to hear.

Perhaps I am satisfied most of the time and can forget my deep longing for Paris because my best friend from college, Amy, lives here. She provides a touchstone for my visits, but just her being here—the very idea of it—calms me. In many ways, her choices are mine if I had stayed, but better because she is endlessly more glamorous than I. She had the daughter I won't after two boys; she finds time to read books I probably won't, either. She floats between English and French easily, saving French mostly for arguments and insults and loving asides to her dashing French husband because theirs are the best words to express passion. I agree and imagine I would do the same.

She holds this space, this transitional space, until I am ready to claim it again. There is always hope, as I well know, and always Paris. Those are constants in my life, and in the best parts of my dreams, they marry.

Maybe that is what draws me to the city in the first place—that it shifts form, changing to suit my needs every time I greet it. We, together, become. It is intimate and foreign all at once, which I think is an apt descriptor of the inner life of an expatriate. Or a stable cancer patient, actually.

And so we become again.

I have been told by many healer-types that I have a tendency toward floating away, that my cerebral nature can take over and leave me with a lack of groundedness in my energy and in my life in general. I have had to teach myself how to remain earthbound, how to listen, how to breathe and stay present. Perhaps this is another reason why Paris feels like home—it is old-fashioned, heady and largely oblivious to the world in which it finds itself. Here, time stands still, conversations linger and swirl in ashy cigarettes. The tension between current style and dedication to tradition creates a vibrant, confusing landscape that holds you while pushing you away.

Actually, that's not a bad descriptor of my relationship to cancer, either.

Paris, *je t'aime.* Thank you for embracing me once again and giving me even more language of hope. *À la prochaine.*

The Symptom of Sadness | Caroline Wright

One of the very hardest parts about having cancer, I think, is something that hides and scars deeper than the illness itself and is indeed more infectious: mental health. Morale. There comes a point when the moment of being a patient, being a sum of symptoms that are managed by a host of chemicals, expands the distance between the you that is recognizable (the one that both motivates and enacts the fighting) and the you that you greet in the mirror or in your mind and that is accounted for by knowledgeable strangers. It makes fighting feel impossible.

I have had these days. I expect them to be ahead, too. The problem is that once the passage into darkness has occurred and becomes familiar, it is so hard to find the way out. And alone and in the dark is not a place to fight a strange battle against the worst parts of your own body, a battle that is harder than any version of you might have ever imagined. The darkness is contagious and deep. I find that avoidance of it through maintenance and a constant, honest dialogue with my inner self is the best way to keep away, sure—but cancer by definition is unpredictable and out of control. The stakes are so high and the sadness isn't too far beneath the surface, so a dip in the rollercoaster can derail the whole thing.

I've found an antidote that pulls me out of the sadness, however. And I recognize that my relative good fortune is a huge, invisible part of my solution, that my energy and outward health has been largely unaffected by my treatment. *(Or is that a product of the fact that I have put mental health in primary focus the whole time? I really don't know.)* Having cancer and feeling sick have been two disparate paths that have only crossed a few times, though can meet in my mind in the very symptom of sadness I am writing about now. It is a very real, very daily struggle and everything I do is in service of avoiding it.

The only thing that helps me when I *do* find myself feeding the saddest, most fearful parts of my mind, is to find real gratitude. I know this thought could sound empty, like a platitude on the wall of a dentist's office, numb without context. But in this place where cancer lives, the smallest truths are significant and reminding myself of them on occasion really helps me. The first and truest one I cling to is being profoundly thankful for this body of mine, for its wisdom and for fighting on my behalf when I am in my own way. It is working so hard and I am so grateful that it is *mine*, that it holds my mess of bones and skin and cells that everyone seems to have taken such an interest in. For every way it has made me feel weak since my diagnosis, there are many more ways it has made me feel strong. My body has impressed me just through basic human functioning in very inhuman circumstances.

Holding this basic gratitude—I mean really holding it, like the precious object that it is and sensing its shape and weight and how it can change over time—is my solution. After that recognition, I find that others line up almost like the metaphysical pillars that they are, such as a gratitude for my husband and children and parents and community and creativity, each for their roles in my strength. None are owed to me in this place where cancer lives. None are obvious here, either.

But I am *here*, lucky me. Holding my children for another day, building Legos with them or cooking for them, none of that is owed to me in this place. I saw that in the hospital and its echo resounds when I find myself in the darkness. Holding tightly to gratitude, I've found, is the antidote to my cancer that really works.

I am here, says my heartbeat as I exhale and refill my lungs with fresh air and clear and calm my mind. *I am here.*

Tests | Paul Markunas

As we prepare for the next MRI and follow-up visit at UW this coming Tuesday, I feel compelled to write some thoughts *before* we know what that MRI shows.

Tests.

As we have all written before, we have seen the best in people from all walks of life and spheres as we have traversed this journey with Caroline and her family.

But it remains poignant to me, after reading her so beautifully expressed journal post "The Symptom of Sadness" the other day, that "tests" are what really define us as a group of people, as a family and as individuals.

It is the tests we face in life that define us. To paraphrase a 19th century political writer, "tolerance is meaningless unless practiced by a fervent believer," so, too, talk about healing and change and cancer is meaningless without the practice of changing one's attitudes, habits and actions to make the most of the available medical remedies and to augment them with psycho-spiritual-physical force of action. This is what Caroline has done.

In other words, she writes a lot. She talks a lot. But she also has reorganized and changed her life in ways which I cannot begin to recognize the old Caroline BT (before tumor).

Without concrete evidence of predetermined success, she has stepped up her game to attack the cancer, to save her life, to save her family's life, all while living in the unknown.

These are the tests that determine who we really are.

I don't know where this really comes from. In religion, everyone ascribes a feeling of hopelessness to giving oneself over to one's faith. But this is more profound than that. In Caroline's case, her initial diagnosis of terminal cancer and 18 months to live only hardened her joyous resolve to get on with living and meet her adversary head-on.

It's not what we are given, but how we respond to what we are given that defines us. Tests. These wonderful tests are the things we'll remember.

So, regardless of MRI results on Tuesday, there is no more bad, sad, or devastating news to tell. Caroline has brain cancer. That we know. And we know how she'll meet the news she's given this week.

And aren't we lucky to be a part of it all.

Roles | Caroline Wright

The roles we play and how we are cast in them is something I think about a lot from here.

I stare at my dad sometimes, this man who comes over at 7 am to spend a cool twelve hours in service of me and his grandsons doing things that exhaust him and often frustrate him, things he never asked to spend his days doing. He is our savior, without question, and his daily selflessness is humbling and incredible.

I can't believe that this man has adversaries, much less ones who have known him his whole life. Then I realize, it's because he's not this person to them—he not only might not behave this way in their lives, but there also isn't space for him to do so because of the role he plays in their narrative. This is true of my brother, too. Yet we all know that no one person can be reduced to a tagline or just one adjective, right? I mean, that's something that feels offensive when it happens to any of us, right? There are colors, nuance and motivations to our choices that no one else sees. Yet we all act like we know everything about someone in order to be able to characterize them, when we know so little about them, maybe nothing at all.

So, these roles are cast rather than earned, then. They are more about the person casting them than the subject itself, because it is being ascribed without their input. More than condemning this behavior—it is human nature and, further, how society functions after all—the more interesting question is *what is it about me that needs this person to play that role?*

I need my dad to be my savior. It gives me control and comfort in some way, specifically in the way that my doctors cannot. It grounds me in the love I've recognized my whole life and it is an important part of what makes this circumstance of ours feel powerful rather than destructive. This means I don't acknowledge his experience of a suffering father on a regular basis, however. That's how the role thing works.

I constantly consider the role I am playing to other people—some are comfortable to me, others are not (and that is telling, too). But they have to do with what that person needs me to be in order to feel comfortable or safe in their own choices, not the me that I know or hold true to my heart. To some, I am a tragedy—a young mother facing a terrible fate with a full life of possibly jilted possibilities. To others, I am a beacon of hope. I am more likely neither or both or something else entirely. I am human.

I spoke about this dynamic with my thesis advisor in Paris and he told me of a class he taught recently. He wanted to play with this idea of how a person's representation of another is delicate and can create a narrative of its own—he didn't allow any student to speak for themselves in class.

He only allowed students to convey their commentary on the assigned reading through someone else, to tell someone their thoughts then have those thoughts relayed. He said that it was rare that the person's thoughts were ever felt to be represented clearly, which didn't surprise me at all.

I thought about this a lot in the first few days of our stay in Paris and Nice as my mind translated English phrases to spit out in French, what thoughts felt possible to express and the others that emerged as approximations or generalizations as a result of my language limitations.

Maybe every interaction is in some way a translation, a way of taking another's experience and filtering it through one's emotional language to then emerge something different entirely, like these roles we are asked to play.

In most cases, this just feels like an unfortunate truth, an acknowledgement of how social constructs form and function in contrast to the inner life of an individual. There is a lot of space in between that no one acknowledges or can even see.

This writing, though, feels like it inhabits that space quite comfortably and so gives me a secret passage to define my own role in terms of my cancer. Here I am able to show so many parts of my heart and mind that wouldn't be able to be expressed—or, alternatively, perceived—in daily life through action. This writing gives my boys a picture of the human that is their mother, and by writing it, my humanity, not my illness, is reinforced.

I am a lot of things and so are you. Thank you for bringing the kindest, strongest ones here as my readers, my support, my community. I become stronger and kinder in the space that this love provides me, and it is translated back to my body as a source of strength I use to fight.

I feel powerful because you make me so.

7 ——— THE GIFT OF HOPE

*All the darkness in the world
can't put out the light of one candle.*

—Confucius

AUGUST 29, 2017

Good News | Garth Wright

Today we went to the doctor for Caroline's 6 month MRI:

- Caroline's blood work continues to be great
- She is tolerating the maximum dose of chemotherapy very well
- Her MRI scan is CLEAN
- Her tumor resection cavity remains as big and the edges of enhancement have decreased

This very good news comes right before Caroline starts her next round (3 of 12) at the maximum dose of chemotherapy on September 4. She is doing so well that we no longer need to see the doctor monthly; her next visit is in 3 months for the next MRI.

What Celebration Looks Like | Caroline Wright

After our incredible appointment with the affirmation of the success of my recent MRI scan results from Dr. Taylor, Garth and my dad were asking me how I wanted to celebrate. We all exclaimed ideas as we spilled inside our yellow house. However, the two boys downstairs in the basement were becoming more feral by the minute (it was dinnertime after all), so I heated the black bean soup I had thawed for dinner tonight. I had pulled it from our freezer before our big day began, before I knew we would have something to celebrate.

I went outside as a rosy gold light spread across the sky and snipped some greens from our raised beds in the front yard, those made for us by our neighbors. I waved excitedly to my dad who was then pulling away in his car. I beamed at him as I wagged my hand back and forth. I could tell from the top of our hill that he was choked up as he drove away.

Inside, the boys had become terrors during my brief aside in the garden. I sling bowls of beans and quinoa at them and we huddle around our kitchen table. *Do I tell them about our day, my news?*, I wonder. I ask Henry if he knew where I was that day.

"The doctor," he replies in between shoveling bites into his mouth. I notice he has a hint of face paint on his cheeks left over from school.

"Yep! Do you have any questions about the visit?" I ask my boy who is more focused on earning a dessert than anything I could possibly have to say to him. He pauses briefly to search my face and in that moment I realize it doesn't matter. Looking at his face, past the dirt smudges that suggest a successful day for an almost five-year-old, I saw that to him I am already forever and as alive as I will ever be. The notion of future lies somewhere after dessert and before his birthday in two weeks. That feels closer to my idea of time right now, too.

I felt like jumping on the table and screaming with joy. Instead I ate black beans that tasted like cold winters in Brooklyn sitting on the floor of our best friends' apartment, while Henry sprawled his dirty feet across my lap. In that moment, they felt like the same thing.

After our bowls are scratched clean of every last spoonful, we chase each other downstairs. I give Henry a bath, then crank some obnoxious music that Henry and I jump around to. He shouts at Alexa, our resident robot courtesy of Amazon, to play the song "Firework" by Katy Perry. (Garth and I joke that we hope Henry is gay to suit his music preferences; if not, his taste may be a source of shame someday. I can't scold or correct his affinity for terrible pop music because I, too, essentially have a gay spirit animal living inside me who occasionally demands such music.)

Igniiiiite the liiiight and let it shiiiiine! We twist and shake our bodies and both bellow the lyrics from somewhere deep in our bellies. *Baby, you're a fiiiirework! Come on let your colors burst!* Shake, shimmy, jump, hug. Theodore isn't sure what is happening, but bops around and clasps my thigh with a huge bean-stained grin. Then my favorite part blares from the speakers, which feels strangely poetic, and we belt it at the top of our lungs while Henry strikes a naked pose. We shout: *maybe the reason why / all the doors are closed / so you could open one / that leads you to the perfect road. / Like a lightning bolt / your heart will glow / and when it's time, you know / you just gotta Igniiiiite a liiiight and leeet it shiiine...*

The crescendo builds, our voices can't hold our volume or excitement. We fall to the floor, kicking like bugs, singing in cracked tone our joyful, silly song.

It was the perfect way to celebrate our beautiful news— with a night like so many others before it, comfortable and wild at the center of our menagerie, squirming on the floor with my lion-hearted boys. A celebration of the beauty of our normal lives together as a family, made different now in the light of the consuming belief that I will be here dancing and singing with them for a long time.

And just like that, with laughter resounding in the basement as the chorus, the key changed from "what ifs" to "could be's."

"I have a talisman I want to show you..."
Paul Markunas

That's what Caroline's head chemo doctor said when she walked into the room after seeing her six month MRI.

She was smiling and flat-out said that this MRI looked better than the last one 3 months ago. She is a very experienced, capable doctor, head of Chemotherapy at UW after a distinguished career in Boston and at Virginia Mason, and she is head of the Tumor Board at UW which reviews pathology weekly to recommend diagnoses.

So after breaking the good news that Caroline appeared to be "cancer free," (at least in this MRI) she brought out the talisman and told the story of her longest glioblastoma survivor, now 19 years. The talisman was a photograph of a young man at the summit of Mount Rainier, arms extended and upright in victory: he had scaled the summit two years after glioblastoma surgery and the subsequent radiation and chemotherapy protocol.

Dr. Taylor explained that, of all her glioblastoma patients over her long and impressive career, his success stood alone. She remained in contact with him over the years, even attending his wedding some years after surgery and treatment.

She went on to say the she saw similarities to Caroline's situation: age at diagnosis, size and shape and construct of the tumor and good results from the initial surgery and removal. She hesitated to use the word, but admitted that, after 19 years of continued life, she would have to say he was "cured" of his glioblastoma brain cancer.

She hoped Caroline would beat his record.

As much as we are thrilled with the clean MRI and the optimistic comparison to a singularly unique glioblastoma, this comparison also pointed out how uniquely and perhaps miraculously Caroline's treatment and success up to this point is. It does not, however, allow any of us to become complacent, let our guard down, change these new and successful habits which are clearly documented showing the increase in success of patients who treat their cancer in a mind-body-spiritual context and not merely as a physical disease.

Most importantly, Caroline's cancer has permanently changed many lives and brought a new perspective to the way we all live and the way we all view life.

More about that later, but for now, we are all committed to continuing to beat all the odds. Caroline has, in our minds, already scaled Mount Rainier. On to Everest and beyond.

What Changes Now | Caroline Wright

Fueled by the optimism of my last MRI, I have been floating and thinking the past few days. Everyone greets me with relief, mirroring mine.

What Dr. Taylor's talisman changed for me was everything and nothing all at once. It changed everything in the sense that the secret whisper of a doubtful voice in my head, the one that chatted to me as I folded Henry's clothes to wonder if I would see Theodore fill them, the very one that made me feel as though I had to start and finish a quilt for Theodore immediately so he would have one just like Henry's and so know that I loved him just as much if I died, is less powerful. I now feel like I will live long enough for Theodore to remember me, which is the biggest gift I could have ever imagined. The doubtful voice, the one I didn't trust before, is quieter now. I ask it to stay now to keep me company and help me remain present.

What the talisman did not change is the protection of my health and routine, my mortality, or the fact that I had a very deadly cancer with a high recurrence rate. My doctor's encouragement isn't a guarantee by any means—there is a lot of time between now and the nineteen years her other patient earned. That's his story and this is mine.

If anything, I am more fiercely committed to my routine and listening to my body because it's been working so far.

It is tempting to feel safe now, to look for bows to tie around the package that is my cancer. The truth from before, the scary one I faced daily then, I still face now—I live in an uncertain place. We all do, really, but I will always have to look over my shoulder and remain a little bit superstitious. It feels disrespectful of the learning I've found within myself and lived since my diagnosis to choose complacency or the illusion of immortality now.

The possibility of time, an idea that had been hidden from me since the discovery of my glioblastoma, is humbling and so hard to let in after what we have all been through. *Is this what a miracle looks like? Do people involved in miracles recognize them?*

Hope is powerful fuel; Dr. Taylor's anecdote refilled my tank a few days ago. I will use it to keep fighting, keep treading this road ahead. I hope it takes me on a long and steady climb and that I always appreciate the journey as I do now.

I will only see the path clearly when I'm much further along—predictions from here will only lead me astray. And, from where I proudly stand now, the time it takes to get ahead are the very days I am fighting to live. I'm in no rush for answers or for time to pass. I'm just here, my eyes and heart wide open.

On Feldenkrais and Balance | Caroline Wright

My dear Heather, my healer and friend who I love to talk about energy with, drove me to and from my reiki practice recently. She helps me find words that describe things in my life that are instinctual and exclusively felt. Things that are truly inexplicable and, in essence, wordless.

Heather also practices Feldenkrais, which she somehow can't even explain well. She told me she was proud that her teacher gave her an explanation of it that she wrote down for me, something that felt concise and accessible. It essentially is this practice that blends movement, a little like yoga, with the student's own bodily capabilities and preferences, as determined through guidance of the practitioner and deep relaxation and spiritual integration on the part of the student. (Easy stuff, you know. And this is even if I understand what Heather is saying.)

Heather credits a combination of Feldenkrais and restorative yoga as her navigation through her own very grave health challenges, including a serious threat of paralysis on more than one occasion.

I asked her if we could practice Feldenkrais together, especially now that Jodi has returned and is available to resume her position as my restorative yoga teacher. Her face lit up, the way I'm learning it does when she has an especially joyful thought like an epiphany.

She continues to explain how interesting it is that I've responded so well to restorative yoga and reiki—they are two practices that access the central nervous system from the spiritual side, activating your parasympathetic nervous system. They work to calm the mind and allow it to relax through the support of energy in the body, accessing things like chakras and relieving places that hold tension. Heather informed me that Feldenkrais is another practice that echoes these principles, but from the point of entry of the *body* rather than the spirit—using physical movement to calm the central nervous system through confidence and a mastery of its own skills. Feldenkrais is the third piece missing from my neurological triumvirate that supports my parasympathetic nervous system.

Learning this gave me a burst of excitement, firstly in finding what felt like a secret to even more capacity for healing, but also a confirmation of the deep trust I've found in listening to my body's ability to help my brain from the inside out.

And then I realized yet another practice I was drawn to before I knew about these other things, the first one I found that accessed this same shared place of deep relaxation— ASMR. Those creepy hypnotic sound videos that I was obsessed with the sleepless week between diagnosis and surgery, remember those? That trance, as it turns out, has felt like home over and over through different practices. That trance is called the "theta state," Jodi and Heather remind me, and it's a place where your parasympathetic nervous system comes in to allow your central nervous system to rest and repair. It's the place where my brain has been working hard to heal itself and relax from the trauma it's been through. I really do believe that these practices, this space, is a very significant source of my brain's health so far.

All of these practices, this way of life of mine now, is rooted in supporting a kindness to my body, knowing that it comes from so many places but, at its center is a conversation between the active mind, the physical body and a soulful knowing.

My "active mind" is satisfied through my writing and boundless creative momentum, and the soulful knowing bit from meditation, reiki, restorative yoga and the general sense of groundedness that I cultivate in my daily life. I am thrilled to have another outlet to support the "body" component to this equation, adding to my gentle yoga class and daily walks.

As fall approaches and the distractions of summer are winding down, I look forward to this new element of learning: the study and practice of true balance. On this subject, I will remain a student forever.

Dad's thoughts post-MRI | Paul Markunas

Good news last week, to be sure, but I've been thinking about the big picture, about the last tumultuous six months and all we've all been through and have a few thoughts to share.

My gut feeling about the latest and greatest MRI results is that I do believe there is a chance that the surgeons were able to remove all of the tumor and cancer growth from Caroline's brain.

The head of chemotherapy told us that this was a rapidly growing tumor, owing to it's contained and spherical shape. The cancer cells (tumor) were attached to the mass of dead tissue the tumor had created as it ate cells in order to live. It is possible that all of the living cancer cells were removed during that initial surgery over six months ago.

However, statistics indicate that this type of cancer (glioblastoma) usually begins its aggressive re-growth about eight months after the cessation of treatment. So, for Caroline, that would mean eight months after the chemotherapy has stopped or about January of 2019. So we cannot and will not let our guard down. Diet, exercise and mental and spiritual therapies will continue for the next few years and probably long after that since these are serious lifestyle changes not just remedies for a possible killer that we believe might reemerge at any time.

So we are lucky. One-tenth of one percent lucky. This is Caroline's story and it is being written even as we spend each precious day and moment together.

That brings me to my next wave of thoughts and probably my last to be shared here for a while. What this has taught me specifically and my family more generally is:

- Enjoy each and every moment, whether alone or with others, no matter what is happening around you. Look for the reason in each moment and your need to call that moment forth to learn, to be present, to be filled with gratitude for all that we have been given.
- Find *your* family. Tell the people you love how important they are to your own well-being and how you cannot live without them. It doesn't matter who they are or how you are, or are not, related, be really with them when you are and let them know.
- Pay it forward. Not everyone is as lucky as we all have been and when we sense an opportunity to help, seize it and do something about it.
- Minimize interactions with negative, phony, or difficult people. People who can't see the truth. People who don't have a sense of the wonderment of the spirit and of life. You can't change them and they only zap your strength and steal your oh so precious time.
- Help a child. They are our future and the future of

our planet. They are our greatest source of hope and inspiration. Make it your mission to make them be all they can be in every way possible.

This, in short, is what I always believed but I know now more than ever. We are so, so grateful to be buoyed by great news and accept that Caroline will live with a diagnosis of terminal brain cancer for the rest of her life.

We know that, because of that diagnosis, each day now counts more than a hundred in the quality of time and love we share together. And, because of Caroline, we know our own little sphere of the world will be a blessed place forever.

Grateful indeed. Blessed for sure.

On Luck | Caroline Wright

I have always believed I was born under a lucky star. Really. I am one of those people whose dreams came true by the age of thirty. I'm married to the love of my life, who also happens to grow more handsome with every passing year. I have a dream job, a dream house in a dream city, and a pair of beautiful brothers I am lucky enough to call my sons.

In fact, just a few days before the phone call from my doctor about my diagnostic MRI results, I actually said to myself while folding laundry, *I love my life so much, something has to give, no one gets all they hope for. This feels like the beginning of a Lifetime movie.*

Boom.

With the explosion of that life, I strongly considered that my lifetime string of good luck had run its course. Diagnosis: cancer. Biopsy of mass reveals it's the most aggressive one. Missing the genes that would make the available therapies more effective.

From where I stand now, stable and holding a perceivably clean recent scan, it might seem as though somehow my lucky streak ordained it so and of course I would be fine. That was absolutely not the case. I don't have that kind of faith.

When thinking about the successes of my early career, I would hand it all to luck. Jeff would always point out that it wasn't a random occurrence—the element I'd failed to consider is that I work incredibly hard on what I choose to invest my focus.

I've been thinking about the roaring return of my luck—or at least my perception of it, since really nothing has changed—since Dr. Taylor's boost. I think it is mostly luck, I do. But I think that, very similarly to how I approach my work, there is magic that can occur in your favor if you are ready to throw all you have at the one tiny glimmer of an opportunity. I've been given a window and I plan to run at it with the confidence of a well-trained athlete.

It's how I got a job with Martha Stewart right out of college and culinary school out of a stack of 7,000 applicants for the same job.

It's how I launched my cookbook career despite having an agent who told me she didn't believe I could sell a cookbook before the age of forty.

I have worked very hard since my diagnosis. I've fought demons I recognized and ones I didn't. I've found love and light every day, even in the darkest corners. I look in the mirror with the genuine pride of both a teacher and student for a day's job well done.

An unspoken piece here that underlies each of my successes—in life in general, but certainly in the circumstance

I now find myself as a medical outlier—is my profound privilege. I have an education that has given me the kind of tools I need to approach my self-care with research and critical thought. My entire care team, from my doctors to my immediate family, are all highly capable, highly educated and detail-oriented. That my social connections brought me to the short list of transfers to the UW surgeons within a week of diagnosis is not luck: it's a complex system of factors that are intertwined with privileges from every stage of my life. That I even have the time to focus on self-care and suddenly find myself with motivated, compassionate and perfect care for my children is an enormous privilege. My loving family is another, one I never had before my diagnosis quite like this. I am deeply grateful for all of it—the brew of luck, hard work and privilege that has produced my current position.

I shouldn't be here by all accounts. I'm not apologizing for the fact that I am. I am humbled and grateful and feel it deep in my soul. It's up to me to make the best of it now, and I plan to.

I am running towards that window at full speed, trained and ready for it to open wide and let me squeeze through.

My Road Map | Caroline Wright

Lately I have been getting a lot of requests for tips, ideas for how I "cured" myself. For the record, I haven't cured myself. If there is even a glimmer of a chance of that, credit would belong to my doctors, likely mostly to my very capable surgeons first and then a team of very diligent specialists that followed.

That said, self-care has been a huge part of my coping and healing and I know it has helped my experience of my cancer, whether or not it was transferred to my cells.

More importantly than the *what* I did—those are extensively documented here, anyway—is the *why*. The *what*, the manifestation of my choices and the details of how I spend my days, are a direct response of my instinct and the dialogue I have with my body and mind. I think that this is critical—there are a lot of stories out there, including this one, that are largely irrelevant and distracting to someone living through their own cancer story. I think that in focusing on someone else's tools and success steals the most beautiful part of this cancer journey that we are given as patients—the opportunity to listen to our bodies and minds very silently, very humbly, and find where our own healing resides.

Here are a few general principles that I deduced over time, themes that were reinforced as important motivators to my choices. I am writing them as bits of advice to someone else battling cancer in the hopes that someone in the early, meandering and fearful stages of diagnosis could feel supported in knowing some things that help me:

First, I feel strongly that doctors should be left to do what they do best: to fight the cancer. Trust them and let them hit it hard with all they have. You, in turn, take care of what you know best: you. If you're like me an already thought you had a balanced life before your diagnosis, consider really stopping everything in your life, like a crisis shutdown. There will be things you miss from your routine and things you won't—listen to that voice.

Find every way to be gentle to your body. It is already working so hard to do what the doctors ask it to do. For me, that involves a lot of yoga, meditation and writing. It also means sleeping well, taking only the medicines that are absolutely necessary according to my doctor. Sticking to a good diet and moving my body with regular, stress-free exercise.

Seek help and conversations with people who are already living awake lives. The sources that feel valuable to you will be different than mine. Starting with practitioners who can diagnose parts of you that the doctors can't see, like a homeopath and/or an ayurvedic practitioner, is helpful. Let them help you find the changes you need.

Focus on where and how your body is strong, not weak, and nurture that source. This pertains to both emotional and physical strength. Mine is my kids and family, my motherhood and my creativity.

In terms of supporting my physical strength, I kept returning to my focus on being gentle to my body. I wasn't fit before my diagnosis—in fact, I gained a lot of weight during the period of my tumor growth. I've since lost almost thirty pounds. I feel much healthier. I believe strongly in walking, even when I didn't want to—actually, especially when I didn't want to. Even if only around the block.

Diet is hugely important to wellness, I believed before my diagnosis as a food professional but has been reinforced personally since. I have maintained a sugar-free, gluten-free, corn and potato-free, anti- inflammatory and alkaline diet full of produce and meats that have been handled with loving hands. No fried foods, no alcohol or coffee. This goes back to the "gentle" idea, too—to let your body work hard on healing itself rather than have it spend valuable energy fighting foods that anger or clutter its clarity on a very basic level. (A naturopath or nutritionist is helpful in finding the most gentle foods for your body if you don't know where to start.)

Remove yourself from toxic sources. Fighting cancer is no time to be a people-pleaser. For those that love you, those you hope to live for, it is important to put yourself first. Those that don't understand that aren't worth your energy.

Support the things in your life that make you feel like you, not a patient. Don't stop doing things that make you happy because you got sick. Letting cancer take over your life is the first step in giving up, which weakens your ability to fight.

Do not look or wait for the side effects that doctors tell you about to show up. It will make you crazy and doubtful. Just live your life as normally as you can until further notice. (That's what I did. As a result, I never noticed any symptoms.)

Get your head out of your phone or computer and be present. It is so challenging these days, but I do think it is an important factor in being able to appreciate the life worth fighting for, to see the beauty of the helpers around you, and listen to your own instincts rather than be distracted by what the world wants you to be or how to think.

There are the prompts I consider with every action I take. I hope it brings comfort to a fellow cancer journeyman.

8 _____ LIFE

GOES

ON

We think that the point is to pass the test or overcome the problem, but the truth is that things don't really get solved. They come together and they fall apart. Then they come together again and fall apart again. It's just like that. The healing comes from letting there be room for all of this to happen: room for grief, for relief, for misery, for joy.

—Pema Chödrön

Birthdays | Caroline Wright

All three men who share my home, the loves in my immediate family, all have birthdays on the 12th and 13th of September. I am now writing this having lived through a gauntlet of intense birthday cake-making and present-wrapping. I always like to say that my uterus only had control of two of the birthdays in this trio, but even I'll admit that the timing is crazy. I guess I was destined to live my life surrounded by handsome Virgos.

I actually thought of their birthday timing a lot over the past few months, thinking that it makes them a sort of close-knit trio of boys after I was gone. These are the kinds of thoughts I had when I imagined Garth pulling a frozen pizza from the oven and the two boys watching him from the kitchen table, with me and my cooking as faint memories for all of them. *They would be close,* I thought. *After all, the boys would never forget their lonely dad who raised them because his birthday is next to theirs.*

These kind of thoughts sneak in all the time, unannounced, and these birthdays were no exception. It's been an emotional couple of days for me. Not only because my little boys are growing up, but because I wasn't so sure I would be here to see it.

Theodore's birthday (shared with Garth) was just like Theodore: a mix of cuddles and insanity. As the boys, small and large, blew out their candles, I was very aware of the gift I am given to be here. *My family, all of this, came from my body. The same one that grew my tumor grew my boys first.*

....

Yesterday morning, Henry's preschool performed a beautifully symbolic ceremony that marked a rite of passage for their school—turning five years old and, so, becoming a guardian of sorts for the younger school kids. This class is called the Owls, presumably for their wisdom. Henry was made an honorary Owl last year when he suddenly shifted from attending three days a week to five because of my diagnosis and treatment. We wanted structure and community for him, and his preschool rose up to meet him (and us) in ways that can only be described as wondrous. (That actually is a characteristic throughout every thread of the school including the teachers there, especially Tara and Teresa, who I honestly consider members of our family now.) Through his school, the connection with his incredible and loving teachers especially when he needed the stability most, we in our family saw Henry transform. He became wiser indeed, regardless of his rank in the preschool forest.

Yesterday it became official, Henry the wise Owl.

Dressed in his cape and crown, I saw him as he gazed at

his peers, his friends, his community as he was inducted as belonging, as a thriving leader. In that moment I was struck with the beauty and grace of this ritual. Especially after all we had been through, my Henry and I. Heart-breaking and beautiful as it's been, we are both wiser for it. Changed forever. Stronger maybe.

As I looked out into a chorus of sweet, softly singing faces, I thought *Henry is one of them, the crowd, any other day. Today he is next to me holding my hand. He still calls me "mama" here and I wonder how long that will last. I wonder if he will ever know how much I love him. At least I have time to show him.*

Then I looked up, overwhelmed with love and gratitude and just simply being alive that tears rolled down my face.

The CBD Experiment | Caroline Wright

A while ago now, my dad and I were told about CBD—the mellow counterpart to THC in marijuana—as a form of medication to flight glioblastoma cells. Dr. Graber at Swedish mentioned that, in a petri dish setting, a dose of 200 mg of CBD oil three times a day kills glioblastoma cells. He also warned that most people can't tolerate that dose, that it makes them lethargic and drowsy.

As a treatment that could be done while I am in this stable place, the CBD regimen appealed to me. I was determined to make it work, despite the hurdles of expense (the first product I sourced was $50 per day) and possible tolerance issues.

I asked around and, to my surprise and fortune once again, found out that someone very close to my friend circle is the proprietor of an organic pot farm. And, even more, that they essentially have a naturopath advisor to consult with in terms of using marijuana as a remedy. (This may or may not be the most Seattle-y sentence I've ever encountered.)

Through this connection, I learned that the CBD dose more commonly used for cancer treatments is 1 gram per day, even more than what Dr. Graber had originally suggested. My friend-of-a-friend's farm was in the process of making their own CBD remedy oil, commonly referred to as RSO oil, but that they had products available that would work in its place until its release.

There was some speculation as to how long the course of 1 gram per day was to go on—some said one month, others three or up to six. There is also research that suggests CBD taken with Temozolomide, the type of chemo I take one week per month, can increase the efficacy of the chemo.

Sold.

My dad and I discussed what we thought to be a logical course of action given the variables we knew. We decided to go with the higher dose of 1 gram per day and the mid-length course of three months. The period we picked, to make it as data-driven as possible, is the exact space between my MRIs. I began the day after my last MRI and have been working my way up in dosage since.

I am at about 600 mg per day now, what Dr. Graber had originally mentioned as the full dose. I will stay here a week or so before the next increase. Taking on this course has involved a number of odd things that I find exciting and funny. Firstly, buying gram after gram of this stuff that people use over many months in portions the size of a grain of rice and I am taking in spoonfuls, feels like I am chugging a magic potion that others only sip. Then, I have to "activate" the product—that is, bake it in a low oven for a short while to make it work—and then divide it into capsules so I have some idea of my dosage through dilution and even distribution. It's a strange mix of feeling like a mad scientist, apothecary and a punk rock rebel-patient. (And I get to preheat the oven, too!)

The wildest part of all, though, is that while I feel these high doses, yes, the feeling is similar to my experience of my seizures. The seizures were far more disorienting, though, and I still functioned (parented! drove!) in their throes. I also find it somehow relaxing to know I am taking a remedy that strongly affects my brain sensations and that whatever I feel between now and my next MRI is only due to CBD. It pushes worry of tumor growth completely off the table.

This CBD experiment is surreal and bizarre on so many levels, but empowering, too. It feels like a gift from my new progressive hometown in that it is even legally available, and a gift from my community in particular that I have such a great, trustworthy source for the product. It also makes me feel like one part Martha Stewart and one part Nancy from "Weeds," from what I remember from the few episodes I've seen. I've laughed at myself as I tossed a capsule into my mouth, *in three months of this I will have a marijuana history of a lot of the teenagers I knew when I was in high school. Bottoms up, Honor Roll Caroline. (I imagine her in Yearbook class right now.)*

I've also enjoyed that, like every other strange footing I've found myself on throughout this whole cancer marathon, I have managed to take something intimidating and unfamiliar and find a way to not only make it work, but make it my own. *This is what I would look like if I had to take weed as a medication. Huh.*

I hope to be up to the full dose of 1 gram per day by the end of the month and then stay there through the fall until my next MRI at the end of November.

Really, it's not that different than my feelings toward my experience of radiation symptoms versus the warnings I was given about them—yes, I can see how people could choose to sleep or slow down from here, but I am busier than that. I have books to write, my sweet boys to raise. And I have a living jet pack of a father to keep up with.

I've fought to be here—there is no way I am missing any moment of this full and strange life of mine now.

Listening to Silence | Caroline Wright

I actually wrote this a few weeks ago, but back-to-school and birthday-ing filled my mind with other thoughts. I had a reiki training yesterday that I experienced in many of the same terms as what I describe my first experience with Feldenkrais, shared below.

I am writing after just having completed my first Feldenkrais session with Heather. I find myself in the same place as I had after experiencing restorative yoga for the first time with Jodi, or reiki with Michael and his team. I wept after both inaugural practices and walked away from it hazy, with a deep sense of intimacy and understanding of my being that is both comforting and confusing. Today, I feel the same. I felt like crying with Heather, my gratitude so overwhelming that it is impossible to process alongside a new experience of my body as, I remind myself, a grown woman. *I want to find the words to explain it, I must. I want to remember, to harness, to hold it. Language is my way, as it always has been.*

It's venturing into a totally silent woods. Under the shadow of the canopy, I feel small as I breathe or step and am reminded of my physical space. I feel immense, too, like the singing of the nesting birds at the treetops are singing just next to me. In the silence of the woods, I am both large and small, inward and out.

In this silence, I am conscious and aware, like the fingers tracing the surface of a calm, clear pool; my body is the rippled gentle waves that follow.

Feldenkrais, like the other body and energy work I've been investing my time and healing in exploring, has changed the perception of my body and mind. It helps me remember the way I moved before my movement became complicated by age, injury and laziness. In these quiet, introspective practices, there is an element of care—both of yourself, for being there, but also on the part of the practitioner as well—that is very healing. There is a kind of intimacy that happens when laying on the ground on a mat, listening to a friend's calm voice and trusting their touch to teach you something. There you let go of thought and distraction to create an immense, quiet forest inside your brain and then walk around in it, just listening. In the woods of your mind, you are both explorer and guide, lost and found. The knowledge that this space even exists within you is empowering enough, but leading yourself there while being literally held by a loving friend is incredibly healing.

It is hard to believe that I didn't know that these practices—restorative yoga, reiki and Feldenkrais—even existed until I discovered my cancer. Each one, along with a great debt to my healers that help me in each of these practices, has helped me find true relaxation and peace. In the woods of my mind, I found the quiet my brain needed to heal and fuel its strongest parts.

I know how to relax now. It only took cancer to figure it out.

The Fall | Caroline Wright

"Dad," I say, bracing myself to utter an absolutely unbelievable set of words, "they found a mass in my brain."
I remember turning the words over as they tumbled out of
my mouth, my eyes wide and hands shaking. I had so little
information, but every fact stretched for the eternity of those
moments. Repeating, stumbling, repeating, crying, silence.

> *7 cm. Frontal lobe.*
> *Supposed to go to the hospital if...*

I have been replaying this moment a lot lately. It's amazing how
quickly my mind can bring me right back to the dark basement
that night, with a recollection so clear that I remember being
thankful that the kids were asleep, in my skin. Even now.

The strangest part of telling my parents is how ashamed
of myself I felt at the time. As if, in stating the words I called
Hawaii to repeat, I knew I was going to change their lives
forever and how sorry I was for it.

It has me thinking about the ownership of news like this,
about how each one has its own written destiny. Those who
own it give it meaning. The ones that have been occupying
me lately are ones from turning points in my story.

One scene I play over repeatedly is from my "diagnostic MRI" as I've come to call it.

I remember joking with the MRI technicians when they pulled me out of the machine to inject me with contrast dye about halfway through the test, laughing and saying, "So you mean to tell me I came in for headaches and you strap me to a jackhammer? Are these noises designed to trigger a headache so you can see something happening in my imaging?"

No chuckles or explanation. Silence, footsteps. A door closes.

After the sequencing was finished, the tech, the one I joked about the stylish backless pjs with as I was set up, returned. She told me to take a minute to sit up. My head was spinning, but I blamed the jackhammer. I sat on the table a minute, then the tech brought me my shoes, almost in a huff. I fumbled to put them on and she refused to make eye contact. She had seen the 7 cm elephant in my brain.

Not very friendly anymore, huh, I thought as I dressed and struggled to recall where I parked. Then I drove home, not knowing that the disorientation I was feeling was that I was having a seizure. The news of my tumor was not hers to share. I've come to accept that and forgive her.

To this day I really struggle with that MRI experience, but especially my memory of that tech. I remember the look on her face vividly; it was the first time I saw that look, the terror. I've seen it so many times now, with every exchange about my cancer or bald head, that is no longer something I notice.

It was the only time I saw it on the face of a medical professional, maybe. The face of Dr. Silbergeld, my surgeon who reported the tumor pathology to me, was different. He seemed more used to the subject of brain tumors, even scary ones like mine.

I didn't see it on the face of my internist because she told me over the phone. "I can't believe I have to tell you this, Caroline," she began. I may have borrowed her phrase in the next few hours as I called everyone I knew.

And now, six months later, the dynamics have completely inverted. I live in a place where sad and terrible news, the kind that destroys families and dreams, lives too. The place where Dr. Silbergeld visits often enough to have been so nonchalant about the pathology. In this place, good, life-affirming news is so rare that Dr. Taylor, the most senior doctor on my team whose career is older (and far more lauded!) than I am, had a twinkle in her eye as she left to fetch her omen to show me.

She only had one that looked like mine, and that guy is still alive.

These moments I replay, the exchange of language and information, have magic to them. They are held, suspended in some colorless preservative, frozen and volatile at once. Thinking about them is as if to peer over a vortex—lean over for a closer look and I'll fall.

Heirloom | Caroline Wright

There was this period where every time I saw my mom she would give me something precious, the kinds of things that she saved for me for some future occasion. I bet she didn't imagine giving me her beautiful opal ring I've always loved of hers at Jonas' birthday dinner lumped in with a stack of manila folders of ancestry information for me to look over, or her beautiful jade bracelet while standing up in my kitchen.

I have now been given my lifetime's worth of trinkets and symbols already. I guess that's something that happens when your daughter is dying. These objects, stuffed from a diet of tradition and hope and both the promise and memory of time, hollow out. In a way they are more beautiful, new again, with the timeline and its expectations lifted.

When the natural order of things is disrupted, the meaning of everything changes. The disruptive stone that is cast causes seemingly infinite ripples.

This is part of the reason why that we, in our family, have sighed with relief after the most recent scan, but there isn't a return home, a return to a familiar place. There isn't such a thing as "normal" anymore. The tokens and symbols here aren't worn at parties.

The idea of an heirloom now, from this place where motherhood and sentimentality have taken on a new hue, are things that hold love over beauty. Over the past six months, I have been consumed with creating spaces for my children to experience their mother that they barely know.

I spent hours recording my thoughts on a variety of subjects, conversations I hoped I would have with them over years as their mother, like what happens after getting their first bad grade or what to do in the face of a bully. Adair and I spent hours recording my thoughts on topics I would draw from a jar so my boys would have an idea of their mother aside from her cancer.

I spend my days writing—here, as well as my children's book projects—motivated by the same factors.

Meanwhile, my parents sold or gave away every belonging they've ever had to move to the smaller urban scale of our Fremont neighborhood, so they can be in walking distance of our house. Belongings I thought I would want to display in my house or wear proudly one day, gone. Heirlooms hollowed of their hope, unloaded onto strangers and released of their expectations.

From here, the only heirloom worth passing along is love. In some ways, I guess love is the hope that belies both parenting and legacy, the idea that a loved one will find meaning and value in something you built for them—whether an experience, as in parenting, or an heirloom album. The point of differentiation between them, of course, is mortality. Only one of these spaces is motherless.

I hoped that these objects I created could mother my boys in my death, that they could hold them when my arms could not.

My thoughts, my words and videos of my animated stories are their heirlooms. And now, from a place of hope in which I likely have time ahead, these heirlooms are hollowed out once again. They remain beautiful, like my mom's ring that now wear on dates with Garth, but their meaning has shifted.

What is left, then, is something far rarer than any antique. Happiness. Togetherness. Presence. Something shared by all of us in our family now, created and nurtured by our bodies, but effecting change for generations to come through our love.

That, more than anything, is what I hope my boys recognize as a signature of my parenting *and* my legacy.

Update | Caroline Wright

Here are a few random thoughts. I like to imagine them swimming in the pool of my resection cavity, doing leisurely laps.

- A very old and dear friend spent her twenties with me in New York. She, a lesbian burlesque dancer then, and I made a fun pair. Scout is as beautiful and intelligent as she is totally ridiculous, which is why I love her. So, we used to talk about her act, supported by great vaudeville performance tradition and Scout's fierce feminism, over bourbon. I was fascinated that my Amherst-educated friend was essentially denuding herself for bachelor parties. To that, Scout would reply, "the only thing more intimidating than a naked woman is a naked woman who talks." And with that, the queen would get on stage naked and read poetry. I've been wanting to sit down with that Scout and that Caroline and let those ladies know that having cancer feels the same sometimes. And I just crawl up on stage and read poetry in my own way. Who knew.
- I actually laughed out loud the other day as I was shaving my head for the second time that week at the idea of "brave" actresses shaving their heads in movies. It's

always portrayed as being so shocking. Demi Moore and that chick from Empire Records come to mind. It's just a Tuesday for me. I want to watch those scenes again now, though, to check out their technique...

· I have suspicions I am losing my hearing in my right ear. It could be a side effect from radiation. *Most likely it is just earwax*, I tell myself, so I will be gross and report back after I see a doctor today.

· Theodore kissed me the other day for the very first time in his life and I was so overjoyed that I was telling my neighbors in the street. *I get more of this.* I am so lucky.

Turns out that having brain cancer doesn't make you less prone to silly thoughts—in my case, surgery only gave them a reason to have a pool party in there.

Reiki | Caroline Wright

I step into the sun-filled house, a cottage in a tree-lined Seattle neighborhood. There is a massage table in the center of the room. I set my jacket, bag and hat on an overstuffed lounge chair tucked into the corner and hug my friends. We giggle as I climb onto the table to lay down, *much softer than other treatment tables*, I realize.

I find quiet, or it finds me. Michael, the master and spiritual guide in this place, sweeps the air around me with his hands. Expression slips from his face and finds his hands instead. I close my eyes and anticipate silence and clarity. It takes over my body as if pushed into my veins through an IV.

Michael settles into that calm, soothing tone of yoga practitioners to explain the flow of energy I feel in my body: a light flowing from the top of my head to drain into the ground from the bottom of my feet. I am wrapped in blankets now, propped up the way I'm used to, swaddled like a child. Someone clasps my feet and pulls my floating mind back from the clouds as if to anchor the ribbon of a balloon bobbing in the breeze.

A physical warmth, a sunshine takes over parts of my body. The darkness behind my closed eyes feels vast and cavernous. Sometimes it is a movie screen with crisp images, sometimes it is lit by colors or patterns of light.

My body hums as if to hover, as if the energy radiating from my sternum could lift me from the table. I feel awake and asleep at the same time. Occasionally my stomach gurgles or I can sense someone's breath.

Energy, light, warmth, my blanket. Thoughts and breath ebb and flow, waves that transport, carrying life's force, pooling in places that ask.

I think about how different this table is to others I've stretched out upon in the past six months. It dissolves, washed into the foam. I see a beach, beloved faces I've never met, flashes of light. It dissolves, replays something I've seen before, I'm not sure. The waves wash.

The sun rises on my right side, now warm and buzzing almost, as if caffeinated. *Or is this a feeling of connectivity, the waves now in my blood and coursing through my body?* Words are useless here. I try to listen and hear surf instead.

Michael asks me politely to return to my body, to the room. Noise of birds fade in, a distant garbage truck, a tea kettle burbling in the next room. The warmth of my friends, here, beaming with the brightness that was just inside my body.

I am clean. The tide brought me to this shore, more human and alive than before.

A Poem | Caroline Wright

I had never given a thought to my funeral, certainly not before my diagnosis. Even after my diagnosis, however, I struggled to imagine what my funeral would have been like. I'm pretty good at planning parties, but this was one I just couldn't pull together.

I was reading a book that my surrogate mother, Margie Meliza, sent me months back called "Earth Prayers From Around the World." I had avoided it largely because of the mention of God on some of the pages and I judged it quickly as likely not having a place in my vocabulary. My yoga teacher read a beautiful passage from it the other day, though, and I became inspired to take it from my bookshelf and give it a chance. I've since marked a few passages and poems from it.

Here is one of my favorites that encapsulates my feeling of death, the feeling I was trying to convey to my boys as a dying mother. It is seemingly unnamed, though the author is credited as Birago Diop. A quick Google search tells me he was a Senegalese storyteller and born the year our house was built.

Those who are dead are never gone:
They are there in the thickening shadow.
The dead are not under the earth:

they are in the tree that rustles,
they are in the wood that groans,
they are in the water that sleeps,
they are in the hut, they are in the crowd,
the dead are not dead.
Those who are dead are never gone,
they are in the breast of the woman
they are in the child who is wailing
and in the firebrand that flames.
The dead are not under the earth:
they are in the fire that is dying,
they are in the grasses that weep,
they are in the whimpering rocks,
they are in the forest, they are in the house,
the dead are not dead.

It's strange to have found this, as if I should put it in a file marked to be read at my funeral. Now I have no idea of where to put it, but I love it all the same.

Reunion | Caroline Wright

I had imagined this moment, what it would be like to see the doctor who found my tumor, Dr. Deans, again. We had exchanged a few emails since my surgery and it was clear that we both are in awe of each other in our own ways. That we both had lived through something incredible and that the other of us played a starring role in the most unbelievable story that either of us had experienced, possibly ever. (Certainly so for me.) We were the only ones who knew and who could still *feel* how it all began.

Walking into one of the treatment rooms at the clinic, I was struck how it looked the same. *My life is unrecognizable, but the office feels exactly as it did that day.* It is all the same, of course, but so different to me. This was the first exam room; I've seen so many now that I wouldn't remember any others.

Dr. Deans enters and it honestly feels like seeing an old friend or a beloved teacher, maybe. An exhale in human form, comforting and life-affirming all at once.

She takes a look at my ears with a twinkle in her eye, saying, "Forgive me, but I don't trust a neuro-oncologist to know what to do with earwax," and then punctuated with a "Yup." She explained what she thought to be a total blockage of both ears by earwax. I was mortified—and very relieved.

Mostly mortified. Many tools were involved, as was a frantic call for backup hands after a scramble in the hallway looking for the right arsenal to go after my last shred of humility.

In that moment, when the lima bean-sized piece of petrified wax emerged, I thought it was lucky to be here instead of with my homeopath. He would have made some comment about my body's tendency to accumulate and hold onto waste and I would have wanted to slide from my paper-lined perch even more than I already did. At least I could hear again.

I hugged her, looked down and noticed her pointed dress shoes. I remembered them from that day, too. Her combination of lab coat and elegant shoes reminded me of my mother in the best way, being fierce and good at your job as a woman among men at work.

We talked some more, each representing to each other a living version of the character whose story they told for the past seven months. She kept using the word "haunted," I noticed with deep understanding, as if the day we both remember so well broke apart into fragments of unhinged imagination that chips at the corners of sanity. Or reality. Or both.

I told her about my continued battle with the memory of that MRI tech. She nodded and agreed with me. We picked apart our unresolved issues from the early days of diagnosis, reveling at our shared luck. It felt good to have one other person who was literally in the same room the last time I was Caroline Wright, the healthy thirty-something mom of two. I wonder what part of Dr. Deans forever changed that day.

As I was making the move to leave, I looked her in the eyes and thanked her. That day, with her as my doctor and talking about the shape of my headaches, my incredible luck began. Right there in that timeless space, our lives converged. It's as if, in our collision, we both cracked and shifted. We are marked by each other now.

With luck, gratitude and intuition. They were there that day too.

Exhale.

Time | Caroline Wright

Part of me thinks that I've found myself in this mess because I didn't know how to relax. I've said it before and it still rings true when I think about it. I needed to learn to do one thing at a time, to be present and patient with myself. I am still learning and try to practice every day.

Turns out that being told you likely have only a year to live doesn't make you want to do one thing at a time, however. Even though I feel like I've genuinely been able to eradicate most of the major stressors in my life and better manage my need for rest, I still have been making endless to-do lists.

Now, with the idea—not the promise, but the very idea—of time ahead takes some of the pressure off of some of my pacing for creativity. The idea of time from here forces me to continue the path that my diagnosis started. *I must relax. Focus on here rather than always looking ahead.*

Is it a combination? Does looking ahead with excitement have to cheapen the present, or could it be that my love for my life, really holding the things that squirm from my grasp like my boys and my writing, is just the beginning of my next story?

I think it is important to be kind to my enthusiastic self. She's well-meaning and big-hearted, too. She just gets in over her head. She loves life, activity, accomplishment. I don't think she's necessarily unhealthy, just easily distracted.

The counterpart to these impulses are ones I've learned through others, the cultivation and practice of deep calm. Hearing the truth in silence. I always thought, and have even been practicing in my own way, that calm is like a switch. A choice between *on* or *off*.

I think I am beginning to see that my goal is to live somewhere in between *on* or *off*, in a space of true balance. I wonder if striving for balance isn't actually striving at all, but walking steadily forward with purpose.

Is this, in a nutshell, one descriptor of growing older? Balance pulling up a chair at your table, finally ready to share its secret, its contentment?

I look forward to nurturing this new relationship, between balance and me. If this is part of what it means to get older—to let go, settle in—I am here, open and ready. To find comfort with the passage of time and confidence in the predictability of life.

This may be the last invisible hold of fear releasing its grasp, finding confidence for balance, the confidence to grow older. No amount of accomplishment, I see here, is a substitute for time.

So now I wait and do and rest and age. I promise to wear birthdays and wrinkles and joint pain like the badges of honor they are. Balance, I am here for you. Humbly waiting and learning and ready.

Confusion | Caroline Wright

While on vacation this summer, I had a dream so convincing that I woke up disoriented and wondering what side of reality I was on. I had dreamed my cancer had been entirely imagined and I was, in fact, as healthy as I feel.

I sat in bed, light pouring in. *But I had that MRI. I had surgery, I remember that. They draw my blood every month and take detailed pictures of my brain every third month.*

It happened. *It is still happening,* I think, I'm reminded as I scratch my shorn head and craggy scar. It's hard to believe, really. All of it.

Just as I had found enough distance from the surgery and the fast-paced diagnostic period and had begun to start processing the trauma of it all, I was told I am not just doing well, but may very possibly *be* well.

It's like waking up again, cataloguing what happened all over again, looking for clues about what is among the *could be's.*

Except now, the expectation seems to be that I am back to "normal," which in its suggestion diminishes the severity of our circumstances. As if because people prayed for me, this success was inevitable or somehow deserved. Neither are true, I know well, and that kind of thinking hurts. It implies control, which none of us have. It is as if relief is the only acceptable feeling—it is certainly all of our primary feelings, without a doubt—and any others aren't allowed to be acknowledged.

I'm thrilled, obviously. But the realist in me—the same one that continued to create and write for my boys even when I knew in my deepest soul that I had some time left—keeps me on track. She reminds me that there are no guarantees and my cancer came unannounced the first time.

I am aware that a comparison to Dr. Taylor's star patient is still a comparison to a stranger with different DNA. I also wonder how he feels about his cancer, what words he uses to describe it, or if he even does anymore after nineteen years.

Or do I have brain cancer anymore? Am I ever not going to be terminally ill? I feel neither ill or even close to death, so words, on top of everything else, are confusing again.

The "new" me I've woken up to from dreaming is generally pretty confused. Maybe it will never make sense. *What would I need to know in order to feel safe in my body or to be able to hold my kids with reassurance?*

Nothing. The answer is nothing, I know that, and wanting more defies human nature. I've seen my own fragility, the boundaries of my own mortality, and nothing can smooth or erase the ripples that are caused by this shift. The silence, the lack of answers, are the same as before, but now it feels more dangerous because of hope.

Hope. When it was generated by me and my instincts, its purity was beautiful. Now, given to me by my doctor, it has been handled by a lot of people and it's hard to hear what my body is saying about it. I'm trying to wipe it clean, to put it back in my pocket, and listen intently for the voice that gave it to me in the first place.

Instead I am being told what my hope and my gratitude and my life ahead looks like from here, which is more confusing, not less.

I don't understand anything about my circumstances, looking around to say *how did I get here*. I don't have answers. It all feels like that dream, the one I wake up from to scratch my prickly and pock-marked scalp in order to remember. *It happened.*

I have faith that time will show me its wisdom, I do. At least I have that.

More Conversations with Henry | Caroline Wright

Today at 5 a.m., also known as The Reveille at our house as determined by the management, Henry sat across from me at the breakfast table. He was feeling particularly chatty, it seemed, and told me of all the day's itinerary for his class trip to a pumpkin patch four days ago. I find his chatter comforting. I tried to stay awake, my head propped up in my hands. *Listen to the words he chooses*, I think. *He is his own person.* I know it will be impossible, the day I no longer recognize this little boy in him. I will survive long enough to experience that common ache of a parent.

"...I mean, Mama, you could just *die*," he said with a characteristic silliness he reserves for his storytelling. I watched the meaning of the sentence register on his face. Sobered, he then starts again—

> **Henry:** Mama, you could die. Really you could. *[His eyes widen and he nods the way he does when he is listing facts.]* From the cancer. You could die sooner than all of us. Even though it makes you sad.

I'm speechless and I nod as tears climb to my shallow eyes. He looks me over one more time, casually and impishly

shrugs his shoulders and scurries downstairs to join
his brother.

And in that moment, watching his ever taller, leaner body
turn for the stairs, I realize this fight will be forever. For all
of us.

The Waiting Room | Caroline Wright

I have been on a big dose of CBD for two entire months. 800 mg per day, to be exact. This experience has taken me to unusual circumstances—at dispensaries before noon, in line with other devotees looking for a feeling.

It reminds me of the period when I made an effort to leave my cell phone at home, unused, as much as possible and everywhere all I saw were people looking down. Now I'm back online and remind myself to stop, to face whatever I want to turn away from in that moment—being bored, being alone, being disconnected.

Dipping into these lifestyle choices as a part of my cancer experience, both that of CBD as well as going off of social media, for example, has shown me how uncomfortable it is for most people to just be. Myself included.

I get it. The daily nature of life, as my dad always says, is hard. Being a human is complicated.

Checking out, anesthetizing, doesn't make it easier, I've seen in myself. Taking loads of CBD like I have been doesn't have a huge effect on my days, but it is a fight to be present. To be awake. Sometimes literally, but certainly always spiritually. It makes my inner voice quiet, which is nice on some days but disorienting on others. My relationship to writing—or, really, finding something to say—has been altered, more sluggish, more work.

The voice I've been looking for, the clear one I trust and usually shows me what the future looks like, hasn't been living in the same places since I started my CBD experiment. That was the day after Dr. Taylor gave me her Hope to add to my own. It's hard to know from here which is the stronger drug, actually.

I've wondered about the relationship of comfort and forgetting from this place. In order to be comfortable, does it require a certain amount of forgetting? Isn't that another, more systemic, version of anesthetizing? So is there a need to escape built into human nature? Where does this impulse sit in relation to being present?

I have been struggling with these questions lately. There is so much I don't understand, but I wonder if this, too, is part of the nature of being human.

Of course it is. It doesn't make it any easier. Or suddenly all "better."

I'm looking forward to being sober again, more readily present again. I'm negotiating my new "normal," on how to hold my experience since my diagnosis without letting it make me fearful or crumble inward. I suppose that's been my battle all along and I'll find my way again as I have before.

I'm not sure there's anything "normal" about it, but that's okay. It's human. And today that's enough.

A New Place | Caroline Wright

The place I find myself most often lately is as unrecognizable as the one I found in February. It's quieter, eerily silent as if before a storm. Something aches in my chest like a part is missing or as if I'm in mourning.

But no one died, I think. *I'm supposed to be happy,* I think.

I am. I am all of the feelings. A new friend told me of her cancer experience the other day and described it so aptly as if the person you were before your diagnosis was put into a blender, emotions and all, and what emerged—your new perspective on life—is like an emotion soup.

Emotion soup, indeed. Stirred into mine, too, are all the feelings of being spared: gratitude like none I've ever known, seeking meaning like never before, the introduction of fear. It is a dense, murky brew.

Not knowing what to say stems from an abundance of narratives. There is so much meaning here that it suffocates the storyteller.

I crave simplicity, purpose, direction. When tending to the boys or on the rare occasion I can hold them, I understand my luck, my purpose, this place. I am not just "mother," but "me" too. The "me" part is the one who's choking on her words in this silent place.

The Parking Spot | Caroline Wright

A silent helper in all of this, a bystander for all of my life's
events over the past near decade, has been my therapist.
(Saying so is probably the last vestige of the New Yorker in me.)
I love her so much and am grateful to have her on my team.
She has helped to guide me through a lot. I haven't spoken to
her very much since my diagnosis—two or three times, really.
I usually have some idea of what she is going to say, but having
her do so is very comforting. I tend to reach out to her when I
need the voice in my head to be spoken aloud.

She is one of my access points for the Truth. She always
has some for me.

I called her to explain my aimlessness lately and I could
almost hear the subtext, *duh*, peek out between her sentences.
Saying it out loud made me realize the depths of what I'd
faced this year. She held my feelings and stories in her loving,
smart way and assured me that this healing, too, just takes
time. And kindness. Less doing, more being.

And here we are again. Same tune, different song.
Nowhere left to hide. Nothing left to do but wait for the
arrival of meaning. It will find me. I'm saving its spot, like
an old lady in Brooklyn who grumbles about the sudden
increase in street traffic. I'm saving a space, front and

center, using the trash and recycling bins. I purge, I wait, I prepare.

Over the past few days, I have begun to find comfort in this silent place now. It helps me listen again. I am ready.

Not Today | Caroline Wright

I look at my wrist and trace the outline of my "not today" tattoo with my gaze.

It reminds me of the days just after surgery when the powerful steroids had me convinced I was going to die any time I closed my eyes to sleep. I would climb into bed and reach for Garth's hand and explain that a part of me deep inside felt like a dog who was looking to hide under a porch to die gracefully.

Occasionally he would ask what I wanted him to do if I stopped breathing. Usually, though, he would just kiss me and lay silently next to me, holding my hand until my racing mind allowed me to doze off.

He was the one who encouraged me to get the tattoo so I could look at it when I opened my eyes in the morning. It helped me believe I would wake up again.

It was a time when I spent my days frantically accomplishing things for my legacy, emailing people in the middle of the night with updates on projects so they knew how to continue without me. No one made me feel crazy, surprisingly. Garth and my parents wondered when my panic would stop. Over time, and by going off of steroids, it did.

I am very fortunate not to live in the light of those fears—sudden death among them—any more. I see not only days but years ahead.

With the shift in my perspective, so has the meaning of my tattoo shifted. I now use it to remind myself to slow down, to slacken the pace of my to-do lists or planning that can take on a pace and consciousness like a ribbon of ticker tape. When I start to obsess over the "could" and "should" do's, I look at my wrist.

Not today.

The tattoo is an indelible reminder of both truths that I hold each day: that I am healthy enough not to die today and that I am learning to slow down. It holds both meanings just like my days do. I am profoundly grateful to have this reminder. It adds strength and meaning to each of my days along with permanent, tender comfort. A gift from my body to my brain.

Strange Things To Be Good At | Caroline Wright

I went to the hospital on Tuesday night. There are a few symptoms I have to track carefully while on chemo— fever, most notably—so I've been paying attention. I vomited all day in between naps and feeling miserable. At around 4 pm, Garth suggested that I call my doctor. In addition to the health storm I was facing, my symptoms amassed to suggest possible neutropenia. (I hadn't heard this word before this week and have heard it probably 50 times since.) It is a condition that could prove deadly to me, as it refers to a person's white blood count being dangerously low.

My cough, 100.8 fever, abdominal pain (from vomiting, but no matter) and "productive cough" (another term I'd never heard before and now can't shake from my vocabulary) were enough to cause my doctors to call me in.

So, Garth and I went to the ER. It was strange to be at the ER without being worried. It occurred to me then how strange it is to be *good* at going to the ER, and how many strange things I'm good at now. Like how to read a phlebotomist to determine whether or not warning them about my tricky veins is helpful or nerve-wracking.

Or having my ID always at the ready in the line in the

blood draw department; those who fumble and slow the line are clearly rookies.

The strangest thing I think I've learned to be good at is acknowledging that I don't know everything about my body. To double-check, just in case.

I was released a few hours later with the confidence that I was sick but not *that sick* and that I'd done the right thing. All in time to crawl into my own bed.

The Power We Have | Caroline Wright

I used to think that "doing good" was relegated to those who demonstrated volunteerism. Like, it only counted to be in the Peace Corps or not at all. Besides, it wasn't something that non-religious families did that much.

And then I got sick and witnessed my first miracle. Each gesture was something I'd done before, but together they shifted, swelled in their collective power. They healed. I believe that.

It wasn't just soup. Or cards. Or a text. They were each flickers, flint, a spark. Ingredients needed to build a roaring flame.

And it didn't require a membership to an organization or vaccines to visit an impoverished country. It changed my life. One life. It could have saved it for all we know.

I now try to think of who I can help with a simple gesture— some soup or some cookies, a hug. It is the smallest way I can change the world right now, bolstering my neighbor. It could certainly change someone's day from being sad or lonely to feeling supported, which is a huge shift in itself.

Instead of just "I'm here," as I used to focus on in belief of my survival, this too has changed in tone. It addresses, invisibly, my community: "I'm here [for you]."

We each are capable of this power, the power to change a day, to help someone worry a little less, to bring a meal to an overwhelmed friend. These ingredients amass to a flame of its own, to heal unseen wounds.

No thanks are necessary because the gratitude is paid forward.

I understand what it means to be changed and, in turn, live fueled in part by gratitude for my community. It healed me.

And I am only one small person.

We each have this capacity, to be both small and large. The difference between them is a matter of perspective.

Resistance | Caroline Wright

When visiting my Sarah in Nashville, as I did a few weeks ago, I am accustomed to finding myself with precious "alone time," as Henry would call it. Her busy schedule and my enjoyment of a corner of a new coffee shop with my notebook are a good match.

Sarah sent me a to a beautiful, slow yoga class one morning. The class was a familiar blend of mind and gentle body work, but still different to my beloved class at home.

The instructor spoke as we intentionally moved our bodies. As she was guiding us through a highly visual meditation, she turned the topic to something that resonated deeply with me. *I sound like someone who talks about a sermon heard at church.*

I guess I kind of did, I realize.

She told us to find a point of resistance in our bodies, a place that was in pain or even just holding tension. Then she told us to imagine a lightness around it, or a bubble of air in its place. The intention of making space for resistance, facing it with honesty and bravery without trying to change it, is a very basic form of loving. She instructed us to meet at the point of resistance within our bodies, to show up and be grateful to it. She said her meditation teacher told her that in that very spot we find our own personal doorway to freedom.

As I sat, stretched and imagined this glow I feel and know in my body, I am grateful for these words that so perfectly describe my experience of my journey towards healing. Love at the center that supports feeling rooted, flexible and strong all at once, like a tree swaying in the wind.

Preach, healer. Preach.

Not Today List | Caroline Wright

Not Today List: *a mechanism of hope and patience. In progress.*

> Walking across the Irish countryside from small town to small town, staying at bed and breakfasts

> Hiking in the Grand Canyon

> Becoming truly fluent in French again

> Living in France again, if only for a summer, with the whole family

> Creating recipes for foods that please me first— celebratory sweets and comfort foods, really

> Planning my re-birthday party in February

> Renew my vows with Garth

> Begin painting with watercolors again without showing the paintings to anyone

Go to India and eat all the (anti-inflammatory and gluten-free) food in sight

Go back to Bapa's yellow house in Michigan and kneel where he is buried

Make quilts for friends' babies

Sing in front of people (on stage) to see if surviving brain surgery actually made me braver

Read all the books I missed in college because I was busy in Paris falling in love

1) Learn how to sew a dress and successfully make one I'd wear 2) Wear it 3) Rewrite this same memory from the sixth grade and my handmade vests.

Go on an artistic retreat, like weaving in Mexico

Actually learn to sail the way my grandfather thought I had (I was infatuated with the instructor and remember none of my lessons other than being a pre-teen in the presence of his shirtless, tan body)

Learn to write poetry

Go on a writer's retreat

Get more tattoos; among them, an infinity symbol shared with Garth

Go on a trip alone with my dad somewhere that appeals to our creativity

Finding my voice as an activist participant in the medical realm, doing my part to fight cancer for those who can't

Latest MRI Results | Paul Markunas

Caroline had her second post-radiation (6 month) MRI today and a follow-up visit with a Chemo-Oncology MD.

Her MRI remains unchanged. No sign of cancer or cancer growth.

Her blood work results are good; she continues to tolerate the chemotherapy well with six more regimens remaining after she finishes the one she is currently taking.

MRIs will be done every 3 months for the next 18 months to assess status. After that, they may decrease in frequency.

Next MRI will be at the end of March.

This year will be an especially Merry Christmas!

Stoner Philosophy | Caroline Wright

I am officially done with my CBD experiment. It was a strange and surreal experience—I'm starting to wonder if I am capable of any other sort now, my guess is not—and it is over as unceremoniously as it began.

It wasn't horrible. I felt mostly like myself, a little sleepier maybe. The only times I felt "stoned" would take me by surprise because otherwise I would forget I was taking anything. These surprise moments would come up when I would increase my dose to reach my goal of 800 mg per day (so, not too big of a surprise there) or when I was concurrently taking my chemo meds. Something about that one-two punch to my brain would take me down every time. Those are the only times I actually allowed myself to nap, as I knew there was no way around it.

A funny side effect of being accidentally stoned and a generally wistful person is that I would leave myself notes about thoughts I felt in the moment were brilliant. (In the worst of those moments I couldn't track conversations or hold onto thoughts for more than a few minutes, which can actually be kind of scary to someone who has suffered brain trauma.) These thoughts would come to me during bouts of especially swimmy headspace, like the inner monologue of a tipsy philosophy major. I now have a phone full of notes from this person. I will miss the feeling of grasping onto thoughts with the clarity of importance, even if fleeting.

I won't bore you with all the partial quotes or scribbled phrases, but I'll share a few here just for fun:

- While reading *Crime and Punishment* over Thanksgiving, I wrote this thought inspired by a debate between characters in the book: "Maybe our needs create our realities. Dostoyevsky suggests that ghosts can only appear to madmen, but also says that it doesn't mean they don't exist. Does God only appear to the devout? Does terminal illness only strike those who can keep the secrets it shows them?"
- Verbatim: "Yoga positions still sound like Harry Potter charms to me."
- New motto: instead of trying to seek control, make life's work to try to create and experience beauty."
- "Imagine if human nature wired us to look for our similarities rather than differences. How different the world would be."

Thanks, Stoner Caroline. See you next month when I'm on chemo again.

Crying Uncle │ Caroline Wright

My mom is in the hospital right now with double pneumonia. She has been since the end of last week and there isn't an encouraging timeline ahead for her release.

I am experiencing now what it's like to be rooting for someone you love to fight for their life while totally helpless. It's horrible. It makes me thankful that I had so many people who were doing what they could do. Everything made such a big difference to me, and I wasn't lying in a hospital bed like my mom is.

It has me thinking again of the word terminal, too. She is in a critical but stable position, been hauled around by ambulances and is hooked up to machines. But no one has used that word. It is unspoken, but I see it there.

This year has been really rough on our family, I think. Then I get a text from my dad and Garth texts back and I send another. My parents are in a hospital just downtown. My kids make them videos, asking when they are going to see Gaba, that they miss Gaba. *There is beauty in that, too*, I think. They are here, we are here for them, and we are grateful for each other. *Small steps, big changes.* There still isn't room for self-pity. Just fighting.

If you could turn your healing thoughts that buoyed me to my mom, I would be so grateful. Today she is hopefully having a procedure that may dramatically improve her course of recovery.

But, enough already, 2017. We have felt your lesson, loud and clear: we are aware we aren't invincible and that every moment counts. Let's all breathe easier together in 2018, shall we?

A Merry Christmas Wish | Paul Markunas

I've been sitting here in the hospital 6 am to 8 pm for the past seven days. My wife is very sick. But it has made me review the year in my mind—all the things we've endured, all the people we've met, all the beautiful kindness and warmth we've experienced.

First, I want to thank on behalf of everyone in our family, all the health care workers who dedicate their lives to those who need them. Some are sick, really sick. Some are just lonely and confused. Others just don't know.

We've seen and gotten to know their loved ones, too. How they care, how they are responsible, how they, in fact, try to take the pain away from the people they love.

I got it. Finally I got it. I got your back.

We all need to know that a person loves us and will care for us, will look out for our interests, even when we can't.

I wish that for everyone.

It may seem surprising to some that this would be my wish. But I've seen too much not to know better. May everyone, everyone, have someone in their lives who has their back.

Caroline has it in spades. Glad has it. Not everyone does. That's my wish.

And a Happy and Healthy New Year for all.

The Gift | Caroline Wright

While driving home on the eve of Christmas Eve yesterday from watching the Christmas parade from Gaba and Gampa's hotel where my mom begins her recovery, Henry chirped excitedly from the backseat. He talked about the last day of his Lego advent calendar being the next day, asking if Santa only ate sweets and why, and wanted to know in great detail what our plans were for the following two days. (Theodore, already in his pjs, had been snoozing soundly by this point for quite some time, having collapsed into his carseat. That night had been the first one he'd seen Gaba and Gampa in about a week and rest was past due.)

Garth and I began to use that quiet, focused moment of conversation with Henry to talk about the most important part of the Christmas season to a five-year-old awaiting Santa: the gifts.

Henry: How many presents are going to be under the tree for me? I hope Santa brings me some new Legos!

Garth: Henry, you are very lucky. Lots of kids only get one present from their parents and maybe another from their grandparents and that's it. You have a lot of people who love you very much and send you gifts. Not everyone is so lucky. Every gift is given to you from someone who loves you a lot, and they want to use their Christmas gift to you as a chance to show you.

Caroline: That's right. That's really what Christmas is about—not how many presents you get or how big the boxes are. Each present shows that the person who gave it to you saw something in a store and thought, "Henry would really like this," and spend money on it so you could have it. Every present represents a lot of time, thought and energy that is being shown to you through that gift. So when it comes time to open presents, remember that. Instead of racing through tearing open packages to see what's next, let's work on being grateful for each gift and trying to see the love in every one and communicate what you see.

Henry: *[Quietly, earnestly.]* I may not use words, but I say it in my heart.

Caroline: I know you do. But how can we hear it from inside your body? Expressing love and gratitude is something everyone has to do their whole lives. It's beautiful that you can say it in your heart, but you should say it out loud, too, for someone else to know.

This sweet exchange got me thinking about my own practice of communicating love. It's actually the place where my values and worldview reside—it's my religion, my compass.

I sincerely believe that humanity is meant to be shared—hence your reading this here—and that kindness, the most basic form of love, has the capacity to change lives.

Giving love, as much and as often as possible, creates space to be loved, too. It can be something small, like a hug or a compliment, or a grand gesture. The muscle grows with practice, increasing its capacity with every effort. The effort of love, however, is different from any other of its kind, I've found—it dissolves through communication.

In replaying this conversation with Henry and all that it means to me (especially at Christmastime, but also as a global truth), I realize that this is the secret to life. It sounds dramatic when I put it that way, but it is really so simple. Drama cloaks its meaning and distracts from the clear, ringing tone that cuts through the mist if you listen for it.

I honestly think I may still be here because I have so much more to give. It's that simple.

A note about my mom, since so many friends are asking: My mom has been released from the hospital to rest and recover while on very strong antibiotics. They plan to stay in a hotel for at least a week, as their cubby is a three-floor walk-up and she can't manage those stairs in her condition. My dad is watching her closely and adhering strictly to directives from the care team for exercise, nutrition and medication. We are hopeful for a steady recovery, however slow, and are grateful to have them among us for Christmas.

Farewell, 2017 | Caroline Wright

Last night, as I rang in the New Year the way Garth and I have since Henry was born (very quietly and alone in a very unglamorous way), my phone was lighting up with a bevy of texts whose messages hovered around wishes for 2018 to be better than 2017. A change of luck, mostly.

Really, 2017 was a pretty amazing year. It was terrifying in parts, but it was equally if not more so beautiful. Last year brought me brain cancer, but it also healed deep wounds, gave me the knowledge of not only my mortality, but my strength, too.

I lived when I should have died. It brought me a miracle.

Everything in my life now is in crisp focus. I try to take nothing for granted; things that I once felt entitled to, like breath or my hair or walking around, I realize are actually incredible privileges. It makes me feel even luckier to be here, not just still living but really alive. I eat an apple now for dessert rather than cake, but I am grateful for its sweetness on my tongue. It was there all along, but I didn't taste it like this before. 2017 brought me that, too.

Everything changed in my life last year. Shifted, amplified, concentrated. Focused. Purified. Distilled.

I feel like the best version of myself, or at least I see what that could mean from a set of values that are so different from ones that propelled me before. Living out loud the secrets I've always held in my heart, truths that I always knew but only were spoken when I needed them.

In Henry's ceremony to becoming an Owl at his school this year, his beloved teacher told a beautiful story about a child choosing his parents from a cloud, by looking down through parted skies. I've returned to this image many times since September, considering a fantasy of choosing our life's narrative in the same way prior to birth. *In this one, you'll get terminal brain cancer...*

None of us would have chosen it. I certainly wouldn't have. And that would have been a shame—it showed me so much beauty, so much friendship, so much love. Way more than most could experience in a single lifetime, I'd wager.

It showed me I could believe in nothing and everything all at once. In myself. And that was enough to possibly save my life and give love value over fear. To keep my kids with their mother for at least a while longer.

That's a pretty good year, I think, as I tear the page off of our calendar. May the ones ahead be as profound and life-affirming.

And I made it so.

Here's to making 2018 the best it can be...

The Stories I Hear Now | Caroline Wright

When I was diagnosed, encouragement was sparing. I get it now. Silence as a form of held breath, waiting to see if I would pass the next threshold, beyond the page of the statistics. It is a very lonely place, that breathless one.

I remember some trying to tell me and I refused to listen, I remind myself.

I haven't even arrived anywhere, passed through yet (*will I ever?*, though my year's prognosis hasn't even come and gone), and already the chatter around me has changed. And me with it. Friends light up and tell me about the young mom they know or their uncle or the one success story they knew of someone with a GBM. (It seems like I was the only one I know without a GBM story like that. *Because it was waiting for me to find it, lucky me.*)

It's strange being treated so singularly now, one of the very fortunate few with results like mine. I still don't know what to say about it or how to feel, and it has made the what ifs from before desperate, dangerous. The thoughts grow fangs if I feed them. So I write and think less about what "could be" and hug my husband and kids more instead. I am given today, and tomorrow and likely next month and I just keep that in focus as I live the life I am being gifted, my gifted life.

I've gotten back to work (not like I ever left, really), and being in practice as a primary caregiver. I'm feverishly baking again. I'm driving a little bit more, though I still hate it. My hair is growing back: dark, shaggy and curly like it belongs to someone else. *(It kind of does.)* I think less about my cancer, because with each passing day it feels less relevant somehow to the life I lead. I am back to being pleasantly objectified in conversation by friends and strangers, comments on how thin I've become or how great I look, which no one tells you when they think you're dying.

It's still silent here in this rarefied setting when I drown out the chatter. I feel separate but strong, not lonely anymore. Not alone in a wood, but part of it. Rooted, listening, aware.

Like the sturdiest, ancient pines I've hugged while crossing their paths aside a trail, I am coursing with the language of the here and now as well as what came before.

Like them, too, I am not going anywhere.

Update on my Mom, Glad | Caroline Wright

I have avoided writing this post because I cried uncle before Christmas, my mom was sick already and it felt like enough then. This week has been hard. Last Friday night, while texting my dad who was waiting in the lobby for an update from the surgeon who was 8 hours deep into a projected 4-hour surgery, I honestly thought she died. I cried myself to sleep after taking my last chemo pills for this course.

We aren't done yet, my mom and I. This year brought us progress to being closer, to having a relationship that revolves around clarity, truth and openness. It has been a process, fighting for this change among all of the others. We would make strides, then she would disappear. Or our lives would carry us apart.

And now, back in a hospital room, we come together again. I stroke her hair away from her forehead, as she did mine, and tell her it's going to be okay. I believe it. And my dad, like before, sits by, willing it to be so with every fiber of his devoted being, talking to doctors and advocating for her as he did for me.

As I said, we aren't done yet. I'm looking forward to having my mom back to begin again, again. I love you, Mom.

Here is an update from my dad about what happened:

Glad left the hospital after eight nights of touch-and-go health just before the holidays with our grand boys. She continued to heal at home and then in Maui for 8 nights (on the plane to and from with oxygen!) which really helped her gain strength and stamina.

When she got back she had hoped to get back to work full-time and had a follow-up visit with her thoracic doctors. The news was not good. Her pleural space had major pockets of infection. They recommended surgery to get her lung fully re-inflated and clean out all the infection.

When they opened her chest, they immediately saw that the lower lobe of her left lung had essentially rotted away. So, eight hours of surgery later, she was left with half a left lung, a cleaned out pleural cavity and four chest tubes draining her lung space. They had to take out one rib on her left side since they couldn't open up her chest because of the scar tissue and the infection.

That was a week ago today and she is still in the hospital but is making a steady but slow recovery.

She is beginning to get back to her old self although she is still very weak and has a long road ahead. But we know now she will be ok.

Anniversaries of Choice | Caroline Wright

A variety of pivotal dates in my story find their one-year anniversaries in the coming weeks. As incessant the pacing of the discoveries to my health were last year (one weekly for a parade of weeks culminating with my birthday in early March), obviously so are the anniversaries of those dates this year. Reflecting on them, holding the space to experience them again from a place of strength and health, is daunting in its own way, too. I've made plans, constructed barriers and boundaries for this processing, knowing that it needs to be faced with pride and love, not fear. Fear could swallow me whole if I let it—as easily today as a year ago. So I won't let it in.

This week I've been raising money for an important personal project, mirroring the timing of when I raised money for *Charlie the Cook* last year. I realize in repeating this experience how sick I was then, how frantic and uncontrollably emotional I was during that time— symptomatic, I mean—even before I found out about the mass. My MRI was the Friday of that Kickstarter week, which is equivalent to tomorrow if assimilating those experiences. (The calendar anniversary is Saturday; I am celebrating by getting a tattoo of a phoenix feather, originally painted by the illustrator of *The Everlasting Creature*, Willow, on my right arm. A new friend from my yoga class is keeping me company while it is seared into me. That night, I am having a nice dinner with my family. It will be my mom's first real venture out in public since her surgery.) It's all very layered—the experience mingling with time and perspective, its transformation from trauma to memory. Its path to meaning—and power, I believe—is of my choosing. I choose joy, love, *life*. Today just like every other this year. Emotional healing, I'm learning, takes as much work and self-care as physical healing does, if not more. I have been writing thank-you notes and making cookie dough in preparation for the systematic acknowledgement of all of the people who helped to hold me in the light, to find my health again, beginning with Dr. Deans tomorrow. It feels good to spread love to my doctors through cookies again, like I did during my radiation treatment and when I introduced myself to them for the first time. Allowing who I am to shine through my anonymity as "patient," letting the light beam from me and reflect onto people who have given their talents to benefit my well-being, feels right.

Focusing outside myself, turning the light outward, makes the world brighter. And less lonely, which is probably the worst (and most defining) characteristic of being a patient.

I am grateful to be here now and hope that each of you hold your piece of that love and gratitude that you deserve. We did it together, I truly believe that.

I hope you'll join me in celebrating these dates in your own way, holding me and our connection in your heart as I dance, sing and cry my way through these wild memories over the next few weeks. My friends and beautiful family are here to hold me and I will let them. Again.

Shifting of Perfection | Caroline Wright

Hi, my name is Caroline. I am a perfectionist.

My *Charlie the Cook* books arrived right before my "rebirthday" brunch. There they sat, their cartons stacked high and covered with tablecloths as loved ones ate cheesy kale-flecked eggs around them.

After the dishes were cleared, I set into motion the cogs of many months of planning: books and contents of Excel spreadsheets spilled onto my dining room table, freshly cleaned of mimosas and gluten-free cake celebrating my survival.

I had no idea how to jump in. I had planned for this moment, but really wasn't sure where to start. Al, the very same one who worked tirelessly here to coordinate soup drop-offs in the early days of my recovery, came over and we worked together to start the process of fulfilling book orders.

It is frustrating when you are someone with very high standards and usually the capabilities to match them and then suddenly your brain makes mistakes. I make mistakes. So, in looking at stacks of papers to guide me and the supplies I had ordered and all of their coordinating materials, I just knew that *something* would be off, I just didn't know what it yet. That's a hard thing to accept because I'm still me—brain surgery doesn't change that.

Luckily, the missteps were all very minor and fixable. Al was there (as usual) to help smooth things over. So, this is my new brain in a professional setting. I'm figuring it out and still so grateful for what I *can* do versus angry about what I *can't*.

Perfection isn't all that it was cracked up to be, I'm learning. From here, I see that perfection has little to do with feeling fulfilled or successful. One is an ideal and the others bloom from within.

I had a great week! All the packages are sent off, I signed a very like-minded agent who sees my vision for future books and is in full support of whatever comes next for me. I'm feeling very capable to meet the future. After what I've been through this year, that isn't a small feat. I don't take it for granted.

Whatever the future brings for me, I still don't know—in terms of either career or health. But I don't think it will be perfect. And that, honestly, is just fine with me.

It will be mine, I will be here, and that is more than I could have ever hoped for a year ago.

My Rebirthday | Caroline Wright

I had a brunch to celebrate the fact that I am still alive. I held it on the day I now think of as my "rebirthday," or the anniversary of my brain surgery, last weekend. (Bapa, my grandfather, called the date of his triple bypass his "second birthday," and I honor him and that idea with this celebration, too.)

People I love, people who looked into the eyes of someone they thought could die and were brave enough to hope that they wouldn't, flowed into my house. Many of them hugged me, admitted the fears they didn't say aloud to me before and cried. Many of them laughed with me and tousled my unexpected curls. They ate food I prepared for them and left wearing a bracelet I made for them, both tokens of my profound gratitude.

And my birthday is this week. Friday. I grew one year older, immeasurably wiser and more alive. I will have had celebrations every week for the past month, great milestones that depict surpassing odds and the honoring of great luck. I prepare for the silence that falls after I stop making cakes, the silence of sitting down and breathing well again.

But I am breathing. I am still here.

Silence has taken many forms in this past year. It has scared me, isolated me, disheartened me. It has met me in the woods. It has met me in my mind. It has found me in a confused slur from drugs. I have found calm in it, peace in it. In it, my feelings manifest to fill the void. Now, content and present, it comforts me because I imagine this writing there as I step further away and resume chasing my boys at every turn. I imagine all of us in that silence together, paddling in the hopes I held for my boys and the words I saw about my life. I see us building castles from the grains of sand that I found here inside my heart, the tiniest hints of strength that grew in our conversations, now wide beaches that stretch in low tide. That silent space connects us and will forever. That silence is the space in which none of us can ever die, but instead live in the truth of our connections.

So, as my life finds a new gait and I continue and go *on*, I hope you'll meet me in that silent place and hold this year, as I will, with gratitude. As I live and you live in our parallel worlds and I no longer think about cancer every day, we can always meet again. We are marked by one another now. The silent unknown is familiar and ours, and I look forward to wading in it with you again.

Dear fellow Statistic,

Sorry, I know now is not the time to make a joke... Albeit not a funny one. At all. All I mean to say is that people will tell you they know what you're going through and don't, but I think I just may have a small glimmer. Let me be the thousandth person to tell you I'm sorry.

When I was in the spot you're in now, I didn't want advice or comparisons to other people's stories at all. I wanted answers and I wanted to find their solutions in my own body. I wanted other people to do the research, filter it, and tell me just the edges of what I needed to know because I was hard at work making hope in a hopeless place. (That is the most important work to you as a patient, really, because it's literally the only control you have. I still am hard at work in service to it.)

Although, with that said, community—real support, not pity—was a huge part of the process of what made me feel capable of The Fight. So, out of that spirit, I wanted to ferry this bit of writing I did on a blog I wrote during the year the doctors told me I had to live after I was diagnosed with my glioblastoma.

Anyway, this is all to say I am sending love to you, as cheesy as that sounds, and believe that there is so much life lived beyond the statistics they tell you. I hope you'll keep that in mind as you learn what's next in your treatment and you find your own story.

Cheers,
Caroline Wright

Acknowledgements for The Caring Bridge Project

The first order of thanks comes to Adair Rutledge, my best friend in Seattle. Adair is a powerhouse and a talent whose creativity made this project—and struggle—feel shared and seen through beauty and humanity. She fostered this project as my collaborator, and took it on with gusto, which is her gorgeous way (and her love isn't even represented in this version of the book now). With honesty and company. I will love you forever.

To Joanna Price, who helped me produce the *Everlasting Creature* with grace and beauty and who turned those amazing talents to produce this book from what was essentially a stack of documents. Thank you for helping me create this part of my legacy.

Aunt Elasah and the whole Smith family, thank you for your support. Aunt Elasah, thank you for your generosity and for sending me the CaringBridge site in the first place. Renée Leshan, it was you who gave me the strength to build it in your model.

To Henry's preschools, FCS and Tara's Tots, thank you from the bottom of my heart for the love and care you gave our Henry during this time in which his spirit needed all the extra love and guidance he could get. It helped me to be able to have space to heal, knowing Henry had access to great love, care and a bit of fun while being seen for who he is. Tara and Teresa, I will love you forever for taking him on the way you did during my diagnosis. Thank you for introducing me to Willow.

To my life-long friend, Allison Taylor, who took on the role as my guardian as I approached my healing with as much grace and kindness as she did in my healthiest and happiest times of my life. You grounded me during my disorientation and made me see clearly, even when my vision was blurry. Your role in this story, which was so very crucial and remains one of the greatest displays of friendship I will ever know, has disappeared from the pages of this book, but never my heart.

To Ellen and Joe Rutledge for being the people whose well of kindness and support was endless and truly transformed those around us. It was incredible and turned this scary situation to being almost comfortable, and especially for my loved ones who were trying desperately to hold it together to focus on my care.

To the medical professionals who let me talk at them while I was out of my mind on medicine and the craziest ride of my life. First to Dr. Deans at Swedish Medical who was diligent enough to catch my tumor in the first place, despite forever giving too much information and actively trying to confuse you about the inner-workings of my brain. And Dr. Ellenbogen for the comfort and kindness in the earliest days of diagnosis. Then, on to all of the medical professionals who helped me during surgery, like Drs. Ko and Silbergeld who did a technically superior job to take out my tumor and made me feel almost human in the process. To Christy, their nurse practitioner, who was kind and wanted to help find a way to keep my hair. To the dignified staff at UW Neurosurgery: Marji, Maggie, Dan (who made my MRI pre-surgery not too scary with music), Kim, Camila, Adrian, Adrienne, Lara, and beautiful night nurse Kate C., Irena and Heidi in the ICU, Dr. Satish and Dr. Harrison Cash. To Davis, the assisting nurse for Drs. Ko and Silbergeld, who removed my staples and helped me stay quiet during my blood pressure readings. Thank you to each of you who smiled at me and made me feel human. To my friends at Alvord Brain Tumor Center, my doctors there: Dr. Tseng, Dr. Taylor, Dr. Shetabi and Dr. Graber; the lovely nurses, Pam and Mandy, among the others who usher me into my appointments and take my blood pressure. My MRI and radiation teams.

To Jodi, Heather and Michael, you brought me back from the world of the wounded to the world of the living. You showed me that my energy is precious and was the first thing to make me an outlier, something the doctors can't see. To my family at Aditi—foremost to Jen, Julie and Sally but all of my ladies, too—thank you for loving and laughing with the most scared parts of me and calling it bravery. I am honored to be part of your community.

To Robin, my stories always begin and end with you. You have saved my life in many ways over many years. I'm forever indebted to you.

To Bernie and Theresa, thank you for seeing the way through my diagnosis and giving me pills to swallow and foods to eat when no one else had any idea of what to do. To Dorothea Delgado, thank you for looking into my broken body and help lead me to a voice there.

To Ira Glass, one of my heros, thank you for telling me about ASMR those years ago. I wouldn't have broken through the awkward wall to know that this would have been such a useful tool if I hadn't heard it from you, and I definitely wouldn't have felt human at all during this diagnosis had I not had ASMR.

To "my ladies" here in Seattle, Katie, Katy and Sam: you are truly among the most amazing women I've ever met and I'm honored to be a part of your sisterhood, to have a band of native Pacific Northwesterners who took me in as your own. Your love made me feel strong, fierce and smart when my brain was suffering and I could have chosen to feel otherwise. To my Soulful Mamas, thank you for having my back all along and listening—Renée, thanks for being the first person I called.

To Adam and Stefanie and my whole Alabamian family, thank you for the support from all the way across the country and for making me feel like you would do anything I asked to help get my ideas from screen to page.

To my beloved chosen family: my Sarah, Teddy, Gillian, Alli, Neil, Dan, Jeff, SJ, Amy, Sasha and Jonas. You made me "me" before this did. I love you endlessly. To "Ma" Margie Meliza, thanks for the weekly love letters while I was healing, they penned so much more than offline connection—they communicated timeless love. Thank you.

To my parents, Paul and Glad, whose love moved mountains and made me feel safe and inspired me to change and grow every day. I will love you forever.

To Garth, the love of my life who gave me my life, my roles as a mother and wife. Who supported me selflessly through everything, through my narrow focus on projects (both sick and well); who did the dirty work behind whatever resembles grace in this story; who loved me without fear even as he worried I would leave him with two little kids to raise.

To my Henry and Theodore, I hope this book gives you the smallest glimmer of an idea of who your mother really is and the kind of I have for you always, but especially during the craziest time of my life. Your beauty is everlasting, just like my love for you. Hold both close to you and never take it for granted. They are my gifts to you forever.